MEA CULPA

Mea Culpa

Lessons on Law and Regret from U.S. History

Steven W. Bender

NEW YORK UNIVERSITY PRESS
New York and London

NEW YORK UNIVERSITY PRESS
New York and London
www.nyupress.org

References to Internet websites (URLs) were accurate at the time of writing.
Neither the author nor New York University Press is responsible for URLs that
may have expired or changed since the manuscript was prepared.

LIBRARY OF CONGRESS CATALOGING-IN-PUBLICATION DATA
Bender, Steven, author.
Mea culpa : lessons on law and regret from U.S. history / Steven W. Bender.
pages cm
Includes bibliographical references and index.
ISBN 978-1-4798-9962-3 (cl : alk. paper)
1. Human rights--United States--History. 2. Regret--Political aspects--United States--
History. 3. United States--Social policy--Moral and ethical aspects. 4. Minorities--Legal
status, laws, etc.--United States--History. 5. United States--Emigration and immigration--
Government policy--Moral and ethical aspects. 6. Discrimination--Law and legislation--
United States--History. 7. Marginality, Social--Political aspects--United States--History. I.
Title.
KF4749.B39 2015
172'.10973--dc23
2014028738

New York University Press books are printed on acid-free paper, and their binding materials
are chosen for strength and durability. We strive to use environmentally responsible
suppliers and materials to the greatest extent possible in publishing our books.

Manufactured in the United States of America

10 9 8 7 6 5 4 3 2 1

Also available as an ebook

To my mother, Irene, who will disagree with some of my conclusions

CONTENTS

ACKNOWLEDGMENTS

I rely on the insights and passion of my colleagues and friends who reviewed early drafts of this book: Hazel Weiser, formerly the executive director of the Society of American Law Teachers, Rebecca White, Todd Bender, and Rebecca Fowler, as well as those who helped me initially frame and shape the project, particularly Richard Delgado, Jean Stefancic, and Margie Paris. Participants in workshops and presentations at Seattle, Gonzaga, and the University of Washington law schools supplied valuable leads and suggestions.

Although I have been at Seattle University School of Law for a few years, this labor of writing spans at least a decade, and I am grateful for the research support of Miranda Larson while I was a faculty member at the University of Oregon School of Law, as well as my Seattle law students Jonathan Segura and Arthur Sepulveda. My new institutional home, Seattle University School of Law, supplied me with the necessary support and encouragement to contribute to the betterment of the human experience. My research librarian at Seattle, Kerry Fitz-Gerald, gave me more than I could expect, and my former assistant Jonathan LeBlanc never questioned the piles of copying I sent his way.

Most of all, I am grateful to my son, Dominic, for giving the project newfound purpose and direction when he entered my life.

Introduction

> We simply do not see many forms of discrimination, bias, and prejudice as wrong at the time. The racism of other times and places does stand out, does strike us as glaringly and appallingly wrong. But this happens only decades or centuries later; we acquiesce in today's version with little realization that it is wrong, that a later generation will ask "How could they?" about us.
> —Richard Delgado and Jean Stefancic

Although this book aims to benefit our time in history, its origins are selfish. As the author of several books extolling the virtues of immigrants and decrying the negative constructions of Latinos/as in the American imagination, I constantly receive criticism to the effect that I am swimming against the current and should realize the dangers that immigration and, specifically, Latino/a immigrants pose to our culture, safety, and economy. With each book I write, and each talk I give, the body of my accumulating work speaks to my identity as a compassionate scholar and, it seems at times and in some venues, as a near lone voice for immigrant dignity.

When my son was born in 2008, I especially realized that my written legacy might live in the memory of future generations. At the same time, the ascendancy of the Internet, particularly Facebook and other social media, helped preserve and broadcast my scholarship and advocacy, and the opinions and prejudices of others, in ways that were not enjoyed by past generations. Consequently, I now think more about what I say, write, and do as a legal scholar tackling contentious issues in an environment where, should I change or come to regret my positions, an indelible electronic record might remain to encapsulate my prior views.

As a legal scholar, I came to question the origins and bona fides of my controversial positions and worried about the possibility of moral blind spots I might become aware of too late, if at all. In theory, a scholar is supposed to reach pristine results untainted by his or her personal views and politics, although this impartiality is far from realistic, as it is also for judges and their decision making. Instead, much of my writing came from my passions for fairness and equality. To situate my compassionate writings in theory and to help guide my conclusions, I began searching for some beacon, or moral compass, grounded in theory and history if possible, for the variety of social issues I regularly engage in my research and teaching. Perhaps that moral compass might save me from embarrassment as enlightened society moves beyond the prejudices of the moment, even those prejudices spanning the generations that came before us.

Having written considerably about the media's role in fostering and propagating stereotypes, I understood a similar dilemma that cultural artists face. How might their legacy endure when viewed by future generations? Might they find themselves on the wrong side of history and their artistry sullied? How might cinematic works such as *Birth of a Nation* (1915) appear to later generations, and presumably to many of us now, who might be repulsed by its glorification of the Ku Klux Klan and its vilification of African Americans, as in a scene where a white woman leaps to her death from a cliff to escape a black man's pursuit? How might we see television comedies from the 1950s, particularly *The Honeymooners* with its thinly veiled references to domestic violence—"right in the kisser" or "straight to the moon, Alice"?

How might some of today's media hold up with their cringe-worthy vilification of blacks, Latinos/as, Arab/Muslims, homosexuals, and other groups? Will today's rap music, relying on a misogyny that reduces women to orifices for pleasure or profit, fall from cultural favor? Will Hollywood regret its constant mocking and demeaning of same-sexuality in today's films? Will future audiences question why cinematic villains always seem to be menacing people of color?

Artists and scholars are hardly all those who might worry selfishly about their legacies. I cannot mount the steps of the Thomas Jefferson Memorial in Washington, D.C., despite its stately beauty, because it celebrates a man who owned hundreds of slaves in his lifetime, even if at the time apparently civilized men acted in the same fashion and probably their economic and social well-being depended on honoring that "peculiar" but awful institution. I wonder about the legacies today of politicians such as California's former governor Pete Wilson, who so callously threw Mexican immigrants under the bus in his aspirations for a second term in the early 1990s by championing anti-immigrant policy, or Arizona's current governor Jan Brewer, who portrayed arriving Mexican immigrants as chopping the heads off Anglos in the desert in their fervent quest to collect welfare, deal drugs, and generally to wreak havoc on a state. Similarly, consider the various politicians who "joke" about effective ways to repel undocumented immigrants by killing them or who equate homosexuality with abominable crimes. Are these politicians the George Wallaces of today, standing at the schoolhouse door promising segregation and inequality forever and ensuring themselves a place in history's hall of shame?

Educational institutions must worry too about their legacy. Slave-owner names adorn schools across the country, and the history of many Ivy League institutions is entangled with the centrality of slave ownership in their culture and economy.[1] Scholars and even athletic coaches like the now disgraced Joe Paterno help form the identity of elite academic institutions. Teachers selecting curriculum and textbooks should wonder what history might think of their choices, which may shape and help sustain prejudices in another generation of youth. Scholars must appreciate the potential for regret in their research ideas and conclusions or, in some instances, their silence in the face of current oppression. The silence of the academy was captured in an article decrying the lack of protest by legal scholars against the internment of Japanese Americans and against other domestic abuses during World War II: "The Dogs That Did Not Bark: The Silence of the Legal Academy during World War II."[2]

Corporations too have valuable identities and reputations that can survive across generations. When JPMorgan Chase apologized in 2005 for the practices of Chase Bank's predecessors, which lent money routinely on the collateral of slaves as lenders today would on houses and cars, it brought home the potential connectedness of company brands and identities with regrettable practices. Might Wells Fargo Bank later regret its role today as a leading shareholder in the private-prison industry, which cages detained, undocumented immigrants away from their families in growing numbers?[3] Years from now, should it survive, how might Chick-fil-A, the U.S. restaurant chain, feel about its strident public opposition to same-sex marriage?

Religious institutions have reputations that span generations as they attempt to attract new members and donations. How might constituents remember the Catholic Church's unstinting opposition to gay equality? Notably, the Catholic Church bucked a poll showing that 60 percent of U.S. Catholics favor marriage equality and spent $2 million in a failed assault on state marriage-equality initiatives in the 2012 elections.[4]

Of the various legal actors and policymakers in the United States, arguably judges have the largest stake in decision making on the right side of history. Given the precedential value of their rulings, wrong-minded policy not only may define them but may have regrettable legal consequences for decades or even centuries to come. Imagine the legacy of the five slave-owning Supreme Court justices, including Chief Justice Roger Taney, when the Court issued its 1857 *Dred Scott* decision calling black slaves "beings of an inferior order" to be owned and sold.[5] Or the three Supreme Court justices who concurred with the Court's 1873 ruling that allowed Illinois to deny women the right to practice law; explaining their vote in a concurring opinion, they declared: "The paramount destiny and mission of wom[e]n are to fulfil the noble and benign offices of wife and mother."[6] Or famous Supreme Court Justice Oliver Wendell Holmes, who, in upholding an abhorrent mandatory sterilization law, quipped regrettably that "three generations of imbeciles are enough."[7]

Even during their lifetimes judges have regretted missed opportunities for justice, as when retired Supreme Court Justice Lewis Powell revealed that his biggest mistake was joining the Court's 1986 decision upholding, by a narrow 5-4 vote, a Georgia law criminalizing consensual sex between homosexuals.[8] Similarly, Justice William O. Douglas expressed regret for his vote supporting the constitutionality of interning Japanese Americans in military detention camps during World War II, admitting "grave injustices had been committed" and that "fine American citizens had been robbed of their properties."[9] When the Supreme Court agreed in late 2012 to consider the legality of California's prohibition of same-sex marriage, my colleague Deborah Ahrens framed the opportunities for legacy by asking whether the Court wanted to write *Plessy*, the now-embarrassing 1896 decision upholding racial segregation, or *Brown*, the monumental antisegregation ruling in 1954 that rejected the inequality *Plessy* had permitted.[10] Despite their professed allegiance to the task of interpreting the Constitution as written, given all the prejudices it reflects, no doubt Supreme Court justices and other judges would be intrigued by the promise of some viable and accurate moral compass by which their legacies (and our own) might be better written.

Apart from the media, scholars, judges, politicians, and other legal actors, everyone has a stake in avoiding regrettable policies and practices. As voters, constituents, protestors, and agitators, we all influence public policy and could benefit from moral guidance. As representatives of our time in history, we might welcome the generational association with fundamental change that contributes to the evolution of humane society. Imagine the fulfillment undoubtedly felt by those today who can look back with pride on the roles they played in prompting the civil rights era of the 1960s. In contrast, consider how one might feel now if one had lived and acted on the other side of history—for example, as the owner of a segregated lunch counter or as a member of the Ku Klux Klan. Will a participant in today's Minuteman Project, patrolling the U.S.-Mexico border in the hunt for undocumented immigrants as if they were wild game, feel similar regret or suffer a stained legacy akin to that of the slave owners of prior generations? Might today's prosecutors look back with horror on their role in fostering the world's largest system of incarceration and one that disproportionately targets people of color? Might schoolchildren of today regret their shaming of gay students, as when 2012 presidential candidate Mitt Romney, as a student, cut the long hair of a crying gay classmate his friends held prone? Everyone, then, has a stake in their own personal legacy and, collectively, that of the current generation.

Moreover, with the advent of public electronic communication through the Internet, as noted above, vast numbers of U.S. residents regularly express opinions on contentious issues using the preserved record of blogs, comments on media websites, tweets, and more. Such a widespread preservable record of thought has never existed before, and therefore more of us have a stake in forming and articulating informed opinions that don't expose us to embarrassment in our lifetimes or beyond, when a legacy of regret is passed on to our descendants.

Toward that goal, in this book I identify and apply a moral compass, steeped in history, that can guide decision makers and all of us on our journey toward an advanced humanity and one that avoids moral blind spots. In doing so, I begin by expressing several limitations. Foremost is that I focus on policies and practices of the United States rather than of other countries. Particularly given my review of past regrettable U.S. practices and official government apologies to help identify a defining moral compass, it is possible that other nations have different histories of regret that may suggest a different lens. Nevertheless, the moral compass I identify has evident application elsewhere, and occasionally I draw on examples from other nations to support its predictive value.

As a related limitation in scope, my focus is primarily on domestic policies and practices rather than on U.S. foreign policy, although the moral framework I identify and apply has potential for application abroad. Many of the policies of regret that I identify, such as current immigration laws and abusive tactics in the ongoing War on Terror, also have international dimensions. Chapter 11 accordingly explores some of the ramifications the moral framework I propose holds for U.S. foreign policy, particularly in our military interventions.

Perhaps most significantly, I focus on policies applicable to groups of individuals and generally not on policies involving science or the environment. In large part this emphasis on humanity reflects the constraints of human knowledge in fields dependent on advances in medical and scientific knowledge. For example, we likely regret having used lead paint and asbestos in constructing buildings given what we know now about the health dangers of these materials to occupants. Our society now appreciates the health risks of tobacco use, alcohol during pregnancy, and high cholesterol. Tobacco is a good example of the difficulties of predicting some harms. If cigarettes were just being introduced in the consumer marketplace today with their risks known, no doubt they might be banned for their profoundly adverse health effects, if only for their second-hand impact on children and other occupants of the home or office where they are smoked. Yet these sorts of risks are extremely difficult to predict. It took years of medical studies to definitively identify and prove the grave health threats posed by smoking, and the knowledge we now have of the dangers of smoking doesn't readily translate to other products and practices. Might eating meat cause cancer, or using cell phones, or failing to sleep sufficiently? We are in large part dependent on science and experience to identify and warn us of risks, and generally these risks are difficult for us to predict in the absence of that experiential knowledge. Moreover, a fundamental difference in moral culpability exists between the questions "How could they have participated in something so terrible as slavery?" and "How could they have failed to know the dangers of smoking?" In regard to slavery, obvious human suffering is apparent. In fact, as addressed later in this book, only through dehumanizing their victims did the perpetrators perhaps blind themselves to the pain they inflicted, as we might stomp on a spider without remorse or moral quandary. The smoking question is more forgiving—the absence of human knowledge at the time meant that the public generally assumed product safety and at worst was negligent in not earlier identifying and acting on the risks as they became apparent.

We are at the mercy of science and experience for confirmation or identification of many of the potential risks that surround us. Environmentalists today might warn us that using fossil fuels rather than renewable energy, continuing our consumption-oriented economy, and failing to reverse or at least slow down climate change will eventually be seen as conduct that, putting regret aside, might seal the fate of the human race if universal recognition of peril comes too late. Animal-rights advocates might argue that our raising of animals for food and our experimentation on animals and use of them for entertainment all amount to an abuse we will regret as we learn more about the animal kingdom, the pain animals suffer, and the viable product alternatives that exist in agriculture.[11]

One of the constraints of scientific knowledge is disagreement among experts. Take, for instance, the subject of climate change, which some scientists believe is neither caused nor accelerated by humans or, if so, is part of a normal cycle that greater earth forces will correct.[12] It is difficult to imagine a moral framework that would resolve this debate, particularly one based on the human experience. While I submit that no informed person could doubt the realities of climate change, it still comes down to which set of experts is believed, and there is no external framework (save perhaps the thermometer and measurements of sea-level rises and ice-cap loss) that supplies guidance in predicting regret for the industrialization and consumerism that drive those global changes. In contrast, I submit that the issues I explore using the moral framework I propose are far less disputable in light of the historical experience of those oppressed by generations before us whose obvious suffering brought those issues into focus. I thus concentrate on policies of mistreatment of our fellow humans.

Despite that focus, many of the historical examples of regret that I examine are in fact interconnected with scientific and medical knowledge. For example, the eugenics movement of the early twentieth century, which prompted anti-immigration policies and compulsory sterilizations in the interest of creating a super-race, was based in part on scientific beliefs about mental disorders and intelligence and their hereditary transmission. Even segregation (and later, integration) of races was connected to advancement of knowledge. In its 1954 decision in *Brown v. Board of Education*, declaring that separate but ostensibly equal public education facilities were inherently unequal, the Supreme Court relied in part on psychological knowledge demonstrating that black children experience segregation as denoting their inferiority— knowledge that may not have existed when the Court endorsed segregation in 1896.[13]

Similarly, current areas of contested scientific knowledge often connect to human suffering and mistreatment. For example, rising sea levels, which many attribute to human influence, are starting to affect, in particular, communities of color near the shorelines of vulnerable nations.[14] Nevertheless, my focus is on policies, particularly federal and state laws, that more apparently and indisputably affect and harm vulnerable human groups.

*   *   *

I begin by surveying various potential frameworks for predicting regret, such as religious teachings and the standards of international human rights law. In considering and rejecting these and other predictive frameworks, Chapter 1 details historical instances of U.S. regret, as identified primarily by official federal or state apologies, for clues that should have been evident to policymakers and participants in such regrettable practices as slavery, lynching, Jim Crow laws, involuntary sterilizations of the mentally infirm, and land theft from and killings of Native Americans in the origins of the United States. The most common predictive thread running through these abhorrent policies and practices is the perceived lesser humanity of those we victimized, such as blacks, Natives, and the mentally disabled.

Applying this predictive framework of subhumanity to identify today's types of subordination, Chapter 2 reveals several current policies and practices that are ripe candidates for future regret. It also argues against any politicized origins of the predictive framework.

Next, I examine each of these potential landscapes of regret in detail, by specifying the nature of the subhuman construction of the particular group, the adverse legal and societal consequences that accompany the dehumanized image, and an agenda for reform should we start to humanize the vilified group.

Chapter 3 begins to apply the predictive framework using today's dehumanization of immigrants, particularly undocumented immigrants from Mexico, whom we construct as "illegals" and "aliens" and subject to restrictive immigration laws that ignore both ardent employer demand and willingness to hire undocumented immigrants and the immigrants' own compelling instincts for human survival. The chapter articulates what federal, state, and local policies might follow from a compassionate view of immigrant workers and their families.

Relatedly, Chapter 4 details the abuses of U.S. farmworkers, who increasingly are undocumented Mexican immigrants. Farmworkers are dehumanized and invisible in the production of our food supply and remain among the most vulnerable of our workers; they are engaged in dangerous and difficult work with scant financial reward.

Chapter 5 more broadly surveys the landscapes of poverty in the United States and concentrates on the two settings most commonly dehumanized and, in the first instance, racialized—welfare recipients, who are stigmatized as lazy, promiscuous welfare queens, and our homeless population, who are seen in subhuman terms as worthless street trash. Articulating a variety of reforms after critiquing existing welfare and homeless policies and practices, Chapter 5 ultimately suggests repairing these inequities by tackling the looming and greater inequity of our time: the spiraling income (and wealth) gap.

Chapter 6 addresses our dehumanization of the sexual identity and personhood of our lesbian, gay, bisexual, and transgender (LGBT) population, focusing on marriage inequality as well as the criminalizing of their sexuality while acknowledging some ongoing progress in legal recognition of the equal rights of sexual minorities.

Chapter 7 tackles the so-called monsters of death row, those criminals whose crimes are so appalling we have slated them for execution. Examining the historical evolution of execution from its racialized application to southern blacks and its use for crimes less severe than murder, this chapter also surveys how the means of execution evolved to include presumably more humane techniques. Nevertheless, the moral compass of subhumanity predicts we will regret our continued reliance on the death penalty, with or without its evident procedural flaws.

As Chapter 8 explains, the post–September 11th demonization of Muslims and Muslim-appearing individuals led to regrettable public and private backlash in the post-attack hysteria. Using religious profiling and a supposed propensity toward terrorism to encompass Muslims and those who appear Muslim, we view this poorly defined group as subhuman and evil. We hold particular disdain for those more particularly and individually accused of terrorist acts or designs, even resorting to enhanced interrogation techniques, a euphemism for torture.

Our progression toward humane treatment for some groups stretches across generations, illustrated here by the long U.S. history of oppressing blacks and women, which is detailed in Chapters 9 and 10. Although we may look back with disdain on past generations that enslaved blacks and denied women the right to vote and own marital property, these chapters question whether we have fully humanized these groups. In light of the current mass-incarceration campaign directed at blacks and the retention of legal control over a woman's body and her reproductive choices, we might ask how far removed, if at all, we are from the oppressive days we supposedly abhor. Chapter 9, in the case of African Americans, and Chapter 10, addressing women, suggest reforms to surmount the current oppression on what has proved to be the long road to humanity for these groups.

Chapter 11 briefly examines the history of our dehumanization of populations abroad, most notably in World War II, when on one front we were fighting Nazi Germany, which oppressed and murdered Jews as subhuman, while on another front we were bombing Japanese cities and civilians, whom we had dehumanized. Lessons examined in this chapter include those insights gained from the dehumanization of combat and the potential fluidity of the subhuman construction of our enemies.

Finally, the concluding chapter begins the task of repairing our generational image by restoring the humanity of these various vulnerable groups and ensuring our prescient legacy in the same process. Touching on the role of the media, government officials, teachers, schools, scholars, and all of us, this chapter assumes that the various compassionate reforms suggested throughout the book are achievable only if we view the target groups as equally human. Ultimately, although there is no silver bullet or magic formula for instilling compassion in the general public, a variety of approaches undertaken simultaneously stand the best chance of achieving success on what is likely a task of humanization that will span generations and that could start with our own.

*   *   *

A note on "we" and "us": Obviously it is problematic to essentialize the current generation(s) in asking how could "we" oppress vulnerable groups. For example, to the extent the reading audience consists of welfare recipients, or LGBT populations, or women, or other subordinated groups, it is important to acknowledge the potential separateness of this audience from those who are facilitating the ongoing subordination of the target group. Yet even dehumanized and subordinated individuals can contribute to the subordination of others—for example, when a gay voter supports restrictive immigration policy based on a misconception about the contributions and humanity of immigrants. Recognizing the imperfection of essentializing the audience of "we," this book nevertheless employs that reference as a reminder that "we" are all to some degree complicit in some or all the prevailing types of subordination detailed below. If not, then humanity has been moved that much forward.

1

Regret

Frameworks for Prediction

Hindsight is always twenty-twenty.
—Billy Wilder

I began this project with a strong sense that our mistreatment of immigrants was at the forefront of U.S. policies we would come to regret, but I lacked a framework to reinforce that instinct or to reveal other regrettable practices. The first few years of this research project, then, entailed a search for predictive clues—some moral compass to guide our policy choices. Below I discuss some of the frameworks I considered and rejected on the road to locating that trusty moral compass.

Having been steeped in Catholicism during my formative education in Los Angeles–area Catholic schools, I considered whether religious teachings might be an effective guide to predicting regret. Among the constraints on relying on religious tenets, however, is the vast array of religious faiths flourishing in the United States. Christianity, the dominant U.S. religion, alone includes the Orthodox, Catholic, and Protestant faiths. These Christian faiths follow the Bible as their religious text, perhaps signaling that we might rely on the Bible rather than, for example, the Quran or the Book of Mormon, as a moral compass for our times. No doubt millions of faithful U.S. churchgoers engage and embrace the teachings of the Bible in numbers that could, and often do, influence policymakers and translate into policies. Yet, as a predictive framework for regret, the Bible is deeply flawed.

Even if one were to ignore the alternate texts of other faiths and the millions of U.S. residents who fail to subscribe to any tenets of organized religion, the Bible is a poor predictor of regrettable practices. The Bible addressed injustices of the time but fails to keep pace with current societal dynamics of injustice, particularly those occurring along color lines. Among other problems, the Bible is full of vague and ambiguous text that can be interpreted to lend support to both sides of contentious issues. Moreover, the Bible can be read to support abominable practices and outcomes that any decent society has long left behind and that any civilized nation should disdain. Although the Bible does sympathetically address some of the contentious social problems raised in this book, particularly our ill treatment of the poor, in other areas it advocates barbaric policies. In both the Old and New Testaments, for example, the Bible embraces human slavery, instructing slaves to be obedient to their masters, "with fear and trembling," as they would obey Christ.[1] The Bible freely advocates death for a variety of offenses—for example: "The man who commits adultery with his neighbor's wife must die, he and his accomplice"[2]—a practice that today would indisputably and justifiably be deemed cruel and unusual punishment under the U.S. Constitution. The Bible suggests a rape victim might be punished by death for not sufficiently protesting her assault: "If within the city a man comes upon a maiden who is betrothed, and has relations with her, you shall bring them both out of the gate of the city and there stone them to death: the girl because she did not cry out for help though she was in the city, and the man because he violated his neighbor's wife."[3] Similarly, the Old Testament provides that "a priest's daughter who loses her honor by committing fornication and thereby dishonors her father . . . shall be burned to death."[4] Homosexuality is equally condemned: "If a man also lie with mankind, as he lieth with a woman, both of them have committed an abomination: they shall surely be put to death; their blood shall be upon them."[5] With the Bible as a moral template, then, we might resort to (or at least tolerate) human slavery and executing adulterers, promiscuous women, homosexuals, and even rape victims, hardly the prescription for decent society.

Proponents of religious scripture might respond that the Bible is a living text that must be interpreted in light of the human experience and that guidance should come primarily from its emphatic commandments, such as the Fifth Commandment's imperative, "Thou shalt not kill." Consistent with this view, the U.S. Catholic bishops in 1999 relied on the flawed experience of capital punishment to call on Catholics and other people of good conscience to reject execution.[6] But because

Catholics do not represent the majority of Christians in the United States, would this Catholic spiritual guidance and interpretation carry controlling weight in the face of contradictory readings? Moreover, are U.S. bishops or the Vatican the most appropriate body for definitive interpretation of Biblical teachings as a basis for U.S. policy?

No doubt religious scriptures, with their ancient origin and often unclear and conflicting directives, are a poor moral compass for predicting societal regret. Still, given our overwhelming reliance on religious faith as a guidepost for social policy and moral values, as is evident in the abortion debate, I occasionally consider what the result might be from religious teachings, either in support of or in contradiction to the moral framework I articulate below.

A human rights framework is another potential moral compass for predicting current policies of regret. As with religious tenets, the human rights perspective suffers from the uncertainty of which texts should govern U.S. policymaking—those that we joined and presumably already implement? What about the many formal expressions of human rights the United States has rejected?[7] Relatedly, there is the uncertainty of which promulgating body establishes definitive human rights standards for this purpose—the United Nations General Assembly? What about other organizations or even conferences such as the 2001 World Conference against Racism, Racial Discrimination, Xenophobia and Related Intolerance, which produced a widely cited Declaration after the United States and Israel withdrew from participation? Either way, reliance on international human rights supposes some consensus among nations on fundamental issues. This can be problematic given that compelling and unbending economic or other justifications often underlie abhorrent policies, as demonstrated by the once widespread embrace of slavery, which is nowhere near completely erased from human practice given the prevalence of sex and labor trafficking. Economic imperatives, in particular, can hamper agreement on human rights precepts and thus present the conundrum that if human rights principles should serve as our moral compass, then presumably we may never face the prospect of change in the prevailing economic order, such as the dictates of capitalism. Moreover, many human rights standards are phrased broadly and allow a nation to boast compliance while in practice flouting the likely spirit of those standards.

Despite my rejection of articulated international human rights as a moral compass to predict regret in the United States, much of the canvas of our regret predicted by the dehumanization model presented below is consistent with the picture that regard for international human rights would paint. Therefore, I often engage intersections with international standards of human rights for additional support of the model. In some instances, however, the dehumanization framework for predicting regret goes beyond existing human rights standards. For example, the international human rights model does not supply adequate protection for equality based on sexual orientation,[8] and human rights standards on the imposition or abolition of the death penalty have been developing only slightly ahead of trends in the U.S. courts and states, as discussed in Chapter 7.[9]

Another possible guidepost for regret is the historical tendency, both in the United States and abroad, for nations to react poorly in times of hysteria. For example, just weeks after Japan's attack on Pearl Harbor in December 1941, President Franklin Roosevelt signed an executive order authorizing the internment, in remote and abysmal detention camps, of Japanese Americans living near the Pacific Coast. The present controversy over torture of suspected terrorists might similarly be seen as a regrettable reaction to the public hysteria surrounding the September 11th terrorist attacks, as reinforced by the violation of international law regarding torture.[10] Similarly, calls today for an impenetrable border wall and Arizona's restrictive laws affecting immigrants and their families may be explained as overreactions to the supposed menace of undocumented immigrants arriving from Mexico. Economic hysteria too has prompted regrettable policies and practices, as during the economic stagnation of the 1880s, when we scapegoated Chinese immigrants and enacted a federal law to exclude their entry, and during the Great Depression and in the 1950s (Operation Wetback), when we aggressively deported Mexican immigrants en masse and even many U.S. citizens of Mexican heritage. Yet not all abhorrent policies and practices stem from public hysteria—for example, the institution of slavery, which survived for generations, was rooted in sustained economic and other supposed justifications rather than in some cataclysmic event or fear gripping the populace and prompting short-term overreaction. Our longstanding policies that subordinated and decimated Native Americans are another example of regrettable actions distinct from overreactions of the moment. Thus, hysteria as a guide may not reveal every moral blind spot.

Yet another predictor of regret is vigilante violence against particular groups, such as the historical record of the lynching of blacks, the domestic terrorism practiced by the Ku Klux Klan, and the modern-day private assaults on border-crossing undocumented immigrants and on LGBT residents. Although many of the policies and practices discussed in this book as landscapes of future regret share the common thread of violence against vulnerable groups, I contend that this violence is a consequence of subhuman constructions. As discussed below, in predicting regret we should more profitably focus on subhuman constructions generally than on their consequences, although the usual coincidence of violence and subhuman images does lend support to the accuracy of subhumanity as a moral compass.

In considering and rejecting the above and other models for a predictive framework of regret, I decided to examine historical instances of regret within the United States for common clues that should have been evident contemporaneously to policymakers and other participants. Initially, however, I had to decide how to identify those policies and practices that are shameful examples of regret. Are official apologies necessary to signal regret, and from which government actors? Might it be enough to claim universal acknowledgment and condemnation of practices now seen as foul? Does it matter that as a nation of individuals we fail to agree on almost everything, particularly on what deserves apology? Indeed some U.S. residents still support slavery, and some, in the instance of sexual and labor trafficking, still practice it despite human slavery's contravention of the rule of law. Pat Buchanan, for example, while not explicitly supporting slavery, echoed other contemporary conservative pundits in suggesting that slavery was a positive experience for blacks because in the United States blacks have "reached the greatest levels of freedom and prosperity blacks have ever known."[11] Supposedly, then, blacks should thank our forefathers who solicited their arrival as slaves. The number of U.S. residents who supported internment of Muslim Americans following the September 11th attacks suggests many still believe internment is justified on grounds of race, religion, and the like, rather than constituting a regrettable historical moment.

With these complications in mind, I looked both to official apologies from government entities and officials and, for confirmation, my own sense of our widespread societal acknowledgment of wrongdoing, to identify several policies and practices we might generally agree as a country were abhorrent and misguided. First, no doubt our nation (the above naysayers excluded) regrets the despicable practice of slavery and the vestiges of slavery enforced in segregationist Jim Crow laws. In 2003, for example, President George W. Bush called slavery "one of the greatest crimes of history."[12] The U.S. House of Representatives apologized for slavery, finally, by resolution in 2008, and for Jim Crow laws, joined by the Senate in 2009. The Senate Resolution recognized that millions of enslaved Africans were "brutalized, humiliated, dehumanized, and subjected to the indignity of being stripped of their names and heritage" between 1619 and 1865. Even after slavery ended, African Americans experienced "virulent racism, lynchings, disenfranchisement, Black Codes, and racial segregation laws that imposed a rigid system of officially sanctioned racial segregation in virtually all areas of life." Accordingly, the Senate Resolution, in acknowledging "the fundamental injustice, cruelty, brutality, and inhumanity of slavery and Jim Crow laws," apologized to African Americans for "wrongs committed against them and their ancestors who suffered under slavery and Jim Crow laws."[13]

Related to the horrors of slavery is the post-slavery legacy of murder by lynching. Carried out primarily in the South against African Americans, the lynchings of more than forty-five hundred people took place from 1882 to 1968, according to conservative estimates.[14] Many of these lynchings were carried out in accord with the terrible sentiment expressed in 1930 by a southern U.S. Senator, Thomas Heflin, who stated, "Whenever a Negro crosses this dead line between the white and the Negro races and lays his black hand on a white woman, he deserves to die."[15] Blues legend Billie Holiday sang tragically of the "strange fruit" of black bodies hanging from southern trees in what *Time* magazine ultimately named the "Song of the Century."[16] State and local governments either ignored or sometimes actively participated in these murders, which were often staged in a festive carnival atmosphere. Finally, the U.S. Senate apologized in 2005 for its failure to pass federal antilynching legislation and for thus tolerating the domestic terrorism of racialized lynchings.[17]

Second, in a similar vein, we can surely lament as a country our mistreatment of Native Americans, although not to the extent of giving up our comfortable residences on once-tribal lands. As acknowledged in a draft resolution reported favorably from the U.S. Senate Committee on Indian Affairs in 2009, the conclusions of which were embodied in the 2010 Department of Defense Appropriations Act, our nation subjected Native Peoples to "official depredations and ill-conceived policies." As outlined in the draft resolution, the United States forced Natives off their traditional homelands onto reservations, caused one-fourth of the Cherokee nation to perish in their infamous forced removal—the one-thousand-mile Trail of Tears, launched bloody attacks such as the Wounded Knee Massacre of 1890, stole tribal land (more than two billion acres acquired in one-sided treaties) and other tribal resources, and forcibly removed Native children from their homes and sent them to distant boarding schools to erase their cultural heritage and languages. Accordingly, Congress apologized in the Defense Appropriations Act "to all Native Peoples for the many instances of violence, maltreatment, and neglect inflicted on Native Peoples."[18] Similarly, Congress by joint resolution in 1993 apologized to Native Hawaiians for the U.S. overthrow of the Kingdom of Hawai'i in 1893 and the resultant "deprivation of the rights of Native Hawaiians to self-determination."[19] Congress, however, has not apologized for the similar acquisition of sovereignty over the island of Puerto Rico in the same imperialistic decade. Unlike the state of Hawai'i, Puerto Rico remains in legal limbo as a U.S. territory. Its residents have neither voting representation in Congress nor the ability to vote for the U.S. president yet are subjected to absolute and plenary Congressional authority to impose laws the islanders abhor, such as the federal death penalty.[20]

Third, the internment of 120,000 Japanese Americans in miserable, isolated detention camps during World War II is another obvious policy of regret, as reflected in 1988 Congressional legislation, signed by President Ronald Reagan, that apologized for this mass relocation and imprisonment, which was motivated by "racial prejudice, wartime hysteria, and a failure of political leadership" and "carried out without adequate security reasons and without any act of espionage or sabotage." Moreover, Congress appropriated funds for public education to prevent the recurrence of such an event and for restitution to those interned.[21] At the same time, however, Congress has offered no official apology for the atomic devastation of Hiroshima and Nagasaki during World War II.[22]

When I began thinking about societal regret, the above three examples from our history— of slavery/lynchings, the annihilation and displacement of Natives, and the internment of Japanese Americans—were foremost in my mind as those historical policies I would regret having facilitated in any way. My study of government apology yielded additional examples of regrettable law (or, in the case of lynching, absence of law) and social policy.

Our immigration history includes the 1882 Chinese Exclusion Act, the first U.S. law to ban immigration on the basis of race or nationality. Effective until the mid-twentieth century and joined by broader laws and treaties known as the Asian Exclusion Laws, the Chinese Exclusion Act also denied Chinese laborers already in the United States the possibility of obtaining U.S. citizenship. More than a century later, in 2011, the U.S. Senate formally apologized for that Exclusion Act, as did the House in 2012.[23]

President Bill Clinton apologized in 1997 for the infamous, forty-eight-year Tuskegee Syphilis Experiment, in which the U.S. Public Health Services withheld penicillin from 399 black men with that venereal affliction, who were dehumanized and used as laboratory rats. Ultimately, twenty-eight died from syphilis and one hundred more from related complications, while some of their spouses contracted the disease and some of their children were born with congenital syphilis.[24] Similarly, the United States intentionally infected hundreds of Guatemalans (mostly prisoners, the mentally ill, and women) with syphilis between 1946 and 1948, aiming to study the disease. In 2010, Secretary of State Hillary Clinton apologized for this international affront to humanity, expressing outrage "that such reprehensible research could have occurred under the guise of public health."[25]

Related to these outrageous domestic and international syphilis experiments were the forced sterilizations conducted in the twentieth century under color of state law. Prompted by the eugenics movement, which also influenced U.S. immigration policy, the idea of engineering some super-gene pool led more than half the states in the early 1900s to enact compulsory sterilization laws covering certain criminals, epileptics, the mentally ill, and the feebleminded. Adolf Hitler copied this heinous social policy in Germany and expanded it to encompass those with physical deformities and alleged hereditary conditions such as blindness, as well as to alcoholics and drug addicts.[26] Performed on tens of thousands of women in the U.S. states as well as on Native American women and on Latinas in Puerto Rico, the practice of involuntary sterilizations slowed considerably in the 1940s as reason took hold.[27] Several states (including Virginia, North Carolina, South Carolina, California, and Indiana) issued apologies for their compulsory sterilization programs. Apologizing in 2003, South Carolina's governor acknowledged that the victims of eugenics under the state law directed at those diagnosed with "insanity, idiocy, imbecility, feeble-mindedness, or epilepsy" were mostly blacks and women.[28] North Carolina's sterilization program, the subject of an official apology in 2002 and a legislative grant in 2013 of compensation for victims, lasted from 1929 to 1974 and encompassed children as young as age ten and, by the 1960s, mostly young black women.[29] California's governor apologized in 2003 for the state's forced sterilization program, which sterilized twenty thousand patients in state hospitals who were diagnosed with lunacy, feeblemindedness, sexual deviancy, or epilepsy, among other conditions.[30] Virginia's governor issued a formal apology in 2002 for the state's sterilization of about 7,450 residents from 1924 to 1979.[31]

Examining these various regrettable policies and practices, all of which prompted official apologies, reveals several commonalities. First, the U.S. Supreme Court upheld most of these practices in their heyday, anointing them with the so-called rule of law. Probably the most discussed case of regret, *Dred Scott v. Sandford*, upheld the institution of slavery and the rights of slave owners over their legal property—slaves.[32] In its opinion, written by a former slave owner, the Court concluded a black slave was not a citizen under the U.S. Constitution and thus could not invoke the jurisdiction of federal courts. Moreover, a Congressional law prohibiting slavery in certain regions, known as the Missouri Compromise, was held void under the Constitution, which "distinctly and expressly affirmed" the right of property in a slave and obligated the federal government to protect that property should a slave escape from his or her owner. The upshot of this 1857 decision was to deny freedom to a black slave who had been taken into territory where slavery was outlawed, thus effectively treating him as a transportable chattel rather than as a human being with prospects for freedom. Later, in 1896, the Supreme Court approved state-mandated racial segregation in its *Plessy v. Ferguson* decision, upholding a Louisiana "separate car" law that required black train passengers to ride in "colored-only" cars.[33]

Native peoples fared equally poorly—for example, under the Supreme Court ruling in 1823 of *Johnson v. M'Intosh,* which is still the law of the land, so to speak.[34] In deciding the preeminence of land title derived from the U.S. government, the Supreme Court justified the U.S. acquisition of Native land by force as a title by conquest from "fierce savages" that the courts were powerless to deny. The Supreme Court thus validated the theft of Native land, supplying the foundation for today's protection of property rights largely to the exclusion of Native peoples. As legal scholar Robert Williams wrote in examining the abhorrent imagery the Court relied on for this ruling, if invoked today the Court's characterizations of Natives as savages "would be regarded as not only being in bad racial taste but as grossly violative of a host of contemporary international human rights standards relative to indigenous tribal peoples."[35] Later, in 1955, the Supreme Court adhered to the *M'Intosh* precedent to deny an Alaskan tribe compensation for timber extracted from land the tribe claimed to own from time immemorial; after "savage" tribes had lost their land by discovery and conquest, they remained in possession only with "permission from the whites."[36]

During World War II, the Supreme Court upheld the conviction of a Japanese American, Fred Korematsu, who was arrested in Northern California after he refused to report to his internment detention camp.[37] Denying Korematsu's challenge to the constitutionality of wartime detention as violating his due-process and equal-protection rights, the Court deferred to the imperatives of military necessity to justify internment.

Rejecting a constitutional challenge to the Chinese Exclusion Act, the Supreme Court in 1889 deferred to the absolute, plenary power of Congress to admit immigrants and wrote that if Congress "considers the presence of foreigners of a different race in this country, who will not assimilate with us, to be dangerous to its peace and security . . . its determination is conclusive upon the judiciary."[38]

During the throes of the eugenics movement in 1927, the Supreme Court, in an 8-1 decision, upheld the constitutionality of Virginia's mandatory sterilization law targeting the feebleminded, insane, and other institutionalized persons.[39] Its decision allowed the sterilization of Carrie Buck, deemed a "moral imbecile" and committed at age seventeen to the Virginia Colony for Epileptics and Feebleminded, the same institution where her certified "feebleminded" mother resided.[40] Carrie's infant daughter, Vivian, was also tested and deemed to be of below-average intelligence, thus prompting the infamous slur from Justice Holmes that "three generations of imbeciles are enough."

Second, another commonality in these regrettable U.S. policies is that justifications in the interest of public health or safety or of the economy were offered for all of them. Often, the Supreme Court articulated these justifications to support its upholding these laws and practices. Even the most objectionable policies had some ostensible rationale for the greater good. For example, in upholding the Virginia sterilization law, Justice Holmes drew a comparison between eugenics and patriotism and also invoked public safety:

> We have seen more than once that the public welfare may call upon the best citizens for their lives. It would be strange if it could not call upon those who already sap the strength of the State for these lesser sacrifices [of sterilization] . . . in order to prevent our being swamped by incompetence. It is better for all the world, if instead of waiting to execute degenerate offspring for crime, or to let them starve for their imbecility, society can prevent those who are manifestly unfit from continuing their kind. The principle that sustains compulsory vaccination is broad enough to cover cutting the Fallopian tubes.[41]

In the Japanese American internment decision of *Korematsu*, the Supreme Court relied on military necessity of "the gravest imminent danger to the public safety" to justify racialized exclusion.[42]

The sometimes ruthless imperative of economic prosperity helped drive the despicable institution of slavery as did the unbelievably paternalistic notion that masters somehow protected their black slaves from worse harm by offering them food, shelter, and medical care in exchange for their labor.[43] Slavery created wealth for many slave owners and their descendants, and Thomas Jefferson, himself a slave owner, acknowledged that "slaves provided the labor that made the southern economy possible."[44] Similar economic justifications underlay the Supreme Court's embrace of Manifest Destiny and of land development to the exclusion of Natives. As Supreme Court Chief Justice John Marshall wrote in the *M'Intosh* decision to justify government conquest of Natives and their land, "The tribes of Indians inhabiting this country were fierce savages, whose occupation was war, and whose subsistence was drawn chiefly from the forest. To leave them in possession of their country, was to leave the country a wilderness."[45]

Third, despite the veneer of some of these once rational-sounding justifications proffered to buttress these policies of national regret, on close examination one compelling explanation underlies their adoption and implementation. It is the thread that runs through all the sad history detailed in this book and the current injustices slated for future regret—the perceived lesser humanity of the targets and victims of the various laws and practices. As illustrated in the *M'Intosh* decision, Natives were seen as violent "savages." Once conquered by white settlers, we governed them, in the words of the Supreme Court, as their "superiors of a different race."[46] Subhuman images demarcated the other victimized groups. A U.S. Senator from California, James Phelan, described Japanese in 1920 as "immoral people" who would mongrelize our country.[47] During World War II, we constructed Japanese as menacing subhuman threats—likened to "monkeys, baboons, gorillas, dogs, rodents, rattlesnakes, vipers, cockroaches, bees, [and] ants," while at the same time superhuman in being "monstrously large or strong, preternaturally cunning and devious; resistant to pain," as well as disloyal.[48] Exclusion of Chinese immigrants under the 1882 Chinese Exclusion Act was based on widespread "yellow" journalism, which depicted the Chinese as willing to consume rats, and Chinatowns as "filthy breeding grounds of depravity, degradation, and disease—in short, a serious and imminent moral and physical threat to public health and welfare."[49] In 1896, Supreme Court Justice John Marshall Harlan explained that the Chinese race "is so different from our own that we do not permit those belonging to it to become citizens of the United States."[50] Relatedly, then-prevailing conceptions of Puerto Ricans as an "inferior race" and of Filipinos as subhuman monkeys underlie the decisions of the Supreme Court in the early-twentieth-century "insular cases," which legitimized U.S. territorial acquisitions and confirmed the subordinate legal status of their inhabitants.[51]

African Americans were regarded as savage, menacing brutes;[52] their subhuman status was no better described than by the U.S. Supreme Court in refusing to recognize them as protected by the U.S. Constitution. Summarizing the subordinate societal regard of African Americans at the time of our founding, in 1857 the Court remarked:

> [They had] for more than a century before been regarded as beings of an inferior order, and altogether unfit to associate with the white race, either in social or political relations; and so far inferior, that they had no rights which the white man was bound to respect; and that the negro might justly and lawfully be reduced to slavery for his benefit. He was bought and sold, and treated as an ordinary article of merchandise and traffic, whenever a profit could be made by it. This opinion was at the time fixed and universal in the civilized portion of the white race.[53]

Thomas Jefferson was of the same mind, writing that blacks were "inferior to the whites in . . . body and mind" and lamenting that blacks cannot utter a "thought above the level of plain narration."[54] A notable Georgia lawyer, Thomas Reade Rootes Cobb, wrote in 1858 that blacks were so mentally inferior that slavery supplied them "the greatest degree of perfection of which [their] nature is capable."[55] Similarly, the eugenics movement regarded the feebleminded as subhuman threats to be institutionalized and sterilized to prevent their taint on the human race.

The connection between dehumanization and odious practices is evident too in recent history's most discussed massacre, the slaughter of millions of Jews and of other dehumanized groups such as Gypsies, the developmentally disabled and mentally ill, and homosexuals, in the horror of Hitler-led Nazi Germany. The Nazi regime carried out its deadly eugenics agenda using, among other methods, lethal injections, firing squads, and the gas chamber; the technology of gas-chamber executions was borrowed from the United States, which employed them to execute death-row inmates. These Nazi victims were deemed "lives unworthy of life."[56] Propaganda in "The Subhuman," a pamphlet distributed to Germans in the millions of copies, articulated how some human beings were not worthy of humanity and fell beneath even animals: "The subhuman, that biologically seemingly complete similar creature of nature with hands, feet, and a kind of brain, with eyes and a mouth, is nevertheless a completely different, dreadful creature. He is only a rough copy of a human being, with human-like facial traits but nonetheless morally and mentally lower than any animal. Within this creature there is a fearful chaos of wild, uninhibited passions, nameless destructiveness, the most primitive desires, the nakedest vulgarity. Subhuman, otherwise nothing. For all that bear a human face are not equal."[57]

More than anyone else, Hitler propagated a subhuman construction by contending that "the Jews are undoubtedly a race, but not human,"[58] in suggesting that marriages between Jews and Aryans produce "monstrous beings, half man, half monkey," and in calling Jews and Aryans as "widely separated as man from beast."[59] Germany ultimately apologized for the slaughter of six million Jews it had once regarded as a "parasitic race" that threatened racial purity.[60]

Surely, as played out globally in other horrific and even ongoing genocides, dehumanization leads to terrible and regrettable consequences. Yet, dehumanization can serve as a moral compass for compassionate policymakers and the public to foresee the potential for societal regret and to thus alter the course of history during the current generation.

2

What Dehumanization Predicts

The Landscapes of Future Regret

What we are now witnessing in the 21st century is the frac-
ture or complete breakdown of families, societies, and governments as a result of centuries of dehumanization that
have taken a toll. More natural disasters (tsunamis, earth-
quakes, hurricanes, tornados, etc.) merely uncover the reality of the natural disasters we have created by granting sanctuary to dehumanization via the law.
—Liza Lugo

Armed with the moral compass of dehumanization, we can readily map
the landscapes of future regret. As explored in subsequent chapters, as
a society we tend to regard undocumented immigrants (the majority
of them Mexican), farmworkers (the vast majority of them Mexican),
welfare recipients and the homeless, homosexuals, Muslims and
Muslim-appearing individuals, and death-row inmates as subhuman.
Although we may not view death-row inmates, commonly seen as vile
monsters, in the exact same way in which we view so-called welfare
queens, at bottom our generalized lack of regard for these and other
dehumanized groups leads to laws and practices that can endanger
and even extinguish the lives, freedom, and dignity of millions of U.S.
residents.

The chapters to follow address each of these dehumanized groups,
with examples of their subhuman construction and discussion of the
legal and societal consequences that flow from these negative images,
along with the possibilities for transforming their treatment should we
soften our views. Preliminarily, in this chapter I address these dehumanized groups together to demonstrate that facially compelling public-safety and economic justifications are proffered to justify the con-
tinuation of policies detrimental to them. Moreover, the rule of law,

often as bolstered by Supreme Court opinions, anchors many of these detrimental policies and practices. Thus, without the moral compass of dehumanization to reveal how we might be mistreating and misjudging these groups, we might readily be seduced by the interrelated combination of compelling justifications and the rule of law to regard our current policies as beyond reproach. Examined through the lens of dehumanization, however, many of our current practices and laws that we take for granted are catalysts for eventual societal regret and must be dismantled if we are to stake our legacy as a compassionate and prescient generation.

Chapter 3 details how we regard undocumented immigrants as menacing subhumans and accordingly imperil them through restrictive immigration laws and practices that aim to repel and intercept these interlopers. Justifications abound for the hostile treatment of undocumented immigrants specifically and of immigrants, regardless of their legal status, more generally. We tend to conflate undocumented laborers with criminals, drug dealers, welfare cheats, and even terrorists, thus positioning them as a danger to public safety and our economic well-being.[1] We regard them as inassimilable threats to a Eurocentric vision of U.S. culture.[2] We view them as taking jobs from U.S. citizens while not paying their fair share of taxes. We designate them as "illegals" for their original sin of unlawful passage or presence in the United States, and once we see them as illegal, we perceive them as inclined to commit any crimes against humanity they may happen upon.[3] Immigrants, whether documented or not, further alarm us because of fears that population growth will imperil the environment. With this laundry list of safety and economic justifications for restrictive border policy and aggressive interdiction of undocumented immigrants within the United States, it is not surprising that our laws and practices mirror and match the fervor of these perceived threats.

Farmworkers, addressed in Chapter 4, are mostly Latino/a and often are undocumented, a situation that prompts some of the same immigration concerns. Longstanding economic justifications rooted in the necessity of having an affordable and uninterrupted food supply also underlie the oppressive treatment of farmworkers; these justifications are grounded in the mistaken assumption that to supply a living wage would imperil the health of other U.S. residents who might no longer be able to afford their grocery bill. Similar justifications accompanied slavery, as some argued that slave labor produced agricultural products—such as cotton, sugar, rice, and tobacco—that were vital to the nation's economy.[4]

Addressed in Chapter 5, America's poor are hampered by restrictive welfare reform, minimum-wage levels far below a living wage, and an inadequate supply of affordable housing. Justifications for their continued ill-treatment are economic growth and fairness as well as public safety. Proposals to shrink wage inequities by raising the minimum wage and taxing the wealthy are countered by economic arguments that the minimum wage (even when well below a living wage) kills jobs and economic growth. Restrictive welfare reforms are said to guard against welfare cheats, and in any event welfare is seen as fostering dependence and shame and thus as detrimental to the poor. Many consider the homeless urban poor a threat to public safety and contend that they should be criminalized and driven from contact and view.

Oppressive policies against gay and lesbian residents are ostensibly justified by concerns for public safety—consider, for example, socialite Paris Hilton's crude insult to gay men in 2012: "most of them probably have AIDS"[5]—as well as unfounded fears for the welfare of children in same-sex families and even for the reproductive survival of the nation.

Capital punishment of convicted murderers is urged for its supposed deterrent effect on heinous crimes. Similarly, torture of suspected terrorists is advocated by many for the greater good of preventing the death of innocents. Racial profiling of Muslims and Muslim-appearing individuals is urged with the same aim: preventing innocent deaths through detecting terrorist plots.

As noted above, past horrors were justified too on public-safety grounds. Proponents defended the heinous practice of lynching blacks in the U.S. South as necessary to protect white women from sexual assault at the hands of black men.[6] In Nazi Germany, Hitler justified the extermination of Jews as a public-safety measure; having constructed the Jews as a "parasite" and a "harmful bacillus," he stated that mass murder was necessary "so that no harm is caused by them."[7] Relatedly, U.S. radio host Neal Boortz labeled Islam, seen by some as a catalyst for terrorism, as a "deadly virus spreading through Europe and the West."[8]

In addition to the above justifications, most of the existing oppressive U.S. policies against undocumented immigrants, the poor, gay and lesbian residents, and other groups are legitimized by the rule of law. For example, as Chapter 7 details, the constraint on cruel and unusual punishment in the U.S. Constitution fails to bar all executions. While over time narrowing the crimes and the defendants for which capital punishment is available, the Supreme Court nonetheless views execution as permissible for some offenses and some offenders, permission several states readily accept. On the immigration front, the Supreme Court defers to the plenary power of Congress and the executive to dictate restrictive immigration policy, which Congress has obliged. As addressed in Chapter 5, the Supreme Court refuses to recognize a constitutional right to housing for the homeless, thus sanctioning their mistreatment on city streets. The Supreme Court has made progress in forging humane policies for gay and lesbian residents, such as by striking down discriminatory criminal sodomy laws and, in 2013, the federal Defense of Marriage Act, which denied federal benefits to married same-sex couples;[9] but other restrictive policies, aside from recent success in challenging state prohibitions on same-sex marriage, have thus far withstood most judicial scrutiny.[10] On the twin fronts of the War on Drugs and the War on Terror, the rule of law singles out communities of color and religious beliefs for profiling, feeding our system of mass incarceration and our propensity to fight terror with our military and law enforcement at any societal cost.

The rule of law sometimes complicates reform, most starkly when undocumented immigrants seek laws to regularize their status and supply a pathway to citizenship. Here, the stain of undocumented status constructs their identity as "illegals" and impedes the compassion needed for reform. Relatedly, the horrible crimes of death-row inmates, in their affront to the rule of law, render them unlikely to garner sympathy and reconsideration of their sentences. Accused terrorists are similarly situated.

*   *   *

In mapping the landscape of regret, it occurred to me that most, if not all, of the reforms I urge on behalf of the various vilified groups

I address are contrary to current conservative platforms (in contrast, the Republican party was founded in the mid-nineteenth century by opponents of slavery who saw the humanity of its victims). The disconnect between my proposals and conservative views raises the suspicion that the reforms I propose are simply a restatement of liberal ideals rather than having a more organic origin that might resonate with conservative audiences mindful of their own legacies. Here I address and rebut that suspicion.

Admittedly, in the aggregate the policies I suggest clash with conservative agendas. In 2013, for example, most Republican politicians opposed legalization for the millions of undocumented immigrants residing and working in the United States, opposed raising the minimum wage to help the working poor, supported the death penalty, and opposed same-sex marriage. Moreover, in regard to the issues discussed in Chapters 9 and 10—the War on Drugs (and the consequent mass imprisonment of African Americans) and reproductive rights—most Republican politicians are "law-and-order" proponents who support restrictive drug laws and their enforcement and who oppose a woman's right to reproductive choice.

Most of the reforms I suggest, however, clash too with the policy agendas of many Democrats. Although President Barack Obama's position on gay marriage evolved between his election in 2008 and 2012, when he became the first president to support same-sex marriage while in office, many other Democrats continue to oppose same-sex marriage, as reflected in the clear majorities of Democratic Senators and Representatives who enacted the federal Defense of Marriage Act in 1996 with the signature of President Clinton. Although more support for the death penalty resides within the Republican Party (73 percent of Republicans polled in 2012 believed that the death penalty is morally acceptable), many Democrats (42 percent in the same poll) favor capital punishment.[11] In regard to immigration enforcement, President Obama's administration has deported more undocumented immigrants than were deported during President George W. Bush's presidency. Like recent presidents before him, President Obama has continued to prosecute the War on Drugs, which devastates communities of color.

Rather than being simply a restatement of liberal ideals, the predictive moral compass I adopt here functions more organically by supplying a framework for societal regret. I started this project with a sense of regret for how the nation treats immigrants, but little else was clear until the lens of subhuman constructions emerged. Indeed, as I discuss in Chapter 7, the moral compass of sub/humanity even clashes, at least in principle, with my own long-held support for the death penalty—a belief I have begun to rethink and move beyond in light of its inconsistency with the respect for humanity and equality that resonates in this book. Relatedly, my own views on the propriety of torture have vacillated over the years, particularly when it is presented alongside the unlikely doomsday scenario of a terrorist plot set in motion with millions at risk, a plot that could be defused should one recalcitrant suspect reveal critical details.

I challenge conservative readers to construct their own moral compass but not one shaped simply by economic and public-safety arguments. As outlined above, even the most reprehensible policies and practices, such as slavery and the internment of Japanese American families, were justified at the time by seemingly compelling arguments of economic necessity and public safety. Those justifications, as I have argued above, supply no immunity from regrettable practices. Rather, the framework would need to derive from those past instances of regret I have described or would need to supply some more viable protocol for identifying examples of past regrettable policies that in turn supports a conservative agenda. For example, one possible framework for regret that conservatives might advocate is based on the value of human life. Presumably on that agenda would be restrictive immigration reform (under the false assumption that immigrants are especially prone to violent criminal conduct) and reproductive choice. Capital punishment is the rub, here, but presumably the supposed deterrent effects of execution on prospective killers would be argued to override the death toll of condemned inmates.[12] By this same logic, however, the past failures of U.S. policy identified above might be justified in similar terms. For example, more lives might be spared through medically experimenting on vulnerable groups, as was done to research syphilis, than on foregoing these practices because the resulting medical breakthroughs might allow others to die or suffer less. The mass internment of Japanese Americans was justified to protect against loss of life through insurrection. Obviously, then, a moral compass that would not have signaled these shameful policies and practices is a flawed predictive tool.

Conservatives who believe that somehow we have already transcended racism and attained a postracial United States might suggest some kind of racialized moral compass that avoids overt racial injustice. Wielding such a predictive framework, they might accordingly point to affirmative-action policies as the most blatant example today of what they would label (reverse) racism.[13] Similarly, conservatives have attacked ethnic studies curriculum as teaching racial hate under the guise of studying white privilege. They might effectively characterize past regrettable practices, such as slavery, segregation, and even internment, as examples of overt racialized injustice. Yet some instances of past regret I have identified are not readily racialized, particularly forced sterilization laws, outside of their often-racial application in the South. In a broader sense, viewing race as a social construction by which society groups individuals together and then elevates or subordinates those groups in relation to each other can explain much of the landscape of regret I map below.[14] For example, society groups homosexuals together in a demeaning way and subjects them to deleterious policies in a manner that mirrors racialization in the past and present. Moreover, even when more traditional racial discrimination along color lines is evident, as with the current attacks on immigrants that thinly veil an anti-Mexican or anti-Latino/a animus, most conservatives believe, somehow, that repressive immigration policies are racially neutral because immigrants might be persons of any background. Any moral compass based on race, then, is problematic as it is too readily manipulable based on how race and racial inequities are constructed at the moment.

*   *   *

The chapters that follow map the current subordination of several groups we have effectively dehumanized—including Mexican immigrants, farmworkers, the poor receiving welfare, the homeless, sexual minorities, murderers awaiting execution, and Muslims and those of Muslim appearance. Describing the contours of the various subhuman constructions, along with deleterious policy consequences and the prospective agendas for reform should we humanize these groups, these chapters paint a dismal portrait of ongoing dehumanization in the United States.

In addition to their shared dehumanization and the other commonalities addressed above, these groups are linked to the recipients of past official apologies by our efforts to exclude them all from so-called civilized and decent society. Depending on our needs, we employed different tactics to effectively exclude their presence and participation in society. For Native Americans, we exterminated many and relocated the rest to reservations away from the prime real estate of Anglo occupation and expansionist designs.[15] We prohibited entry of Asians through harsh immigration laws and interned many Japanese Americans in remote detention camps. For the mentally ill, we excluded them through restrictive immigration laws outlawing entry of persons of "psychopathic inferiority," which once additionally encompassed homosexuals.[16] We imprisoned homosexuals for expressing their sexuality, thereby excluding them from normal lives in our communities, and we involuntarily sterilized the mentally ill and infirm, hoping to exclude later generations with these supposed hereditary conditions from sharing our communities. We delivered the ultimate message of exclusion to those convicted of capital crimes—their execution. We killed suspected terrorists instead of capturing them, or we tortured them and kept them in secret detention. For others, however, particularly those groups on which we depended for labor, exclusion was more challenging. Although we once considered the prospect of deporting freed black slaves to Africa, our agricultural labor needs prevailed. Yet we kept blacks away from whites through segregation in schools, neighborhoods, restaurants, and more, and today by their mass incarceration in the U.S. prison system as often lighter-skinned immigrant groups replace their labor. Our efforts and desires to exclude Mexican immigrant laborers, particularly farm laborers, are balanced by our cyclical and even seasonal dependence on their labor; the result is the pattern of invitation and forced exile detailed in Chapters 3 and 4. Although we might exclude poor immigrants through immigration laws denying entry of "public charges," our economy seems reliant on the payment of low wages, a practice that impoverishes many U.S. families while it recruits vulnerable and desperate undocumented immigrants. Part of this bargain of economic dependence is that generally we don't formally exclude the poor from our landscapes, at least our occupational ones (apart from the gate-guarded havens of the rich), unless the poor become homeless and thus are effectively considered criminals because of their homelessness. As detailed in Chapter 10, we once even excluded women from the workplace outside the home and from higher education and the voting booth. All these exclusions, when viewed together, signal that we kill those from dehumanized groups whom we can, keep others out of sight or control them in prisons, and tolerate the rest when they serve larger societal needs, especially for labor. Finding and forging humanity, however difficult against this background, initially demands recognition of those in our presence whom we have dehumanized, some for generations. The following chapters begin that task.

3

Aliens, Illegals, Wetbacks, and Anchor Babies

The Dehumanization of Immigrant Workers and Their Families

No human being is illegal.
—Howard Zinn

Foremost in my mind in drawing this broad canvas of societal regret is our shameful and demeaning treatment of undocumented immigrants as less than human—as "aliens," "illegals," and "wetbacks"—as what a California state senator, William Craven in 1993, meant in referring to the children of undocumented immigrants as a people "perhaps on the lower scale of our humanity."[1] During the previous two decades, when I championed the legacy of immigrants to the United States, documented or not, I had no doubt about the humanity of immigrants and therefore the virtues of my promoting compassionate immigration policies. Ignoring vicious hate mail that told me to go back to Mexico, despite the reality of my birth in East Los Angeles to U.S.-citizen parents,[2] I believed that my life work on behalf of immigrants promoted the dignified side of history.

By no means is mine the sole voice contending our current immigration policies, and hostile attitudes toward immigrants, are a national embarrassment we will come to regret. As the *New York Times* warned in a 2008 editorial, "Someday the country will recognize the true cost of its war on illegal immigration. We don't mean dollars, though those are being squandered by the billions. The true cost is to the national identity: the sense of who we are and what we value. It will hit us once the enforcement fever breaks, when we look at what has been done and no longer recognize the country that did it."[3] Similarly, writing in 2007 for *The Nation*, Peter Schrag forecasted national regret while comparing our current treatment of immigrants to the Red Scare of the 1920s or the McCarthy era of the 1950s, "when the nation became unhinged; politicians panicked; and scattershot federal, state and local assaults led to unfocused, and often cruel, harassment."[4]

Despite these influential voices of reason, overall the dialogue on immigration remains decidedly vicious toward newcomers. Although some voice hostility toward all immigrants, regardless of their origin and legal status, much venom today is directed particularly at Latino/a immigrants, especially undocumented Latino/a immigrants. For the most part, these groups are conflated into the image of the menacing Latino/a immigrant, an image that dominates discourse on current U.S. immigration policy. Although the discussion below suggests that as a nation we will come to regret our disdain for undocumented (Latino/a) immigrants, the restrictive and repressive U.S. immigration policies prompted by these derogatory constructions negatively affect other groups caught in the draconian enforcement net and prevailing anti-immigrant sentiment. These include documented immigrants from all backgrounds and even U.S.-citizen Mexican Americans and other citizen Latinos/as because attacks on undocumented immigrants, ostensibly race neutral, are sometimes intended and deployed to reach all Latinos/as.

As discussed below, throughout the history of U.S. immigration, we have isolated certain target groups for backlash and abusive immigration policies. Today, that group is Latino/a immigrants, particularly those from Mexico. The derogatory moniker "wetback" singles out undocumented immigrants crossing into the United States from Mexico by swimming or floating across the Rio Grande or other waterways such as the treacherous All-American Canal, called the most dangerous body of water in the United States because of the many immigrant lives it has claimed.[5] The slur continues to have currency. As Alaska's sole congressman, Don Young, recounted in a radio program in 2013, his father's farm in California once had "50 to 60 wetbacks to pick tomatoes." Although the equally demeaning slurs of "illegal aliens" or simply "aliens" or "illegals" reach beyond Mexican immigrants to those arriving from any direction and by any means of entry, the current use of these terms by the media, politicians, and others is aimed most squarely at Mexican undocumented immigrants.

Undoubtedly these derogatory terms connote a lesser humanity—a subhuman and evil presence coming to harm the U.S. economic and cultural fabric, and worse. Metaphors wielded in today's immigration debate reflect the ominous threat posed by immigrants—expressed in subhuman terms of dangerous water events such as tides, surges, flows, floods, or tsunamis;[6] as dangerous insect and animal intruders such as swarms (of ants), hordes, and packs; and as militaristic threats such as invaders,[7] terrorists, and attackers carrying out a "reconquista" mission to reclaim the U.S. Southwest for Mexico. Even Supreme Court justices have embraced these familiar metaphors for immigration, particularly Mexican immigration, in their judicial opinions, warning of the "silent invasion of illegal aliens from Mexico"[8] and the "northbound tide of illegal entrants."[9] Undocumented immigrants are routinely equated in the media with menacing, disease-carrying animals, such as rats, birds, or swine. In this disturbing vein, hate-radio commentator Michael Savage frequently invokes foreboding imagery in describing the so-called immigrant threat, for example in his blaming of Mexican immigrants for a U.S. outbreak of swine flu in 2009. As Savage put it, "Make no mistake about it: Illegal aliens are the carriers of the new strain of human-swine avian flu from Mexico."[10] Savage even connected another popular subhuman image of undocumented immigrants—as terrorists aiming to hurt the United States or as being aligned with terrorists—to the swine-flu outbreak, querying whether that epidemic was a terrorist attack implemented through Mexico: "Could our dear friends in the radical Islamic countries have concocted this virus and planted it in Mexico knowing that . . . [Homeland Security] would do nothing to stop the flow of human traffic from Mexico?"[11] Lou Dobbs, then a CNN news anchor, claimed further that "illegal aliens" were behind an alarming rise in U.S. leprosy cases, a claim that has since been definitively debunked.[12] Supreme Court justices have jumped on this bandwagon to describe the threats posed by undocumented immigrants as national health risks, for example in writing that "illegal aliens pose a potential health hazard to the community since many seek work as nursemaids, food handlers, cooks, housekeepers, waiters, dishwashers, and grocery workers."[13]

The emphasis in U.S. media and political debate on the original sin of the undocumented border crossing or, in many cases, on remaining in the United States after a lawful admission has expired,[14] is evidenced by the familiar reference to undocumented immigrants as "illegals." Few people realize that it is not a federal crime to remain in the United States after a lawful admission expires, such as overstaying a tourist or student visa.[15] Although those who cross the border without proper documentation do commit a federal crime—a rarely prosecuted misdemeanor for first-time offenders—their presence in the United States is not itself a continuing crime unless they were previously deported. Yet however they came and as long as they remain, we brand undocumented entrants as criminals for their grasp at economic survival for themselves and their families.

The subhuman construction of "illegals" or "illegal aliens" does not stop with their immigration status. Rather, it extends to their supposed propensities, once in the United States, toward criminal behavior and beyond crime to moral turpitude, undue reliance on government support, and disdain for personal hygiene. Evidence of the popular image of undocumented immigrants, particularly Mexican migrants, as criminals is this campaign statement from one of the drafters of the 1990s' anti-immigrant Proposition 187, adopted in California, that aimed to punish Mexican immigrants and their children: "Illegal-alien gangs roam our streets, dealing drugs and searching for innocent victims to rob, rape, and in many cases, murder those who dare to violate their 'turf.'"[16] More recently, Arizona Governor Jan Brewer painted savage imagery of undocumented immigrants from Mexico beheading innocent Anglos en masse in the Arizona desert, presumably to justify her state's draconian treatment of immigrants.[17] Yet scholars have soundly debunked the threatening construction of immigrants and undocumented immigrants as more prone to crime than other U.S. residents.[18] Undocumented immigrants in particular tend to live in the shadows and to lay low, seeking to avoid government and especially police contact.

Negative images of Mexican immigrants extend beyond their imagined criminal proclivities. Obviously directed at Spanish-speaking immigrants, this "poem" read into the California legislative record in 1993 by Republican assemblyman Pete Knight depicts immigrants as poaching welfare resources and engaging in immoral procreation:

> Write to friends in motherland, tell them come as fast as can. . . .
> They come in rags and Chebby trucks, I buy big house with welfare
> bucks. . . .
> Everything is mucho good, soon we own the neighborhood.
> We have a hobby, it's called breeding.
> Welfare pay for baby feeding.[19]

These derogatory images of undocumented Mexican immigrants often encompass documented immigrants and even U.S.-citizen children of undocumented immigrants, who are dehumanized as "anchor babies." Moreover, these negative conceptions of Mexican heritage have endured for decades. During U.S. Congressional hearings in 1930 on a proposed bill to virtually eliminate immigration from Mexico, a submitted report associated Mexican immigrants with animals, thieving coyotes, and lowly swine in contending:

> Their minds run to nothing higher than animal functions—eat, sleep, and sexual debauchery. In every huddle of Mexican shacks one meets the same idleness, hordes of hungry dogs, and filthy children with faces plastered with flies, disease, lice, human filth, stench, promiscuous fornication, bastardy, lounging, apathetic peons and lazy squaws, beans and dried chili, liquor, general squalor, and envy and hatred of the gringo. These people sleep by day and prowl by night like coyotes, stealing anything they can get their hands on, no matter how useless to them it may be. . . . Yet there are Americans clamoring for more of this human swine to be brought over from Mexico.[20]

Mexican immigrants are accused of posing additional threats. Whether because of the sheer numbers of immigrants or their supposed disdain for the environment, some U.S. environmentalists have warned of the threat of Mexican immigration to our quality of life.[21] Some scholars too decried Mexican immigration as threatening Anglo-Protestant culture, especially the late Harvard professor Samuel Huntington, who contended that Mexican immigrants fail to assimilate and might therefore undermine the American way of life.[22]

These longstanding negative conceptions of Mexicans connect to oppressive immigration and deportation policies directed against Mexicans; these policies date to the early 1900s and replicate even earlier backlash policies against other immigrant groups, as discussed below.[23] Although ostensibly excluded from restrictive 1900s' immigration limits pursuant to a Western Hemisphere exemption that survived until 1965, Mexicans were at the mercy of shifting federal and even local prerogatives to encourage (such as through the Bracero Program, described in Chapter 4) or repel (such as through Operation Wetback)

Mexican immigration. When the U.S. economy waned, federal immigration authorities might flex administrative requirements for admission such as the literacy test and the prohibition against immigrants likely to become public charges, thereby controlling Mexican immigration like a faucet.[24] In more dire economic times, the United States, with the cooperation of local officials, would round up suspected undocumented Mexican immigrants and deport them to Mexico. During the economic downturn of 1921–1922, for example, police and local-government officials terrorized and displaced Mexican workers and their families, while vigilante mobs ran them out of town. During the Great Depression, federal immigration officials launched raids while city officials, such as those in Los Angeles who organized special trains, helped transport those caught in the net back to Mexico. Oklahomans threatened to burn Mexicans out of their homes, while signs in Texas warned Mexicans to leave town. Overall, estimates of those deported to Mexico during the Depression range widely from 350,000 to more than 2 million.[25] Relying on racial profiling, this Depression-era deportation campaign swept up undocumented as well as documented immigrants and many U.S.-citizen Latinos/as. An even more massive deportation, derogatorily known as Operation Wetback because it concentrated on Mexicans, accompanied the mid-1950s' economic downturn. Implemented as a military-like campaign, Operation Wetback deported more than a million (most estimates fall within 1.3 and 3.7 million) Latinos/as, mostly Mexicans, and even included U.S. citizens caught in racially profiled sweeps through the borderlands and Latino/a barrios.[26]

When U.S. labor shortages arose during World War II, the emphasis shifted to recruiting Mexican workers to journey to the United States under the abusive Bracero Program, detailed in Chapter 4, evidence of the thrust of U.S. policy toward Mexican laborers as one of "invitation and exile" based on our labor needs.[27] This policy of convenience was akin to treating these workers as inanimate farming implements to be used only when needed but kept handy.

While the federal government remained silent, in 2005 the state of California finally apologized for its role in the Depression-era repatriations—acknowledging that the raids targeted people of Mexican ancestry as "illegal aliens" even when they were U.S. citizens or permanent legal residents, that Mexican families were forced to abandon property

sold by local officials as "payment" to the government for their deportation expenses, and that the deportation raids wrongfully coerced
Mexicans to leave under threats of violence. California thus apologized
for "fundamental violations of [the deportees'] basic civil liberties and
constitutional rights committed during the period of illegal deportation and coerced emigration."[28] In 2012, the Los Angeles County Board
of Supervisors apologized for its own lead role at the epicenter of the
Depression-era repatriations of Mexicans and Mexican Americans.[29]
As noted, the federal government failed to apologize for its actions in
the many aggressive repatriations of Mexicans, particularly under the
federally orchestrated Operation Wetback, and the United States has
not apologized for any other abusive policies over the years that have
affected Latinos/as, although plenty of candidates exist, from the acquisition of Puerto Rico to the U.S.-Mexican War and the consequent shifting of land titles from Mexican ranchero owners to Anglo speculators.[30]

Similar to the vilification of Mexican and other Latino/a immigrants,[31] past negative conceptions of other U.S. immigrant groups
imagined those immigrants, documented or not, as subhuman, leading
to deleterious legal consequences. For example, at different times in our
immigration history, Irish, German, Jewish, and Italian immigrants,
among other European groups, were racialized and deemed of "different and inferior racial stock."[32] U.S. newspapers described them as "an
invasion of venomous reptiles," as Europe's "human and inhuman rub-
bish," and as "the very scum and offal of Europe."[33] The junk science of
eugenics emerged in the early 1900s to support these demeaning characterizations by somehow classifying "new" immigrants from eastern
and southern Europe, along with Asians and other disfavored groups,
as intellectually, physically, and morally inferior to Nordic stock. One
prominent psychologist and eugenicist of the time, Henry Goddard,
determined that 60 percent of Jews entering through Ellis Island were
intellectual "morons."[34] These negative constructions carried legal consequences ranging from state Official English language laws to the
restrictive U.S. immigration quota in effect from 1924 to 1965 that limited the entry of Jews, Italians, Slavs, and Greeks, among other disfavored groups.[35]

Even more demeaning constructions of Asian immigrants reinforced
viciously exclusionary U.S. immigration laws in the late nineteenth and

the twentieth centuries. Setting the stage for these restrictions were the prevailing subhuman views of Asian immigrants reflected in a California Supreme Court decision in 1854, in which the Chief Justice called the Chinese a "race of people whom nature has marked as inferior, and who are incapable of progress or intellectual development beyond a certain point . . . between whom and ourselves nature has placed an impassable difference."[36] Adding to the negative imagery was the "yellow journalism" of William Randolph Hearst's newspapers, which portrayed Chinese immigrant settlements in the United States (Chinatowns) as zones of "unbridled lawlessness, licentiousness, and unchecked evil" and as "filthy breeding grounds for depravity, degradation, and disease."[37] Among other threatening images during that period, Chinese immigrants were described as possessing culinary preferences "just short of cannibalism" in their alleged appetite for puppy dogs and even rats and mice.[38] Similar to current constructions of Latino/a immigrants as menacing threats, an 1873 California Workingmen's Party pamphlet titled "The Chinese Invasion" portrayed Chinese immigrants as invaders. Ominously, Chinese migrants were "constructed in the American imagination as more akin to a hive of insects than to human beings."[39] Chinese were often linked in the media, and by scientists, to dreaded infectious diseases.[40] A prominent California doctor published a report in 1862 that warned of scourges of "syphilis, mental alienation, and epidemic diseases" spread by Chinese immigrants.[41] Unsubstantiated Congressional testimony linking Chinese immigration to leprosy further constructed the Chinese as "walking time bombs of infection."[42] Chinese immigrants, given their supposed racial inferiority, were seen as unable to assimilate with other U.S. residents.[43] Tapping this fear, Congressional testimony warned that the Chinese "are incapable of attaining the state of civilization the Caucasian is capable of."[44]

The anti-Chinese immigrant frenzy sparked hateful mob violence in the 1880s against Chinese residents throughout the West. This backdrop of threatening images also prompted the 1882 federal Chinese Exclusion Act, which denied the entry of Chinese into the United States—the first U.S. immigration exclusion based on race or nationality—as well as widespread discriminatory state and local laws regulating Chinatowns and subsequent restrictive federal laws directed at Chinese immigration and residents.[45] Similarly constructed in menacing terms, Japanese immigrants faced their own immigration exclusion in the form of the 1907 Gentlemen's Agreement, by which Japan promised not to issue travel documents to its citizens who wished to visit the United States. Broader anti-Asian sentiments culminated in a 1917 U.S. law excluding all Asians emigrating from the so-called Asiatic Barred Zone, including those from India, who had begun to immigrate to the United States in sizeable numbers;[46] and the Immigration Act of 1924 prohibited immigration of "aliens ineligible [for] citizenship," which effectively meant Asians.[47] Asians, then, were both barred from entry and, for those Asians already living in the United States, barred from acquiring citizenship and its privileges, such as the ability to vote, because they were not viewed as sufficiently "white." The Supreme Court in turn backed these racialized exclusions.[48] This U.S. approach to restrictive, race-based immigration caught even Hitler's attention; he referred to it fondly in *Mein Kampf*: "There is at least one state in which feeble attempts to achieve a better arrangement are apparent[:] . . . the United States of America, where . . . they refuse to allow immigration of elements which are bad from the health point of view, and absolutely forbid naturalization of certain defined races, and are thus making a modest start in the direction of something not unlike the conception of the national State."[49]

These restrictive U.S. laws remained effective for decades, until relaxed for Chinese in 1943 (when China became a U.S. ally in World War II), Filipinos and Indians in 1946, and other Asians in 1952.[50] Finally, in 1965, Congress eliminated the vestiges of anti-Asian immigration policy that continued to constrain Asian immigration through exceedingly small numerical allowances.[51] Later, in 2011, the U.S. Senate passed a resolution apologizing for the discriminatory 1882 Chinese Exclusion Act, joined by the House in 2012. Earlier, in 2009, California's legislature apologized for its own historical record of discrimination against Chinese residents and for the active role of California politicians in lobbying Congress to enact the Chinese Exclusion Act.

*   *   *

In the few decades since Mexicans, documented or not, have become the face of immigration, the subhuman image of these migrant workers has prompted especially egregious immigration policies, practices, and proposals designed to squelch the so-called Latino/a threat. These responses implicate the federal government, as well as state and local government, vigilantes, voters, politicians, employers, and, effectively, all of us. Next, I survey here some of the more inhumane prevailing immigration policies, most aimed directly at impeding or punishing Latino/a immigration.

As discussed below, current immigration policy leads to frequent deaths during treacherous U.S.-Mexico border crossings. Presumably no policymaker would intend this outcome, which nonetheless is caused by the border-armoring policies implemented most notably during the Clinton administration. Yet some politicians and radio commentators have explicitly advocated or belittled the death of immigrant border crossers. For example, Kansas Republican lawmaker Virgil Peck equated hogs and immigrants by suggesting in 2011 that "if shooting these immigrating feral hogs [from helicopters] works [in Kansas], maybe we have found a solution to our illegal immigration problem."[52] Although explaining later that he did not intend to advocate violence, Alabama state senator Scott Beason proposed during a Republican Party breakfast in 2011 that the way to confront undocumented immigration was to "empty the clip, and do what has to be done."[53] Also in 2011, Republican presidential hopeful Herman Cain invited the death of immigrant border crossers by different means in advocating a lethal, electrified U.S.-Mexico border fence, with alligators in a moat fronting the fence.[54] In a 2010 candidate forum, Georgia state representative John Yates suggested that U.S. officials "shoot to kill" undocumented immigrants at the border, comparing immigrants to an invading force and reminding the audience that "stopping Hitler was worth the price."[55] And a Republican gubernatorial candidate in Texas callously proposed that borderland ranchers be allowed to shoot "wetbacks" on sight.[56] Beyond the border, Michael Savage once implored that hunger-striking Dreamers—undocumented college students seeking regularization of their immigration status—be allowed to starve to death, thereby effectively solving the problem of their need for green cards.[57] Police have similarly dehumanized immigrants, with Knox County, Tennessee, Sheriff J. J. Jones threatening in 2013 to stack undocumented immigrants in his jail "like cordwood" if the federal government did not authorize his deputies to help enforce federal immigration laws.[58]

Coinciding with the subhuman construction of immigrants and the calls, whether in jest or not, for violence against immigrants, is the spike in hate crimes against Latino/a immigrants. Reporting in 2011 that hate crimes against Latinos/as had increased by 52 percent in recent years, the news outlet AlterNet attributed that increase to unceasing "right-wing vituperation" and to "caustic rhetoric" dehumanizing undocumented immigrants as "illegals."[59] In my book *Greasers and Gringos*, I detailed the killing in 2000 of an innocent Mexican border crosser by a white Texas border resident who shot him from behind after rejecting the dehydrated immigrant's plea for water. I discussed the death of a twelve-year-old Mexican boy in 1990, shot near San Diego while crossing the border with his family, by a U.S. resident, high on methamphetamine, who wanted to "shoot some aliens." And I recounted the horrific beating on Long Island, New York, in 2000 by skinheads, one admittedly high on LSD, who attacked two undocumented Latino workers with a posthole digger and a knife. Unbelievably, a New York legislator remarked the next year that if his town were inundated by undocumented immigrants, "we'd all be out with baseball bats."[60] In another book, *Tierra y Libertad*, I detailed unjustified beatings of suspected undocumented Latino/a immigrants by U.S. ranchers patrolling their borderland properties.[61]

These hate crimes escalated in the late 2000s. For example, a white Long Island teenager stabbed Marcelo Lucero, an Ecuadorean immigrant, to death in 2008 as part of a gang attack on immigrants "for kicks."[62] In 2010, a federal jury convicted two Pennsylvania teens of a hate crime for their role in brutally stomping in the head of a Latino immigrant, Luis Eduardo Ramirez Zavala, while a larger group encouraged the murder by yelling slurs such as "Go back to Mexico."[63] Also in 2010, a man who told police he "hated Mexicans" used a wooden stake to stab to death Martin Reyes, a Honduran immigrant and father of six.[64] And, in 2009, a leader of the Minuteman American Defense anti-immigrant group raided the Arizona residence of suspected undocumented Latino/a immigrants, killing a father (Raul Flores) and his nine-year-old daughter Bresenia, who pleaded for her life, and shooting the girl's mother who survived only by playing dead.[65] These are just a few of the egregious examples of hate crimes singling out Latino/a immigrants in the current anti-immigrant climate.

Despite the awful details of these murders, their numbers are vastly eclipsed by the thousands of undocumented immigrants who have died while on their journey to a U.S. workplace or field of dreams. A 2009 report by the ACLU estimated that fifty-six hundred undocumented immigrants had died during their Mexican border crossing since the U.S. government implemented its border-build-up strategy in the mid-1990s.[66] For every one of the thousands of bodies recovered, untold others are literally swallowed up in the desert, making these tragic border-lands estimates conservative at best.

Border security became the mantra for politicians of both parties following the terrorist bombing of the World Trade Center in 1993 and the outcry in California over visible urban crossings of undocumented immigrants near San Diego; the San Diego crossings helped re-elect Governor Pete Wilson and aided the passage of the anti-immigrant citizen initiative Proposition 187 in 1994.[67] With President Clinton's support, Congress enacted the Illegal Immigration Reform and Immigrant Responsibility Act of 1996 to arm the border at urban entry points, such as Tijuana/San Diego (where the campaign was known as Operation Gatekeeper) and Ciudad Juárez/El Paso (Operation Hold the Line), with additional Border Patrol agents, fencing and walls, and advanced detection devices such as underground sensors. Presumably the U.S. government expected that this dramatic show of force would dissuade undocumented border crossers, whose desperation for a chance at economic survival would not lead them to undertake vastly riskier entries in the desolate border terrain far from the safer urban crossings of past decades. But U.S. employers kept calling and undocumented immigrants, both Mexicans and migrants from Central and South American countries, kept coming, now substituting routes through perilous desert and mountain terrain for urban crossings. A considerable number of deaths ensued from extremes of heat and cold, as well as fire and torrents of water. In one grisly example, a group of fourteen Latino men and teen-agers died in 2001 from scorching heat near the Cabeza Prieta National Wildlife Refuge in a remote Arizona desert when their guide lost his way. In April 1999 a freak snowstorm dumped a foot of snow and claimed the lives of eight migrant crossers. Eight Mexican migrants drowned just inside the Arizona border in 1997 when a fifteen-foot-high wall of water carried them off after a downpour. Twenty-six migrants died in 2000 alone in the swift-moving All-American Canal along the California border. Vulnerable migrants died in the 2007 wildfires that swept through the outskirts of San Diego. Migrants choosing to cross the border in the cargo holds of semi-trucks or rail cars sometimes suffocated; in October 2002 a grain-elevator worker in Iowa discovered the skeletal remains of eleven migrants inside a sealed rail car arriving from Mexico.[68]

Migrants crossing the border must brave not only the elements. Those caught by the U.S. Border Patrol routinely face cruel treatment such as denial of water, food, and medical care, and verbal and physical abuse.[69] Border Patrol agents have even killed rock-throwing Mexicans in the borderlands—meeting rocks with bullets. Of late, on their journey north, migrants have been robbed, raped, and murdered by members of Mexican drug cartels and other criminals. The most poignant example of the mounting violence threatening immigrants crossing the border occurred in 2010, when seventy-two mostly Central and South American migrants heading for the U.S. border were massacred on their journey through Mexico, likely by a Mexican drug-smuggling cartel the migrants refused to assist.[70]

Enacted by Congress in 2006 with the votes of then Senators Barack Obama and Hillary Clinton, the Secure Fence Act aimed to ensure the eventual fencing and walling of the entire two-thousand-mile U.S.-Mexico border. Later bogged down by a lack of Congressional funding, the contemplated border wall is a monument to the prevailing policy of excluding Latino/a undocumented workers at any financial or moral cost despite their financial desperation and the economic reality that Latino/a immigrants come to the United States only when jobs beckon them.[71] The wall is primarily a testament to the view that Latino/a immigrants are undeserving of border passage. One writer to the editor opined, "Building a fence between us and Mexico has to rank right up there with putting our Japanese citizens in camps during World War II. It's something we're going to be embarrassed to remember. Our southern neighbors deserve better." Another remarked that the border wall "represents a moral failure and is an embarrassing spectacle—the richest nation in the world building a wall to keep its poor neighbors out. Shame on us."[72]

Once safely across the borderlands and inside the United States, undocumented immigrants must still survive perilous journeys toward employment in the South and other regions of the United States. In 2003, nineteen undocumented immigrants, including a five-year-old, died by suffocation inside an eighteen-wheeler while being transported within Texas.[73] Numerous tragedies occurred in collisions on U.S. highways, with undocumented immigrants stuffed into transport vehicles and huddling without seatbelts; for example, a collision in 1999 near Albuquerque that killed thirteen migrants, most from the Mexican states of Chiapas and Oaxaca.[74]

Having reached their destination within the United States, undocumented immigrants are vulnerable to a variety of injustices, from exploitation by labor and sex-slave traffickers who essentially hold their victims in involuntary servitude,[75] to miserable crowded and substandard housing conditions, to the ever-present threat of a workplace deportation raid or a traffic stop that might reveal their lack of a U.S. driver's license. Obama has presided over the deportation of hundreds of thousands of Mexican immigrants despite the promise and hope in his first term of immigration reform that would address the status of approximately eleven million undocumented residents, most of them laborers and most of them Mexicans.[76] Many of these deportees were torn from their U.S. families in workplace immigration raids. Occurring under the Bush administration, a notorious round-up by Immigration and Customs Enforcement (ICE) of 398 suspected undocumented immigrants at a meat-packing plant in Postville, Iowa, in 2008, is the most egregious example of the abuses of immigration enforcement. Those arrested in the Postville raid were mostly Mayans from Guatemala. Only five had (minor) criminal records.[77] The arrested immigrants were charged with aggravated identity theft, a felony, in a tactic akin to the antics of Arizona's Sheriff Joe Arpaio, who charged undocumented migrants with the felony of conspiring with coyotes (people who smuggle migrants across the U.S.-Mexico border) to smuggle themselves.[78] The Iowa workers were forced to appear in a makeshift court on the showgrounds of the National Cattle Congress in Waterloo, Iowa. There, without adequate legal representation, the majority pled guilty and were sentenced to imprisonment followed by deportation, while their employer escaped prosecution. This fast-track, "cattle-call" criminalization entailed images of "poor immigrant men and women being dragged away in handcuffs and ankle chains as if they were killers and terrorists," viewed by the wrenching "faces of children separated from their parents."[79] Children are often the most unfortunate victims of these immigration raids. It is especially tragic when undocumented parents hope to return to the United States after deportation and thus leave their children behind in the care of relatives, neighbors, and even landlords pending their treacherous journey back to U.S. workplaces. A National Council of La Raza study found that in the wake of ICE raids younger children interpreted parental absence as abandonment.[80] More than 5.5 million U.S. children, 4.5 million of them U.S.-born citizens, live in families with at least one undocumented parent; this situation suggests the vast potential for devastation of U.S.-resident families that deportation can pose. Indeed, between July 2010 and the end of September 2012, almost one in four deportations removed parents of U.S.-citizen children.[81]

Children born in the United States are U.S. citizens under the constitutionally-based doctrine of birthright citizenship.[82] This fact, however, does not prevent the deportation of their undocumented parents. Nevertheless, several politicians have undertaken to abolish or thwart birthright citizenship, most notably former Arizona legislator Russell Pearce. Later ousted by voters, Pearce introduced state legislation in 2011 that envisioned a compact among states to issue separate birth certificates for children born to undocumented parents and that would have created a state citizenship status within Arizona, while excluding and stigmatizing such children. Although approved by a Senate committee, the Arizona Senate rejected these birthright-citizenship bills. Still, the campaign at the state and federal levels to abolish birthright citizenship continues to gain momentum, sparked by the dehumanizing and inanimate construction of these U.S.-citizen children as "anchor babies." This "anchor" phrasing equates human beings with "mere lumps of lead" who "are now things, to be stripped and packaged and used as the majority wills" to justify reactionary immigration and citizenship laws.[83] As Berkeley law professor Ian Haney-López suggested. "Whether 'anchor baby' frightens you depends on which immigration tradition you believe in. [One tradition respects our nation of immigrants.] [But] if you're convinced that some people are so far inferior that they can never be one of 'us,' then of course the anchor baby is a terrifying spook—the same spook as the tar baby, the savage Indian, and the yellow hordes. Or, for that matter, the many European groups once barred by immigration laws as 'beaten men from beaten races.'"[84]

Augmenting the federal border build-up and workplace- and home-invasion raids, state and local governments have joined the effort to identify, arrest, and repel undocumented immigrants. When conducted in concert with the federal government pursuant to 287(g) agreements, cooperation with local law enforcement has Congressional blessing.[85] But the negative construction of undocumented immigrants and the Latino/a face that now accompanies the immigration debate prompted many states and communities to put out their own enforcement tentacles and implement restrictive measures against resident undocumented immigrants. Illustrating the staggering number of local laws regulating immigration, in the first quarter of 2010 alone, almost twelve hundred bills and resolutions introduced in state legislatures addressed immigration and immigrants.[86] Although a few of these proposals honor the dignity of immigrant laborers, such as by offering the same college tuition rates as are charged other state residents, most scapegoat and vilify undocumented immigrants by restricting their driving, housing, employment, voting, and education. Leading the way in demarcating the immigrant as unlawful and illegal is Arizona's S.B. 1070, which criminalized the presence of undocumented immigrants in that state and spawned copycat legislation elsewhere. Previously, Arizona voters had enacted initiatives denying undocumented immigrants any recovery of punitive damages in civil actions, such as for personal injuries,[87] and requiring proof of citizenship for voting and, in the spirit of California's former Proposition 187, proof of lawful immigration status to receive public benefits.[88] Although the U.S. Supreme Court struck down much of S.B. 1070 in 2012, including the state's criminalization of undocumented immigrants, it left intact the core "show me your papers" provision. With racial profiling inherent in the implementation of this S.B. 1070 provision, which requires police to make a "reasonable attempt" to determine immigration status during stops and arrests if they reasonably suspect the person is undocumented, Arizona staked its claim as the Mississippi of our times in abusing human rights and establishing a legal apartheid for Latino/a undocumented residents. Harkening back to the days of vicious state laws regulating blacks, in dissenting from the Supreme Court's invalidation of other parts of the restrictive Arizona law, Justice Antonin Scalia invoked the memory of state antiblack laws: "Notwithstanding 'the myth of an era of unrestricted immigration' in the first 100 years of the Republic, the States enacted numerous laws restricting the immigration of certain classes of aliens, including convicted criminals, indigents, persons with contagious diseases, and (in Southern States) freed blacks. . . . State laws not only provided for the removal of unwanted immigrants but also imposed penalties on unlawfully present aliens and those who aided their immigration."[89]

Adding to Arizona's sorry record against Latinos/as and immigrants in the 2000s was Sheriff Joe Arpaio of Maricopa County, Arizona. Arpaio notoriously initiated a campaign to terrorize and racially profile the local Latino/a population. Presiding over the state's most populous county, the self-proclaimed "America's Toughest Sheriff" employed abusive immigration round-ups, desert patrols, tent prisons in sweltering heat, street parades of shackled migrants in pink uniforms, and bread-and-water diets.[90] Arpaio's egregious civil rights violations eventually prompted the federal government to pull his 287(g) certification and even to sue him in federal court for widespread constitutional violations against Latinos/as and immigrants.[91] Among other alleged abuses, Maricopa County jail officials called Latino/a prisoners "wetbacks" and "stupid Mexicans" and kept limited-English-speaking Latinos/as in solitary confinement for their inability to understand commands in English. Supervisors verbally equated Mexicans with dogs, and county police officers, in seeking out undocumented immigrants, conducted unconstitutional immigration raids and sweeps in homes and workplaces while racially profiling Latinos/as.[92] A federal judge in 2013 concluded that Sheriff Joe impermissibly engaged in racial profiling of Latino/a drivers in pursuing undocumented Latino/a immigrants.[93] Moreover, the same day in 2012 that President Obama affirmed the innocence of undocumented children by announcing administrative deferment of deportation for young "Dreamers," Sheriff Joe's rogue officers arrested a six-year-old girl from El Salvador, suspected of undocumented immigration, and turned her over to ICE authorities.[94] Arizona seems far removed from the human rights sentiment embodied in the

Declaration of the World Conference against Racism, Racial Discrimination, Xenophobia and Related Intolerance, which urges police to
treat migrants "in a dignified and non-discriminatory manner,"[95] and
from the dictates of humanity that infuse the U.N. Convention on the
Protection of the Rights of All Migrant Workers and Members of Their
Families.

Arizona's ruthless assault on Latino/a undocumented immigrants
extends to Latinos/as generally, as evidenced by the state's vendetta
against an ethnic-studies curriculum, especially Mexican American
studies, that resulted in vaguely worded legislation in 2010 outlawing
any school curriculum that promotes ethnic solidarity, overthrow of the
government, resentment toward a certain group, or is designed for students of a particular ethnic group.[96] Obviously anti-Mexican in its adoption and its enforcement and in targeting the successful Tucson Mexican American studies program, the law was signed by Governor Brewer
hours after U.N. human rights experts decried it.[97] The law essentially
communicates to Mexican residents the same sentiment as did pre-Civil
Rights Act business signs that dotted the Arizona landscape and much
of the Southwest declaring "No Dogs or Mexicans Allowed."

Evidencing the trend among states, Alabama's anti-immigrant legislation draws on Arizona's restrictive laws to similarly victimize
Latino/a immigrants, also including within its scope an ominous provision requiring schools to record the immigration status of incoming
students and their parents and to supply that information to the state.
U.S. states cannot constitutionally deny K-12 education to undocumented immigrant children;[98] but this law presumably was meant to
scare undocumented families away from Alabama public schools and
residential neighborhoods.[99] A political cartoon compared Alabama
schools under this law to segregationist "Whites Only" schools in 1963
Alabama, but this time with the sign on the schoolhouse door reading
"No Latinos."[100]

Proposed legislation in Ohio in 2012 effectively conveyed the subhumanity of undocumented workers by mandating their ineligibility
to claim worker's compensation or recovery for their employer's negli-
gence if injured on the job. Instead, by working without authorization
the undocumented worker would simply assume the risk of a needlessly
dangerous workplace.

At the community level, tirades against undocumented immigrants tend to be launched by forceful local officials who scapegoat undocumented (Latino/a) immigrants for local woes, whether criminal or economic. Best illustrating this local hate is Lou Barletta, the mayor of Hazleton, Pennsylvania, who championed laws in 2006 that prohibited rentals of housing to undocumented immigrants and outlawed their employment.[101] Barletta rode the backs of undocumented immigrants all the way to Congress after his tough immigration policies gained national attention. Communities throughout the United States such as Farmers Branch, Texas, similarly targeted immigrant housing.[102] Immigrant employment was targeted in other communities, such as the prestigious California oceanfront community of Redondo Beach (Spanish for round, or perfect), which outlawed day laborers, most of them undocumented, from soliciting work on street corners; this law was ultimately held an unconstitutional violation of their free speech rights by a federal appeals court.[103]

Augmenting vicious federal, state, and local laws and enforcement are discriminatory practices by employers, landlords, and other private actors who take advantage of the apparent open season on abusing undocumented immigrants. In 2009, the Southern Poverty Law Center released a report documenting the miserable experience of Latino/a immigrants in the South, finding many had suffered wage theft and sexual harassment at the hands of unscrupulous employers, with many Latina immigrants revealing their bosses used their immigration status as sexual leverage. As the Center's director lamented, "We're talking about a matter of basic human rights here. By allowing this cycle of abuse and discrimination to continue, we're creating an underclass of people who are invisible to justice and undermining our country's fundamental ideals."[104]

*   *   *

Next I sketch what immigration policies would look like if we valued the human rights and humanity of immigrants to the United States, documented or not, and Latino/a or not. The Conclusion of this book details strategies toward this critical humanization, which might trigger such compassionate reform. For purposes of this exercise, readers might imagine that some of their own family members, with hungry children, reside in another country (or even another U.S. state) and that local work exists well suited to their talents and aspirations. How might immigration policies honor their dignity and protect their safety during the journey and once in their new community?

Primarily, immigration policies that embody compassion toward migrants would ensure that they experience no more deaths or violence in transit. Instead of adding to the gauntlet of risks undocumented border crossers face by advocating deadly force against them through the use of guns, electric fences, and other treachery, compassionate policymakers would ensure an immediate halt to the borderland deaths and assaults of migrants. Given the unrealistic notion that we can somehow curb our appetite for cheap, mobile labor forces or that transformative economic growth in all feeder countries such as Mexico will soon and permanently stifle migration, the only feasible option for stopping the body count is to reform our immigration limits. Today, only a few immigration visas each year accommodate low-wage workers seeking passage toward U.S. jobs in construction, factory work, housekeeping, and similar occupations.[105] Only sixty-eight thousand guest-worker visas are available to immigrant farmworkers, just a small percentage of the workers U.S. agribusiness demands. Because most undocumented entrants come for these low-wage jobs, the type solicited on street corners and through labor subcontractors, meaningful reform must permit sufficient visas for work-based immigration, which for decades has exceeded legal allowances. Not only will aligning visas with labor demand ease the border body count, it will reduce the exploitation and abuse undocumented workers currently face in the workplace, as well as from landlords, local police, and others. To avoid the historical abuses in temporary guest-worker programs, such as the Bracero Program discussed in Chapter 4,[106] an opportunity for the eventual citizenship of workers who wish to pursue an American Dream is crucial for any labor program that honors the human rights of migrant workers and their families.

Immigration reform must address not only migrant workers who come in future years but also the eleven million undocumented workers currently living in the shadows of our prosperity. Most proposals for the regularization of these immigrants insist on some significant financial penalty to atone for their undocumented status and on a touch-back requirement that they briefly and ceremoniously return to their country of origin.[107] Moreover, these immigrants would then need to step to the back of the line for eventual citizenship, which, in the absence of family reunification, would be extremely unlikely given stingy immigration limits. Even President Obama, who at times claims to champion the rights of immigrants, demanded in proposing reform that to hold undocumented immigrants properly accountable they must "admit that they broke the law . . . pay their taxes, pay a fine, and learn English. They must get right with the law before they can get in line and earn their citizenship."[108] Although immigration proposals aimed at Dreamers—undocumented college students and military person-nel—and at farmworkers usually contain more meaningful pathways to citizenship,[109] proposals addressing immigrants who fall outside these categories sometimes allow them to lawfully and temporarily continue working in the United States but deny them the realistic prospect of long-term stability and recognition in the U.S. economy and culture through citizenship.

Immigration reform that honors the humanity and contributions of immigrants to our economy would ensure an opportunity for citi-zenship for both resident undocumented immigrants and those future migrants with an American Dream. Before the passage of the 1965 Immigration and Nationality Act, which imposed the first numeri-cal limits on Western Hemisphere immigration, Mexican immigrants enjoyed the special good-neighbor relationship of the Western Hemi-sphere exemption from fixed immigration limits.[110] As Senator Robert Kennedy saw it, that longstanding Western Hemisphere exemption from rigid immigration limits was "a great experiment to see whether the societies which are rich and free can help those who are less free and poor."[111] Mexican laborers, through the Bracero Program and oth-erwise, routinely answered the frequent call of U.S. employers in critical industries without meaningful acknowledgment of their contribution. Compassionate immigration reform with the humanity of Mexican immigrants at its fore would return us to the good-neighbor relation-ship that once prevailed and permitted unlimited immigration from Mexico and other Western Hemisphere countries. Experience with the European Union model, which allows citizens of member nations free movement for work opportunities, debunks fears that returning to open hemispheric migration would prompt mass migration from the poor global South to the rich North.[112] Particularly suggestive of natural constraints on Mexican immigration in line with our prevailing labor needs is the experience of the net zero Mexican migration across the border that coincided with the U.S. economic downturn that started in 2008. When jobs beckon, experience shows that Mexican immigrants, given the economic desperation of some, will come by any means, documented or not, to serve those demands. When our economy languishes, immigration slows to a crawl, and those Mexican undocumented immigrants already here either return to Mexico or, if border security is too intense for a safe return trip when the economy recovers, remain in the shadows in wrenching living conditions to await renewed labor demand.

Additional compassionate-immigration reforms benefitting immigrants regardless of their countries of origin would flow from the humanization of immigrants and their families. Despite current allowances for family reunification, under the prevailing restrictive immigration limits a huge backlog exists for separated families from Mexico and other countries with significant immigration demand.[113] For example, in November, 2009, more than one million Mexican residents awaited a family-reunification visa, a number vastly exceeding that of any other country.[114] A compassionate immigration policy would increase immigration visas regardless of the country of origin to accommodate demand for family reunification.

Humanizing the children of undocumented immigrants, whether born outside the United States and thus undocumented themselves, or as U.S.-born and thus U.S. citizens, suggests additional reform measures. At a minimum, compassionate immigration reform would embrace the equality principles of Dream Act proposals by conferring a pathway to citizenship and the opportunity for in-state tuition rates for resident undocumented youth. Additionally, once humanized from their subhuman conception as "anchor babies," U.S.-born children of undocumented immigrants should be freed from localized attacks on their citizenship status.[115]

Compassionate reform consistent with immigrant labor demand by U.S. employers will ease the compulsion for workplace and residential immigration raids, which tragically split families apart. Although undocumented immigrants may still enter despite increased allowances for lawful immigration, their numbers would be far smaller and fail to warrant today's abusive and costly immigration sweeps.[116] Rather than having enforcement officials scouring homes and workplaces for targets, emphasis could be placed on just those undocumented immigrants who enter the criminal justice system for serious crimes and thus present themselves for deportation.[117] In anticipation of Obama's assuming the presidency in 2009, an Arizona professor, Roberto Rodríguez, urged that Obama immediately end immigration raids: "On this path, it is not simply the undocumented who would begin to be treated as full human beings, but just as importantly, it might contribute greatly to the rehumanization of our entire society."[118] In his first term Obama failed to persuade Congress to implement this call for humane immigration enforcement, choosing instead to deport more immigrants annually (almost 410,000 in fiscal year 2012) than under the preceding Bush administration, while continuing abusive federal raids.[119] As part of that deportation process, suspected undocumented immigrants may be held without bail in detention centers until their cases are resolved. A 2012 report revealed that immigration detainees can wait weeks or months to see a doctor, be thrown into solitary confinement for minor rules infractions, be served inedible food, and be shipped to detention centers far from their children.[120] At the same time, in 2012, Obama embraced Dreamers and blocked the deportation of certain productive young immigrants, a decision that so enraged Supreme Court Justice Antonin Scalia that he lashed out at Obama for exempting these "illegal immigrants" from enforcement.[121] Scalia thus resurrected the sorry ghost of Justice William Rehnquist, who, in arguing against what became a 5-4 decision in favor of public education for undocumented immigrants, referred to the predominantly Mexican children as "wetbacks."[122] When his colleague Justice Thurgood Marshall compared that epithet to what he had been called as a black man, Rehnquist claimed no disrespect, as wetbacks was a common term where he came from: he practiced law for many years in the current epicenter of immigrant hate, Arizona.

By any measure, much remains to be accomplished to enact and implement compassionate immigration reform and to humanize the face of U.S. immigration. As an immigrant-rights scholar observed, "How a nation treats the immigrant speaks volumes about the nation."[123] Humanizing immigrants, then, might help deliver the breakthrough that humanizes the rest of our society and at the same time fundamentally establish our generation as one that respected human rights, finally.

4

Beasts of Burden

Farmworkers in the U.S. Field of Dreams

What do you get when you cross a Mexican and an octopus?
Got me, but it can sure pick lettuce.
—Familiar "joke"

All my life, I have been driven by one dream, one goal, one
vision: To overthrow a farm labor system in this nation
which treats farm workers as if they were not important
human beings. Farm workers are not agricultural implements. They are not beasts of burden—to be used and
discarded.
—César Chávez

We labor the fields, we bring the fruits to your table, and the
sparkling wine, and yet you do not want to give us the right
to go home and sleep on a Beauty Rest mattress.
—Former migrant worker

The largely negative societal view of Mexicans, Latinos/as, and
particularly Latino/a immigrants, readily extends to farmworkers.
Although early in the twentieth century "Okies" represented the face
of the U.S. farmworker in the West, as did black laborers in the South,
along with a variety of immigrant groups such as Japanese and Filipinos
in the Far West, over time Mexican immigrants replaced these workers
in all corners of the United States. For example, California's agricultural
workforce, less than half of which was Latino/a in 1965, became over 97
percent Latino/a, the vast majority of Mexican background, by the mid-
1990s.[1] Confirming this shift nationally, an Agricultural Workers Survey
conducted by the U.S. Department of Labor in 2001–2002 found that 75
percent of U.S. farmworkers were born in Mexico and that 81 percent

speak Spanish as their native language.² Most farmworkers (53 percent) are undocumented.³ Thus, farmworkers today are readily saddled with the prevailing negative construction of Mexican undocumented immigrants, despite the critical role they play in harvesting our national food supply. The face of the U.S. farmworker in the American imagination, like the face of the undocumented immigrant, is now a Mexican one.

The farming industry has always relied on the most vulnerable workers rather than being willing to pay wages commensurate with the rigor of the work. In the South, for example, after the end of formal slavery, Black Codes—amorphous laws regulating vagrancy and other stated misconduct—allowed black prisoners to be placed into forced agricultural labor.⁴ Relatedly, contract labor laws in the South obligated ostensibly voluntary workers under penalty of law to work for a complete season for a certain employer, subject to the denial of wages for offenses such as arriving late or missing work. Farmers also preserved the southern plantation culture through debt peonage and sharecropping by black workers; this system helped maintain a beholden workforce through loans for seed, supplies, and household needs.⁵ As black workers and other groups, such as Okies who migrated west during the Great Depression, made modest advances through legal reform or other means, the agricultural industry turned to other vulnerable groups. Mexicans increasingly fit this bill throughout the twentieth century as corporate agribusiness displaced the family farmer and the U.S. farm-labor population shrank from the time of the country's founding, when 90 percent of U.S. labor was involved in agriculture, to today, when farming employs only 2 percent of the U.S. workforce.⁶

Regardless of their immigration status and citizenship, Mexican farmworkers have always struggled to be seen as fully human and to garner the respect they deserve from farmers, politicians, and the consuming public. U.S. Senator George Murphy claimed in the 1960s that only Mexicans were suited for the stoop labor of picking lettuce and other crops, as "they're built so close to the ground."⁷ Previously, a Harvard-educated historian and author wrote in 1927 about the "great reservoir of the cheapest and most docile labor" in Mexico. Advocating their utility to U.S. employers in subhuman terms, he observed that "the Mexican 'peon' (Indian or mixed-breed) is a poverty-stricken, ignorant, primitive creature, with strong muscles and with just enough brains to obey orders and produce profits under competent direction."[8] These attitudes portended and help explain the reliance on Mexican labor by U.S. agribusiness, which readily employs the most vulnerable of Mexican workers—undocumented immigrants.

Icons of the farmworker struggle for dignity and co-founders of the United Farm Workers (UFW) union, César Chávez and Dolores Huerta lamented the attitude of growers toward the agricultural workforce that became mostly Mexican. In 1969, during the national grape boycott, Chávez wrote a letter to the alliance of California grape growers, arguing for the human rights of dehumanized workers:

> The color of our skins, the languages of our cultural and native origins, the lack of formal education, the exclusion from the democratic process, the numbers of our slain in recent wars—all these burdens generation after generation have sought to demoralize us, to break our human spirit. But God knows we are not beasts of burden, we are not agricultural implements or rented slaves, we are men. And mark this well . . . we are men locked in a death struggle against man's inhumanity to man in the industry that you represent. . . . We hate the agribusiness system that seeks to keep us enslaved and we shall overcome and change it . . . by a determined nonviolent struggle carried on by those masses of farmworkers who intend to be free and human.[9]

Dolores Huerta detailed some of the specific abuses of farm labor that dehumanize the workers:

> Growers dehumanize their workers. Why would you refuse to give workers a toilet? Because if you don't give them a toilet, then they're not human beings. Why would you allow workers to be sprayed with pesticides? Growers view farmworkers as tools. Workers give the growers their entire adult lives, yet they won't even pay them a fair wage for all their hard work. They don't consider the horrible poverty these workers suffer. Why? Because their goal is profit and they don't care about the people.[10]

Foremost in the legacy of farmworker exploitation is their inadequate pay. Farmworkers are among the poorest of the poor, facing the highest poverty rate of any occupation, and they have remained so for decades. Their abysmal pay is directly linked to their substandard housing, if they are fortunate to be housed at all; their inadequate health care; and the dismal educational prospects of their children. A U.S. Department of Labor survey found that the average income of an individual farmworker in 2001–2002 was between $10,000 and $12,499, while the income for a farmworker family averaged between only $15,000 and $17,499.[11] More recently, the average annual income for crop-worker households from 2007 to 2009 was reported as between only $17,500 and $19,999.[12] Migrant farmworkers are even worse off. Despite sometimes pooling wages from multiple workers, more than two-thirds of the U.S. migrant farm-labor households live in poverty, as do 80 percent of farmworker children.[13] In 2000, the median income of migrant and seasonal farmworkers was only $6,250 a year, a figure that explains their staggering poverty.[14]

Rather than passively accept their fate, farmworkers have consistently rebelled against low wages,[15] most prominently in the 1960s strike and the accompanying national boycott, led by Chávez and Huerta against Delano, California, grape growers.[16] As historian Rodolfo Acuña recounted the stark economic focus of that dispute, "The strike demands were simple: $1.40 an hour or 25¢ a box."[17] Delano grape pickers were making only $2,400 a year at the time of the strike, when the poverty line for a family of four was considerably more—$3,223.[18] Little has changed. Journalist Marc Cooper wrote in 2005 of the continuing inequities California field workers endure:

> Wages among California's 700,000 farm workers, 96 percent of whom are Mexican or Central American, more than half of whom are undocumented, are at best stagnant, and by most reckonings are in decline. With almost all workers stuck at the [California state] minimum wage of $6.75 an hour, it's rare to find a farm worker whose annual income breaks $10,000 a year. "Twenty-five years ago, a worker made 12, 13, 14 cents for a bin of oranges," says economist Rick Mines . . . . "Today that same bin pays maybe 15 or 16 cents — in spite of 250 percent inflation." Virtually no workers have health insurance or paid vacations. The cyclical nature of the crops throws most out of work for two or more months per year.[19]

The economics of migration explain why farm labor attracts Mexican immigrants despite the dismal pay and despite the fact that it is a terrifically strenuous and dangerous occupation.[20] In the early 1990s, for example, the pay range for farm laborers working in west-central Mexico was the equivalent of between only $1.60 and $8 per day.[21] As has been well documented, the North American Free Trade Agreement (NAFTA) and the government subsidies paid to U.S. farmers devastated the Mexican agricultural industry, which did not enjoy the same government largess; as a result many rural Mexican residents came north to opportunities in the United States.[22] No doubt many of the estimated eleven million undocumented residents currently in the United States who aspired to the higher, although still paltry, wages paid in the U.S. fields of dreams were casualties of NAFTA.[23]

U.S. farmworkers were excluded for years from federal minimum-wage protections, as they were from the rest of the New Deal–era labor protections. The Fair Labor Standards Amendments of 1966 mandated for the first time a minimum wage for many agricultural workers (excluding those employed on small farms). But farmworkers nonetheless remain exempt from federal overtime-wage protections that could help compensate for their long days in the field during the short harvest season. Despite the potential boost in wages, the federal minimum-wage guarantee enacted in 1966 was of little practical benefit to farm laborers and did not prevent agribusiness's race to the bottom as it pursued vulnerable Mexican immigrant workers to replace other worker groups. Among other shortcomings, the federal minimum wage failed to keep pace with the rising cost of living. The minimum wage stood stagnant at $5.15 an hour for ten years, from 1997 until a newly Democratic-majority Congress boosted the rate in 2007 to $7.25, still, when adjusted for inflation, far below the effective wage that was guaranteed at the inception of the already inadequate farmworker wage protections in 1966.[24]

Farm-labor contractors are notorious for taking undue advantage of Mexican immigrant workers, whose immigration status and language barriers render them vulnerable to exploitation. Workers are often overcharged for extras, such as job transportation (either to the fields or into town when workers are housed far from services), meals, substandard housing, and work equipment such as gloves; these charges erode the already-minimal wage protections.[25] Unscrupulous contractors may simply refuse to pay lawful wages, unilaterally lower the hours claimed by a worker to conform total pay to minimum-wage laws, and threaten to call la migra (federal immigration officials) should workers complain about their rights or unionize to ensure oversight. Some farm-labor contractors effectively enslave immigrants, taking advantage of their susceptibilities. In one example, immigrant farmworkers transported from the Arizona desert to Florida orange groves were threatened with beatings if they left work before repaying their steep transportation debt. Each week, the labor contractor paid the Florida workers only a tiny sum after deducting for their housing, work tools, and their cross-country transport.[26]

Other factors unique to farm labor suppress income. Workers may be idle for days without pay until field conditions are right and may suffer months without pay during off-seasons. Farmworkers were excluded from unemployment insurance benefits for years, despite the seasonal nature of their work. Today, in part because the undocumented status of many workers denies them benefits, only 39 percent of farmworkers are eligible for unemployment compensation.[27] California farmworkers finally secured unemployment coverage in the 1970s under Governor Jerry Brown, who succeeded Governor Ronald Reagan, a notorious enemy of farmworkers who called the 1960s grape strike immoral and vetoed unemployment compensation three times while in office.[28] Although we may lack compassion for farmworkers whose employment is seasonal and gives them considerable time off, compare their situation with that of most teachers, who make sufficient salaries from just nine months of teaching to support themselves and their families throughout the year. Teachers perform the vital function of educating our youth, but farmworkers feed them.

Unions have secured wage increases in other industries and are vital for exerting collective pressure on growers and labor contractors. The permission afforded other workers under the federal National Labor Relations Act to join unions and to strike was denied farmworkers, however, whom Congress excluded from that Act out of fear of disrupting the nation's food supply. Farmworkers thus remain vulnerable to being fired if they join unions.[29] Farmworker unions have long faced insurmountable odds in organizing unprotected workers given the readiness of even more needy immigrants to supplant strikers. Against these challenges and factors, such as globalization, that ravaged unions across the economy, by 2005 only 2 percent of California's field workers were represented by a union.[30]

Woefully deficient for decades, farmworker housing reflects the inadequate wages in the agricultural industry. The classic exposé of Dust Bowl–era conditions for Okie farm laborers in California, *Factories in the Field*, published in 1939, detailed "indescribably wretched" housing: a two-room cabin with forty-one occupants; housing without plumbing, prompting the workers to bathe and drink in irrigation ditches; shacks constructed of cardboard and linoleum; and tent cities pitched in a sea of mud.[31] Housing of Mexican bracero laborers (those allowed into the United States for a limited time) in Texas during the 1950s included a single building sheltering two hundred Mexican workers in continuous bunks of stretched canvas; bracero workers elsewhere lived in decrepit trailers, train cars, and chicken coops.[32] In 1966, Senator Robert Kennedy and other members of the U.S. Senate Subcommittee on Migratory Labor toured worker housing in Central California, visiting a farm-labor housing camp consisting of one-room tin shacks without toilets or water. Republican Senator George Murphy denounced the camp as "shameful,"[33] but housing conditions experienced little improvement. A more recent study of California farmworker housing found severe overcrowding, with laborers using structures not meant for residences, such as garages and tool sheds.[34] Even worse, many migrants lived in fields, cars, and holes dug into the ground. Some California migrant workers who slept in cardboard-lined holes bathed only when a ranch foreman hosed them down while he watered the crop.[35] As one California worker opined, "The owners don't care how we live. We are like burros to them."[36] In southern California, some farm laborers were using cardboard and plastic for housing to cover themselves;[37] such conditions are reminiscent of those during Chávez's early years, when, at times, his migrant laborer parents were forced to shelter their children under a tree with a piece of canvas overhead or inside the family's Studebaker automobile or a waterlogged tent.[38] One of my Seattle law students, spending the summer of 2012 visiting farm-labor camps in southwest Washington, discovered that most housing consisted of sheds or large buildings divided by bare plywood walls into small rooms that were accessed through shower curtains. Four or five farmworkers lived in each tiny room, sweltering in the tin shacks without cooling and suffering shared bathroom facilities that were dirty on arrival and often clogged. Nationally, many migrant laborers today live in pickup truck beds, in cars, on flattened cardboard in the dirt, or in a garage or other tiny dwelling stuffed with a dozen other workers. U.S. residents might ask themselves whether any other vital U.S. workers live in cars and holes in the ground.

More than miserable wages dictate the shameful living conditions of farmworkers. Undocumented immigrants may have spent thousands of dollars on their border passage and surreptitious transportation within the United States. Although farmwork may be seasonal, they must remain in the United States during the off-season rather than suffer the costs and hazards of multiple border migrations. Given these costs and hazards, the immigrant laborer likely has left behind family in Mexico, whose survival depends on remittances from the worker's U.S. wages. Mexican immigrant farmworkers thus tend to be solitary men who left their wives and girlfriends behind in Mexico for a lonely existence in remote U.S. fields. As detailed above, wages are inadequate, stagnant, and fail to account for migration costs unique to undocumented immigrant laborers. Field work tends to be seasonal, and given the short durations of some picking seasons many workers must be mobile and travel around the country at their own expense to follow the harvests. They cannot take advantage of discounts for longer-term housing rentals. Moreover, some hotbeds of agricultural labor are expensive real estate, such as California's Salinas Valley, the nation's top vegetable-producing region, which the New York Times labeled in 2005 the least affordable place to live in the country.[39] Housing may be scarce in rural locations far from urban apartment communities. Thus, farmworkers renting squalid trailers in Immokalee, Florida, often pay more than renters of condominiums in the resort area of Naples, Florida.[40] In light of these factors, immigrant laborers often make the wrenching but justifiable choice to disdain habitable housing and choose the cheapest option, which may be a spot in the dirt with a sleeping bag and a tarp. Finding that migrant workers bypassed a Napa Valley campsite costing only ten dollars a day, a journalist wrote, "To almost any U.S. citizen, that's a helluva bargain. But if you're from a little mountain village in southern Mexico, $10 is real money. . . . Down there, that's a month worth of corn and beans, or a few hundred pounds of charcoal, or a down payment on an irrigation pump. . . . [So sleeping by] the river is a reasonable alternative."[41]

Those farm laborers with the dignity of a roof over their head nonetheless often face overcrowding and safety issues that imperil their health and their family members. Because about one in five live in employer-supplied housing, complaining may prompt dismissal and thus eviction from their squalid housing.[42] A 2001 national study of farmworker housing found that almost one in ten dwellings lacked working toilets, and more than half offered no access to a laundry machine, a vital safety measure for farmworkers laden with pesticides yet with few changes of clothing. Many housing units in the study suffered rodent or insect infestation and fire safety issues such as frayed wiring.[43] Illustrating the miserable housing conditions farmworkers endure is this account of farm laborers in northern California who lived in structures "that included a burned out two-story building where about 20 to 25 single men slept on the floor every night. . . . The septic system was overflowing and there was raw sewage all over the place. There was no potable water supply. . . . As soon as [the workers] complained they lost their jobs."[44] Tragedy sometimes results from these dangerous conditions, as when a Latino tobacco farmworker's wife and two young children died because an extension cord running a portable heater in an old mobile home without central heating started a fire on New Year's Eve, 2003, while the worker was laboring in the Ohio tobacco fields.[45]

Job conditions are often as hazardous and substandard as farm-labor housing. Farm-labor unions have struggled for years with limited success to ensure that employers supply adequate toilets and drinking water in the fields, as employers sometimes ignore the scant legal requirements. Farm laborers are routinely doused with pesticides. The Environmental Protection Agency estimated that some three hundred thousand farmworkers annually suffer pesticide poisoning, with some ten thousand to twenty thousand of those workers suffering acute illnesses.[46] One incident reveals the dangers farm laborers face. In 1998 José Antonio Casillas, a seventeen-year-old Mexican immigrant farmworker in Utah, was accidently soaked by pesticides sprayed from a tractor. The next day, he was found dead from a brain hemorrhage that caused white foam to stream from his nostrils.[47] Many labor activists (and researchers) believe a connection exists between pesticide exposure and the higher incidence of cancers—brain, leukemia, skin, stomach, uterine, and others—among farmworkers as compared with other Latinos/as.[48] Birth defects and stillbirths run higher among children of farmworkers, evidenced by a boy born without limbs to a San Joaquin Valley farmworker exposed to pesticides, and an infant, born to a Florida farmworker, who had no nose, one ear, one kidney, a cleft lip and palate, and no visible sex organs.[49]

Farm labor is perhaps the most dangerous job in the nation. In 2002, for example, the National Safety Council reported 730 deaths (a rate almost six times higher than the rates in all other U.S. industries) and 150,000 disabling injuries among farmworkers.[50] In 2010, the fatality rate of farmworkers was more than seven times higher than that for other U.S. workers, and the injury rate was more than 20 percent higher.[51] At a time when the average U.S. life expectancy is 77.6 years, the life expectancy of migrant farmworkers is only 48 years.[52] Every year field workers die from thirst and heat exposure because of the often inadequate water and shade provided them. For years the UFW has urged legislation in California to impose criminal sanctions on employers whose farmworkers die or suffer injury from preventable exposure to extreme heat, mindful that California law already imposes criminal penalties on animal owners in similar circumstances. As the UFW asks, shouldn't farmworkers have the same protection as animals?

Reflecting their inadequate compensation, most farmworkers lack health insurance despite the deleterious effects of farm labor on their health. In 2000, only 15 percent of migrants and seasonal farmworkers had health coverage.[53] Despite the Supreme Court's upholding of the Obama-supported Affordable Care Act in 2012, most farmworkers are unable to share its benefits given their undocumented status. A California study found a third (32 percent) of male farmworkers had never seen a doctor in their lives, and half had never been to a dentist.[54] Another study found 18 percent of farmworkers had suffered a disabling back injury.[55] State workers' compensation programs tend to exclude the dangerous occupation of farmwork, with coverage mandated in only twelve states.[56]

Symbolizing the prevailing and historical disdain for the welfare of the U.S. farmworker is the legal and political saga of *el cortito*, the short-handled hoe. Only twelve inches long, the hoe forced laborers to bend over to weed fields and thin out rows of lettuce. Medical evidence established the hoe would cause abnormal degeneration of the spine, resulting in permanent disability and chronic back pain, yet California farmers fervently resisted its prohibition. Finally, after a seven-year struggle in the 1960s and 1970s to bury the short-handled hoe in the courts and administratively, California regulators prohibited the vile tool.[57]

Female farmworkers routinely face the tragedy of sexual harassment and brutal sexual assault at the hands of supervisors who exploit their vulnerability. These silent victims fear they may lose their job, or even suffer deportation when they are undocumented, if they report sexual violence to authorities.[58] A 2010 survey of Central California farmworker women found that 80 percent had experienced sexual harassment.[59]

Farmworker children pay their own special price for their parent's occupation. Many work in the fields, as U.S. law provides a special exemption from child-labor laws to allow young children to work in agriculture outside of school hours.[60] An estimated one hundred thousand children annually suffer agriculture-related injuries in the United States, as many use dangerous tools, labor near heavy machinery, and work with pesticides.[61] Exposed to pesticides in their homes and the fields and sometimes the victims of birth defects, they must overcome the obstacles poverty poses to an adequate education. Some must work to help support their families. Many immigrant farmworker parents are poorly educated (on average, the highest grade completed by crop workers is the seventh grade[62]) and illiterate. Given the added burdens of their long hours of work and the harshness of their employment, they can offer little help with their children's schoolwork. The migratory nature of much agricultural work further imperils children, who may be moved from school to school and who may suffer inadequate housing and lower-funded rural schools. As a result of these factors, dropout rates for migrant children sometimes exceed 50 percent.[63]

Obviously, the undocumented status of many farmworkers renders them uniquely vulnerable to the abuses in pay, housing, and occupational safety detailed above. Yet even documented Bracero Program workers, who came in the millions from 1942 to 1964, suffered many of these same indignities.[64] Ostensibly protected by a guest-worker accord between the U.S. and Mexican governments, these Mexican migrant workers came as needed to pick crops and labor in other critical industries. Strenuous farmwork defined these *bracero* laborers, translated literally as "those who work with their arms." The shabby treatment of Mexican bracero workers despite their government protection further confirms the shameful and ongoing history and experience of Mexican immigrant farmworkers in the United States. As one commentator summed up the bracero abuses, "They were routinely paid as little as twenty cents an hour, subjected to hazardous working conditions, and fired if they dared so much as to speak with labor organizers. They were promised pensions and benefits that they never received. They were confined by law to a contract system that conditioned their entry on working a single crop for a single employer, so they were not free to shop around for better wages and working conditions."[65]

Despite their vital work in U.S. fields to replace laborers (some of them Mexicans) fighting in World War II, bracero workers were subjected to discrimination and segregation. They were barred from restaurants and other businesses on the same terms as other Mexicans and Mexican Americans in the Southwest.[66] In the fields, as one bracero laborer described it, they were treated "like animals."[67] The 2010 documentary *Harvest of Loneliness: The Bracero Program* details how employers dehumanized bracero workers as slaves or animals. They were routinely sprayed with crop insecticide, supplied inadequate water in the fields, and assigned to back-crippling labor using the short-handled hoe. Forced to come to the United States alone without their spouses and children, upon entering the United States bracero workers faced the indignities of being herded naked through physical inspections, poked in the testicles in these humiliating medical exams, and sprayed with DDT to fumigate them. If they became hurt or sick they would be returned home to Mexico, so workers simply wouldn't report their injuries. Wages were less than promised, as the workers ended up paying excessive amounts for substandard housing and bad food. As one writer described it, the catering companies cut corners freely, supplying for dinner sheep heads and chicken necks that became the next day's moldy lunch leftovers.[68] Housing was substandard and miserable.

In Arizona, for example, 250 bracero workers were crowded into super-heated aluminum barracks with stoves inside but no air conditioning; their sleeping quarters thus replicated the inside of an oven. Growers evaded even the minimal wage requirements of the Bracero Program by continuously luring undocumented Mexican workers willing to work for lower wages. When renewal of the Bracero Program stalled in 1947 over Mexico's insistence on higher wages, U.S. immigration authorities even acted in concert with U.S. growers to allow undocumented Mexicans to cross the border into the waiting trucks of farmers.[69] Upon termination of the Bracero Program in late 1964 at the behest of labor leaders such as Chávez, religious organizations, and civil rights groups, these even more vulnerable undocumented workers replaced the braceros as agribusiness continued to require cheap labor.

*   *   *

Farmworkers work very hard. . . . They deserve better. The people who feed us should earn enough so that they can nourish their own bodies. Growers live all year from a seasonal harvest. Farmworkers should be able to as well.
—Dolores Huerta[70]

It's not just a question of [farmworker] wages. It's . . . a basic question of hope for the future.
—Robert Kennedy[71]

I like to tell people, if you had to be on a deserted island and you could only take one person with you, who would you take, an attorney or a farmworker? Right? . . . Because farm work is the most sacred work of all and yet farmworkers are so looked down upon.
—Dolores Huerta[72]

Enacting protective laws for farmworkers has always been a daunting proposition. Agribusiness is a formidable lobby against any measure that might increase labor and production costs. As summarized by one commentator, "Growers' organizations have consistently fought legislation designed to raise workers' wages, improve safety regulations, provide field sanitation, regulate pesticides and herbicides, and provide protections for farmworker organizing."[73] Stereotypes against Latinos/ as have been routinely employed to resist measures to benefit field workers, such as when opponents defeated an initiative proposed to California voters by the UFW in 1976 that would have added farm-labor protections to the state constitution. One opposing advertisement tapped into notions of the criminally minded Mexican to portray the possible outcome if Latino/a union organizers were allowed to enter farms to recruit workers. By showing a woman peering nervously from a farmhouse window, it, in effect, gave the message, "Do you want a Mexican on your property attacking your daughter?"[74] Similarly, in justifying the exclusion of farmworkers from the National Labor Relations Act in the 1930s, a former president of the Farm Bureau Federation explained it was "because they [the farmworkers] were Mexicans and coloreds."[75]

Because farmworkers are excluded from basic worker protections at the federal and state levels, a farmworkers' bill of rights, aimed merely at equalizing the rights of farmworkers with the rights of those in other occupations, is a meaningful goal to be sought in whichever regulatory venue—federal, state, or local—has traction. In his book on the value of migrant farmworkers, Daniel Rothenberg asks, "If those with politi-cal influence were to see farm laborers as people like themselves, could they accept the current status of America's migrants, here in our coun-try, where we ostensibly believe that those who work hard should be able to provide for themselves and their families?" Rothenberg goes on to imagine equality for farmworkers: "If farmworkers were viewed as similar to those with greater social power, what freedoms, rights, safe working conditions, decent wages, or adequate health care would the larger society feel comfortable denying them?"[76] Despite the imposing political battles ahead to establish an equitable future for farmworkers, it is evident what these laborers deserve as valued contributors to our economy and health. In short, we owe farm laborers sufficient pay to support a decent standard of living, housing, and heath for themselves and their families. Farmworkers deserve overtime pay and protection from discharge when they seek to unionize and collectively bargain with their employer. They deserve workers' compensation when they are injured on the job. Farm laborers should have the benefit of a safe working environment that values their welfare by minimizing exposure to pesticides and by supplying adequate water, protection from heat, and rest breaks, and that guards against sexual violence and harassment.[77] Moreover, whether accomplished through federal legislation specific to farm labor or through broader immigration reform, undocumented farm laborers who have been picking food for our dinner tables deserve the opportunity to regularize their immigration status and pursue U.S. citizenship should they choose. Currently, only sixty-eight thousand guest-worker visas are available to immigrant farmworkers, a number far below the agribusiness demand for immigrant pickers.[78] Regularization of their immigration status will help deter human rights abuses in the fields where vulnerable workers fear reporting wage theft, sexual harassment, and other injustices.

Ironically, adequate pay consistent with the rigor and danger of the work may ultimately lure U.S. citizen workers back to the fields. The UFW initiated the Take Our Jobs campaign in 2010 to draw attention to the miserable conditions and wages of agriculture work, offering the services of immigrant (and likely undocumented) workers to train U.S. citizens in farm labor.[79] The premise, confirmed by the meager response, was that few U.S. citizens would actually want to undertake the grueling career of field work, even in the throes of a recession. This outcome reflects the shrewd strategy of the agricultural industry—to attract the most vulnerable workers while paying scant wages rather than supplying sufficient incentives to draw any able-bodied worker to these difficult and often short-term jobs.[80] But paying significantly higher wages, whether as mandated by law or on the initiative of agribusiness, might actually lure U.S.-citizen workers who fall outside the vulnerable groups, and they might displace undocumented workers. This outcome, of course, is no excuse for retaining the prevailing conditions of labor oppression on the grounds that undocumented farmworkers somehow are better off than they would be in Mexico despite the miserable pay and conditions. Indeed, the Convention on the Protection of the Rights of All Migrant Workers and Members of Their Families, ratified by Mexico and other nations of the South, but not the United States, demands in Article 25 that "migrant workers shall enjoy equal treatment not less favorable than that which applies to nationals of the State of employment." By recognizing and honoring the humanity of migrant workers and their families, rather than focusing solely on their output as laborers, the Convention serves as a blueprint for compassionate reform. Consistent with this standard, the United States must aspire primarily to ensure the human rights and dignity of its entire workforce, restoring order in its own house, regardless of how cheaply immigrant laborers may be willing to work. Then, the United States can begin to tackle poverty in immigrant-feeder countries in the spirit of a good neighbor and even as the party responsible for a fair share of that hemispheric poverty. In the case of agriculture, stimulating the rural economies of Mexico might include terminating some of the government programs of largess to U.S. farmers that, through NAFTA and the U.S. export of subsidized staple crops such as corn, devastated Mexico's agricultural markets and rural workforce.[81]

Ending grower subsidies and adding labor costs through increased worker pay would no doubt prompt the typical response to such proposals: poor people in other occupations in the United States would suffer if food costs increased, as food is the ultimate necessity. The reasoning of this argument is that farmworkers who harvest the food, and their families, should endure some misfortune so that the rest of us can eat cheaply. There are two fundamental flaws in this logic. The first flaw is that increasing wages does not always result in prohibitive or even discernible costs at the grocery store or the restaurant. An example is the lengthy struggle over inadequate wages paid to Florida tomato pickers in the South Florida Everglades community of Immokalee. Most of the town's residents are Latino/a, with most of them Mexican. To tackle the daunting social and economic problems of the community and its households, local workers organized in the 1990s to demand a pay raise that echoed the goal of the UFW in the 1960s' Delano grape strike—the Florida tomato pickers, supplying nationwide Taco Bell restaurants, wanted a penny more for each pound picked. At the time, farmworkers were being paid from thirty-five to forty-five cents for each thirty-two-pound bucket they picked, so the wage demand would nearly double their income. For consumers, their Taco Bell chalupas would cost only one-fourth of a penny more.[82] By framing the wage struggle as a human rights campaign and attracting the support of college students, the workers succeeded in 2005 in obtaining their penny per pound increase. If the workers supplying every ingredient for the chalupas and those cooking and serving this tostada at the restaurant were paid fair wages, the cost might noticeably increase, although one study estimated that increasing the then-average hourly wage of $8.83 paid to U.S. farm-workers by 40 percent would still cost the average household just $9 a year.[83] This possibility raises the second and more fundamental flaw in the argument that labor costs must be kept low to ensure that the poor and even the middle class can afford food.[84] What the poor in every occupation really need is increased income to afford the necessities of life. Instead, they face an employment market that increasingly mimics the farm-labor model, in which employees are dehumanized and commodified:

> Increasingly, many American workers are starting to look more like farm laborers. American workers providing basic services and manual labor are increasingly employed under conditions that strongly resemble the farm labor system—working in uncertain, shifting, temporary jobs that provide no benefits and often do not pay enough to keep workers and their families above the poverty line. Industries of all types are now turning to [labor] contactors and subcontractors, allowing even the largest and wealthiest of companies to . . . creat[e] a world of structurally disempowered nonunionized workers who earn low wages and receive no benefits.[85]

Rather than pursue a race to the bottom and institute a crushing circularity in which field workers must suffer so that (for example) hotel maids can afford food, and hotel maids must tolerate low pay to ensure the affordability of transient housing for the field workers, we need to create a system of humanized employment in which there is enough wealth to go around. The next chapter tackles this problem of the growing inequality of wages and the attacks on welfare and the homeless that the U.S. labor-market dysfunctions have created. As with food, there is enough money to go around to supply basic human dignity if we are sufficiently moved to ensure that equity.

5

The Wages of Poverty

Inequality, Welfare Queens, and the Homeless

Poverty is the worst form of violence.
–Gandhi

Farmworkers, many of them impoverished, are the poorest of U.S. workers and demonstrate that our residents may have jobs but still suffer poverty. Our farmworkers tend to remain invisible within U.S. rural settings, as does the so-called underclass that services the cities, from dishwashing in restaurants to mowing lawns and cleaning hotel rooms. Hurricane Katrina briefly exposed the broad swaths of poverty extending into our urban landscapes, manifested during that crisis in the divide between those with the means to depart and to afford temporary housing and those left behind. Whether invisible or exposed, working or not, our poor garner little sympathy and compassion in this land of so-called rugged individualism, where they are readily dehumanized if they seek public assistance or are homeless.

Despite the promise of the 1960s' War on Poverty, we never won that war or even any battles. This chapter accordingly explores the current rise of U.S. poverty and its characteristics, along with the stark realities of poverty, which result in the need for welfare assistance and the dire possibility of homelessness. In sum, we will come to regret our ill regard for the impoverished and our public policies and private practices that foster or tolerate or even punish poverty and impede human dignity.

In this land of opportunity we view the poor as having failed through their own shortcomings and defects. Particularly evident in our disdain for the homeless and so-called welfare queens, both discussed later, is the image of the undeserving poor as those whose inferior culture contributes to their demise while they exploit government assistance. This negative image, resonating with the lesser perceived humanity of minority groups such as Latinos/as and African Americans, who are disproportionately poor, encompasses a perceived lesser work ethic (laziness); a lack of educational aspiration, ability, and achievement; loose morals that result in single parenthood; criminal proclivities; an inability to delay immediate gratification; and a propensity to abuse alcohol and drugs.[1] Anthropologists such as Oscar Lewis reinforced this perception by suggesting that cultures of poverty distinguish the poor from others.[2] This derogatory societal construction is readily debunked: many of the impoverished are the working poor whose grueling jobs do not sustain them financially. Their children often lack educational opportunity, rather than potential, and criminal statistics are fueled by the relationship between economic despair and petty theft and burglary and by the longstanding criminalization of poverty, manifested today in aggressive panhandling laws and status offenses of the homeless. The roots of the problem are largely structural, then, rather than the product of individual choice and culture. Nevertheless, the negative construction of the poor as an undeserving underclass is readily invoked to deny them dignity and adequate government assistance and to hinder economic reform and other vital structural changes.

Related to the blame directed at the individual poor, which aims to deflect attention from structural inequities, is the accusation, leveled most recently by the conservative Heritage Foundation, that the U.S. poor aren't really poor at all, especially when compared with the impoverished in other countries.[3] Apparently the fact that some of the U.S. poor have air conditioners, wide-screen televisions, and cars and wear clothes better than rags justifies the conclusion that they aren't worthy of compassion or help. The reality is that given the inadequacies of public transportation a car may be a working poor person's vital link to continued employment. Many perceived luxury items such as televisions and electronic game boxes are cheap yet still rented from oppressive rental centers, rather than owned, and are routinely repossessed. Clothing is relatively affordable here, prompting conservative scholar Victor Davis Hanson to dismiss the high number of people living in poverty given its invisibility in some venues, where the "windbreaker from Wal-Mart looks no different than the Wall Street tycoon's informal wear."[4] As Barbara Ehrenreich observed more sympathetically, thanks to consignment stores and Walmart, "the poor are usually able to disguise themselves as members of the more comfortable classes."[5]

Rather than being measured by the cheap cost of clothing, electronics, and appliances manufactured by underpaid employees, often in the Third World, the true impact of U.S. poverty is seen in the substandard housing, health care, and education of the poor. Moreover, although the U.S. poor may appear better off than the Third World poor because of the amenities most enjoy, such as running water and televisions, the United States must be held and aspire to its own standard of equity. Our poor are deprived of the basic securities and opportunities that the United States could readily supply them if we simply had the will, and that is the standard by which our tolerance and even disdain for the poor should be judged.

Although poverty has long been engrained and widespread in our economy, it is worsening. Based on measures of poverty that are themselves unrealistically low,[6] U.S. poverty has risen so much it erased gains from the 1960s' War on Poverty and returned us by 2011 to a poverty level (15 percent of the U.S. population; 46.2 million impoverished) last seen in 1965.[7] Analysts predict this alarming poverty level will plague us through at least the end of 2014, spurred by expiring unemployment benefits and weak job and wage growth.[8] As Peter Edelman, former aide to Senator Robert Kennedy, wrote in 2012, extreme poverty, defined as people living below half of the already-low poverty line, is rising fast: 20.5 million U.S. residents lived in extreme poverty in 2010, with 6 million having no income aside from food stamps.[9] Edelman suggests the reach of U.S. poverty is vast, especially when adding the near poor, whom he defines as those with incomes falling below twice the poverty line (which in 2010 was $22,000 for a family of four and was $23,550 in 2013); in 2010 the number of poor and near poor in the United States exceeded a whooping 103 million.[10] That staggering figure follows from the reality that the median full-time, year-round job in the United States paid only about $34,000, and a quarter of U.S. jobs paid below the poverty line for a family of four.[11] In 2014, Walmart stores, for example, paid cashiers about $8.54 an hour, above the federal minimum wage but still resulting in an annual salary of only about $17,000.[12]

Poverty disproportionately affects residents of color, women, the disabled, and children. Although white U.S. residents constitute the largest numerical group of the impoverished, Latinos/as, blacks, and Native Americans are disproportionately poor—facing close to three times the white poverty rate.[13] The situation of these groups elevates poverty in the United States to a compelling civil rights issue. For example, in 2011, the black poverty rate was 27.6 percent while the white rate was 9.8 percent.[14] One-third of female-headed single-parent households live in poverty,[15] and women comprise three-fifths of the adult impoverished population[16] with their poverty rate in 2010 the highest in seventeen years.[17] Many of the poor are disabled, and the disabled are disproportionately poor, suffering a poverty rate in 2011 of 28.8 percent.[18] The United States has the highest child poverty rate among industrialized nations,[19] with almost sixteen million children, many of them black or Latino/a, living in poverty, and seven million of them in extreme poverty.[20] As Edelman wrote, "We are the wealthiest country in the world; that we should have poverty at all is oxymoronic, and that we have the highest child poverty rate in the industrialized world is downright shameful."[21]

An estimated fifty million Americans go to bed hungry each night,[22] many of them children. Hunger results from food being one of the few flexible items in a household budget—rent and utilities are constants, leaving the food budget to yield to the dictates of and variances in meager finances. Lacking a balanced diet, these children can be at elevated risk of contracting diabetes, asthma, dental problems, cancer, and other afflictions, all affiliated with poverty.[23]

*   *   *

I went down this morning to sign up my Dog for welfare. At first the lady said, "Dogs are not eligible to draw welfare." So I explained to her that my Dog is black, unemployed, lazy, can't speak English and has no frigging clue who his Daddy is. So she looked in her policy book to see what it takes to qualify. My Dog gets his first check Friday. Is this a great country or what?
—E-mail "joke" forwarded by a Republican official in Virginia[24]

How come you never see an African-American family portrait?
    Because when the photographer says, "Say cheese," they all run to the welfare center and form a straight line.
—"Joke" in early 1990s calendar sold by Waldenbooks[25]

Restrictive welfare reform was inevitable once the longstanding conception of the undeserving poor was racialized in the second half of the twentieth century both by the image of the welfare queen, which became code for African American unwed mothers, and by the Mexican face of poverty as large numbers of low-wage immigrant workers arrived from Mexico.[26] The 1996 Personal Responsibility and Work Opportunity Reconciliation Act (PRWORA), championed by President Clinton and discussed below, was the result of this antipoor, antiblack, and anti-immigrant animus, which viewed welfare recipients as abusing the system and obtaining financial rewards for their unlawful or immoral behavior.

Wielded by Ronald Reagan, among other politicians, the imagery of the welfare queen evoked stereotypes of black women dating back to slavery, when images of lazy workers were proffered to help justify their despicable treatment and punishments. Conjoined to conceptions of black women as promiscuous, which is another stereotype from the era of slavery, when white owners raped their female slaves at will to ensure propagation of the labor force, the lazy, promiscuous construction of welfare recipients took firm hold in the American imagination. As one commentator put it, we see welfare mothers "as dishonest and irresponsible individuals who purchase bottles of vodka with food stamps intended to help feed their children, or as immoral and promiscuous individuals who are said to breed children to rip off the welfare system for more benefits."[27] Racially coded by welfare critics, the derogatory moniker of *welfare queen* became the popular reference for "'young, inner-city black mother[s]' who stay on welfare for many years and pass on their 'bad values' to their children, who become 'future welfare mothers, unemployed males, and criminals,'" a description that presumes a cycle and culture of poverty.[28] Intelligence factored into the debate, as the infamous *Bell Curve* authors equated poverty with low intelligence in suggesting welfare encouraged the wrong members of society to become mothers and arguing that our welfare policy "subsidizes births among poor women, who are also disproportionately at the low end of the intelligence distribution."[29] Public opinion eventually accepted this image of the lazy, unentitled, and promiscuous welfare recipient, with studies finding that only 31 percent of those surveyed felt welfare recipients who could work were trying to find jobs, and another finding 59 percent believed most able-bodied recipients preferred to sit home and collect welfare.[30] Augmenting this negative image was the false perception that black residents accounted for a majority of U.S. welfare recipients.[31]

Regarding immigrants, particularly evident in the 1994 campaign that led California voters to approve Proposition 187, which denied public benefits to undocumented immigrants, was the perception that immigrants come to the United States for the social-welfare net, both for themselves and for their children.[32] Apparent in that political debate was how "illegal alien" became a code phrase for Mexican immigrants, who are saddled with longstanding anti-Mexican and anti-Latino/a conceptions of laziness, fertility, unintelligence, and criminality. Scholars have debunked the view that our public benefits are a significant lure to immigrants, finding instead that jobs and economic opportunity draw immigrants from Mexico and elsewhere.[33] But these misconceptions still prevail.

Race and the undeserving poor, thus conjoined, became an irresistible target for politicians even though the entire construction was built on myths, such as the perception that welfare mothers fail to work or to seek work.[34] Reagan, in a presidential primary, famously invoked imagery of the welfare queen in discussing a "woman in Chicago" who allegedly had "80 names [and] 30 addresses," thereby "collecting welfare under each of her names."[35] Implicating immigrants in the alleged welfare free-for-all, Republican Senator Phil Gramm contended in 1996, "Immigrants should come to the U.S. with their sleeves rolled up, ready to work, not with their hands out, ready to go on welfare."[36] A master spin doctor, Reagan was able to dehumanize welfare recipients with negative connotations, while simultaneously constructing the receipt of welfare as a dehumanizing experience for the poor. He argued in his first inaugural address as governor of California that "we are not going to perpetuate poverty by substituting a permanent dole for a paycheck. There is no humanity or charity in destroying self-reliance, dignity and self-respect . . . the very substance of moral fiber."[37] The conflation of recipients of color, laziness, and the supposed debilitating side of government assistance was particularly evident in the 2012 presidential campaign, with Republican vice presidential candidate Paul Ryan calling welfare a "culture of dependency," and Republican presidential hopefuls Newt Gingrich and Rick Santorum contending respectively that "the African-American community should demand paychecks and not be satisfied with food stamps" and that we should not "make black people's lives better by giving them somebody else's money: I want to give them the opportunity to go out and earn the money."[38]

Debating welfare reform that was enacted in PRWORA, in 1995 U.S. Congressman John Mica from Florida likened welfare recipients to animals in suggesting that supplying unnatural feeding fosters the dependency of alligators that would otherwise gather food for their young. Wyoming representative Barbara Cubin compared welfare recipients to caged wolves that are given elk and venison and lose their dignity and ability to hunt.[39] Around the same time, the Heritage Foundation published a report in 1994 warning of the alarming growth of so-called behavioral poverty—defined as severe social pathologies including "an eroded work ethic and dependency, the lack of educational aspirations and achievement, an inability or unwillingness to control one's children, as well as increased single parenthood, illegitimacy, criminal activity, and drug and alcohol use."[40]

With these dehumanized constructions of welfare recipients blaming the poverty victim and the doublespeak of promoting humanization through preventing welfare dependency, the stage was set in 1996 for restrictive welfare reform directed at vulnerable single mothers and immigrants. Under the then-existing welfare program of Aid to Families with Dependent Children (AFDC), families were able to continue receiving government aid as long as they were in need. Scrapping the AFDC system, PRWORA welfare reform in 1996 established the aptly-named replacement program, Temporary Assistance for Needy Families (TANF). TANF monies are distributed through the states with a mandated five-year lifetime limit on receipt of benefits regardless of child-care issues; an additional requirement generally mandates that single mothers receiving TANF benefits begin working a minimum of thirty hours weekly within two years of starting to receive benefits. As a result of this law, which Democratic President Clinton declared would "end welfare as we know it," several mothers had to abandon their children,[41] while others were forced into homelessness. Even worse, impoverished families who still qualified for poverty assistance began to forego seeking help because of the stigma now attached to government aid.[42] Despite Clinton's 2006 told-you-so editorial in the *New York Times* declaring the success of PRWORA,[43] that "mission accomplished" euphoria soon turned sour as the great recession, the mortgage meltdown, and the global economic crisis emerged to reveal the holes in the safety net that Clinton erected.

PRWORA reform also scapegoated immigrants, who are thought to be lured to the United States by welfare despite the recognition by almost every immigration scholar that immigrants come primarily for jobs.[44] PRWORA denied most federal benefits to undocumented immigrants, with the exception of a few programs such as immunizations, and also terminated many federal benefits to documented immigrants, including supplemental security income (SSI) for elderly and disabled immigrants, food stamps, TANF welfare assistance, and Medicaid. Although Congress did eventually restore SSI and food stamps for some documented immigrants, those immigrants arriving after 1996 are ineligible unless financially-strapped individual states supply these basic staples of government aid.[45]

The upshot of 1990s welfare reform is that immigrants and single mothers, among the most vulnerable members of the low-wage workforce, were left without a safety net when the great recession arrived a decade later, sending many to the streets. Here, longstanding disdain for the homeless population relegated them to being subject to our regrettable treatment of the homeless who dare to step out of the shadows and expose their poverty to the masses. Other homeless remained hidden in the shadows, such as the undocumented workers who huddled in blankets in what they called "Devils Cave," a four-foot-high crawlspace under the porch of a New Jersey home abandoned by its owner in the economic crisis that began in 2008.[46] Once the economy recovered, they could emerge to resume their contributions to our economy, working low-wage, miserable jobs in the shadow economy of the undocumented and poor.

*   *   *

[People] look at you like you're nothing but a piece of garbage.
—Eddie, a homeless man in Binghamton, New York[47]

> I was conditioned at a very young age to view homeless people as worthless alcoholics and drug addicts. They were not human—they were thugs and murderers and a burden to society. Or so I thought. Until I got "the look."
> —Homeless man forced to spend a winter night on the New York City subway, describing a contemptuous stare from another rider[48]

We reserve our most vile constructions of the poor for the homeless. As one writer described it, the homeless body in the American imagination is a "body of decay," a "degenerate body," one seen as "sick," "scary," "dirty," and "smelly," in essence "street trash," and one marked by disease and feces, urine, and bacteria.[49] As with the poor generally, the homeless are often seen as making their own concrete and cardboard beds—as somehow choosing their lifestyle through an aversion to work or by their voluntary addictions to alcohol and drugs. Justifying his attack on federal low-income housing programs, Reagan invoked this perception in stating that those living on the street choose to be there.[50]

Despite the foul contention that the homeless somehow desire to brave the daunting urban elements outdoors, homelessness is inexorably tied to poverty. As poverty rose during the great recession, so too did homelessness as the mortgage-foreclosure crisis forced many families onto the streets. Even before that crisis, the trend of growing homelessness since the Reagan presidency led the National Coalition for the Homeless to estimate in 2006 that approximately 3.5 million Americans, about 1.3 million of them children, were homeless at some time during the year.[51] Youth and women are particularly vulnerable, with youth susceptible to sexual assault and many women fleeing from domestic violence.[52] Countering the stereotype of the homeless man, the fastest growing homeless population is families, many of them led by single mothers,[53] who are likely to be refugees from welfare reform. A considerable number of the homeless in some areas are employed but earn insufficient income to afford the outrageous cost of housing in cities such as New York City, which in 2012 experienced its biggest wave of homelessness since the Great Depression, an increase that coincided with cuts to a government rental-subsidy program.[54]

With their degraded image, the homeless are treated shabbily in most U.S. cities. Conservative writer John Derbyshire mocked those compassionate jurisdictions that instead honor the dignity of their homeless;

he suggested that we incarcerate the homeless until they cease being a nuisance through their defecating in public places, shrieking gibberish, and exposing themselves to female passersby.[55] True to the prevailing construction, most jurisdictions vilify the homeless, effectively criminalizing their status and giving them a criminal record, which could prove fatal to procuring the employment and stability they need to escape poverty's clutches. Given the dubious constitutionality of most local ordinances targeting the homeless, which keeps many of these laws mired in litigation, communities tend to experiment with a variety of oppressive approaches. Some have outlawed sitting down or resting in public places; such laws are invitations for the police to selectively enforce their application not against the tired tourist but against the entrenched homeless resident. Some jurisdictions outlaw camping on public property and may routinely destroy the possessions of the homeless in evicting them from unlawful camps.[56] In one survey of cities, 17 percent outlawed camping citywide, while 30 percent barred sitting in certain public places. Others outlawed panhandling, which raises free speech concerns, or enacted antiloitering laws, which are in effect citywide in 19 percent of the surveyed cities and that are often challenged as unconstitutionally vague.[57] A few jurisdictions even prohibit so-called enablers of the homeless—humanitarians who give food to the hungry in public places.[58] Some, such as Honolulu, which replaced transit benches with concrete stools, and cities that run sprinklers at night in parks, craftily avoid legal challenges by discouraging rather than outlawing the homeless. Overall, these local restrictions render everyday life effectively impossible for the homeless and arguably violate international human rights law, discussed below, in addition to U.S. constitutional standards and our own sense of decency.[59]

Regardless of their dubious legality, these criminal ordinances, combined with the prevailing negative images of the homeless, invite vigilantism and hate crimes directed at the vulnerable homeless, who are frequently attacked and killed for sport or spite. In 2009, for example, forty-three homeless persons were killed, and countless others were attacked, such as a homeless man in Pompano Beach, Florida, whom two teens dragged down the street by his ankles while laughing and filming the beating for a YouTube video. Similarly, in 2006 teenage attackers in Fort Lauderdale, Florida, beat a homeless veteran to death with a baseball bat while he slept on a park bench; the attackers explained that they assaulted the homeless for sport.[60] These attacks by the common perpetrators (young men) targeted the common victims (middle-aged men) in this spiraling violence against the vulnerable homeless where they live.[61] But women are vulnerable too, as evidenced by the horrible assault in 2012 of a sixty-seven-year-old homeless woman in Los Angeles who was set ablaze by a young man while she slept on a bus bench.

*   *   *

Consider what the United States would offer its residents if we respected the dignity of all workers and those unable to find work or physically or mentally unable to work. From a human rights perspective, the Universal Declaration of Human Rights, adopted by the U.N. General Assembly in 1948, ensures that "everyone has the right to a standard of living adequate for the health and well-being of himself and of his family, including food, clothing, housing, and medical care and necessary social services, and the right to security in the event of unemployment, sickness, disability, widowhood, old age, or other lack of livelihood in circumstances beyond his control."[62] The Bible, too, is replete with commands to assist the poor; these commands are directed particularly at the wealthy, who are beseeched to give generously to the needy—namely, "It is more blessed to give than to receive."[63]

Yet in many instances the poor simply desire decent pay for their hard work. Given the reality of our working poor, who cannot comfortably live on a minimum wage despite working full time, an adequate standard of living demands higher base wages that are compelled by federal, state, or local government.[64] Thus the foremost priority should be to raise income levels to a living wage.[65] Reversal of declining federal support for low-income housing is needed to tackle homelessness, along with more compassionate welfare laws that abandon arbitrary lifetime limits on the receipt of benefits and recognize the need for a financial safety net for immigrants who undertake the jobs most U.S. residents won't do. Tackling the structural roots of poverty will require increased investment in education by government to ensure opportunities for higher education, which is so crucial for income attainment. Each of these reforms is addressed below.

Minimum wage is among the most contentious mandates of government, despised by free-market advocates and proponents of trickle-down economics such as Reagan. Resistance to the minimum wage prompted its stagnation; the federal wage remained at $5.15 an hour from 1997 to 2007, when a newly Democratic Congress increased it to $7.25 by July 2009, supplying a raise to almost 4.5 million workers.[66] The federal minimum has since stood still, remaining below the effective wage, adjusted for inflation, of decades ago. Although as of early 2014 twenty-one states mandated a higher minimum wage,[67] the federal floor prevailed in most states. Working a full-time, forty-hour week for fifty-two weeks of the year, a person earning the federal minimum wage would generate an annual salary of only $15,080. Most readers can imagine the difficulty of supporting a single person, much less an entire family, on this salary. Even raising the minimum wage to $10 an hour would result in only $20,800 annually, below the U.S. poverty line for a family of four and roughly aligned with the federal minimum wage in 1968, as adjusted for inflation.[68] Still, some wealthy business leaders advocate lowering or eliminating the minimum wage, with Peter Schiff, CEO of Connecticut-based Euro Pacific Capital, suggesting in 2014 that without the minimum wage U.S. employers could pay workers their fair worth, with the "mentally retarded" deserving just $2 an hour![69]

Contrary to the popular belief that only teenagers working summers are paid the minimum wage, jobs across the economic spectrum, particularly those held by immigrants, documented or not, by persons of color, and by women, tend to pay the minimum wage or, in any case, still less than a living wage.[70] As other writers have suggested, when thinking of typical minimum-wage workers, think of "women working in garment sweatshops and chain stores," "farmworkers, fast food workers and cannery workers," and "janitors and housekeepers cleaning the homes, offices and hotel rooms of people who make more in a day than they make in a year."[71] Once the province of women and teenagers supplementing family income with part-time jobs, low-paying retail and fast-food jobs today are far more likely to be filled with family breadwinners. This new reality explains a much-publicized 2013 McDonald's video in which a long-time employee earning minimum wages was counseled to supplement her meager income for her family by obtaining food stamps and visiting food banks.[72]

Given the high prevailing rates of unemployment despite millions of people looking for work, job creation is vital. However, opponents of minimum-wage hikes routinely contend that businesses, particularly small businesses, will simply refuse to create new jobs if labor costs run too high. To complement a minimum-wage hike, then, requires the creation of a considerable number of jobs by the government, each paying a living wage. Vital opportunities exist across the country to create jobs rebuilding infrastructure, and doing so can ultimately boost the economy. Modeled after the job-creating initiative of the Depression-era Works Progress Administration, government jobs could foster economic growth in areas such as infrastructure renovations (beginning with government buildings such as schools and offices and encompassing roadways) to ensure energy efficiency and earthquake-readiness in certain regions.

Despite the outcry that accompanies demands for minimum-wage hikes in small businesses, major employers reap enormous profits from maintaining low pay rates. For example, the typical full-time retail cashier makes just $18,500 a year.[73] A 2012 report urged the nation's top retailers (those with at least one thousand workers) to raise their full-time wages for all employees to just $25,000 annually; this change would alone lift 734,075 people above the federal poverty line, as well as help even more who hover just above poverty. The report explains how such an increase would create new jobs in the U.S. economy as well as ultimately increase store revenues. It further demonstrates how companies could fund the wage increase through profits alone, with negligible impact on the household budgets of retail shoppers.[74] Yet Walmart and most other retailers fervently resist such wage initiatives whether implemented voluntarily or mandated by law.

In addition to the removal of lifetime limits for welfare recipients unable to find work and the provision of benefits to immigrants, documented or not, who perform our hardest jobs, single-parent low-income wage earners need workplace day-care programs to facilitate their entry into the workplace; the Center for American Progress proposed in 2007 that federal and state governments guarantee child-care assistance to families with annual incomes under $40,000.[75] Overall, the United States spends less on social welfare as a percentage of its gross national product (GNP) than Western European countries do, a statistic mirrored by the inequity inherent in the fact that the United

States, which enjoys "virtually the highest GNP per capita in the world," has higher levels of poverty than rich countries in Western Europe.[76]

Federal investment in low-cost housing is essential, yet the federal housing-assistance budget decreased 48 percent from 1976 to 2004.[77] In no state does the minimum wage supply sufficient income for adequate housing; for example, in Hawai'i a minimum-wage laborer would need to work an impossible 175 hours weekly (the week has only 168 hours) to earn enough to achieve the standard 30 percent of income needed to rent two-bedroom housing.[78] The amount of affordable housing in the United States suitable for the nine million households earning between only $11,000 and $18,000 annually falls far short of the amount necessary.[79] Meanwhile, federal and state governments choose to invest in a different type of housing for low-income residents—prisons, which are fed by criminalization through campaigns such as the War on Drugs that help ensure the entrenchment of poverty in U.S. landscapes. Local governments and charities supply housing for the impoverished in temporary shelters, which, although crucial as a safety net, undermine the dignity and privacy of occupants.[80] The impoverished need additional stable housing and job opportunities to attain their human right to decent housing, despite the Supreme Court's refusal to recognize housing as a constitutional right.[81] As a group of poverty commentators suggested, what the impoverished deserve is "a massive infusion of federal funds into low-income and affordable housing, part of a 'Marshall Plan' to rebuild American cities," including "sums for the construction of new public housing, maintenance and rehabilitation of existing public housing, and encouragement of not-for-profit, community-based housing production, ownership, and management."[82]

Household poverty is a significant contributor to dismal educational achievement and to students dropping out of high school. Yet completing the cycle of poverty is the reality that financial stability increasingly depends on graduation from college, which boosts earnings some 65 percent.[83] Because the likelihood of obtaining a four-year college education is less than one in fifteen for children of poor families,[84] generational poverty and struggle are virtually guaranteed. As college tuition skyrockets, the federal government must supply sufficient financial aid, especially through tax credits and loan forgiveness, to foster educational opportunity within the lower classes.[85] Yet complicating the equation "education equals financial success" is the reality that the number of U.S. residents with doctorate degrees receiving public assistance increased more than threefold between 2007 and 2010,[86] suggesting defects in the creation of meaningful, full-time employment at a living wage for those with any level of education.

Obviously, meeting the above requirements for compassionate treatment of the working class to defeat poverty demands considerable government spending. Conveniently, there is a ready source of that revenue that springs from one of the staggering injustices of our time—the spiraling wage gap between the average U.S. worker and the super-rich. In addition to the dubious distinction of having the highest rate of child poverty in the industrial world, the United States also has the greatest gap between rich and poor among major industrialized nations.[87] The poster children of the ridiculous excess fueling the U.S. wage gap are not athletes or celebrities or even CEOs but hedge-fund managers. In 2011, a down year for these overpaid magicians of finance, Ray Dalio, only the forty-fourth richest U.S. resident, earned a whopping $3.9 billion as manager of the world's largest hedge fund.[88] The average income-earning U.S. family (earning almost $50,000 in 2009) would need over 75,000 years of employment to equal that feat! Put differently, a smallish city could live comfortably on one U.S. man's yearly earnings. As demonstrated in the aptly titled book *How to Make a Million Dollars an Hour: How Hedge Funds Get Away with Siphoning Off America's Wealth*, other managers enjoy similar success.[89]

After decades (from the early 1930s through the late 1970s) during which the income share of the wealthiest U.S. residents remained stable or fell, Reagan's presidency helped launch a sustained push of income that skyrocketed inequality. Rather than all boats rising, middle-class income stagnated and poverty blossomed as Reagan guarded against any increase in the federal minimum wage, while the super-rich became richer. Intertwined with income disparity, the wealth gap is equally unequal. Having 1,500 times more wealth than the bottom 40 percent of U.S. residents in 1983, the wealthiest 1 percent widened that disparity by 2001 to more than 4,400 times.[90] Today, the wealthiest 1 percent is estimated to hold nearly 50 percent of our country's wealth, with the richest 20 percent holding 84 percent of our nation's wealth.[91] By 2007, the upper 1 percent of U.S. earners received nearly 24 percent of U.S.

pretax income,[92] their largest share of income since 1928; the Occupy Wall Street movement was created on behalf of the other 99 percent of income earners. The great recession failed to significantly impede the wage (and wealth) inequity, as the median compensation in 2010 for CEOs of large U.S. corporations was still almost $11 million.[93] CEO salaries previously jumped almost 500 percent between 1980 and 1995, during what one commentator dubbed the Great Divergence period,[94] while company profits increased only 145 percent and the average factory worker gained only 70 percent in pay, not enough to keep pace with the 85 percent increase in inflation.[95] Based in Illinois, McDonald's food chain paid its CEO $8.75 million in 2011; at the same time Illinois fast-food workers earned just $8.25 an hour, the state's minimum wage; a single worker would need to work more than one million hours to reach the CEO's yearly salary.

Tax reform holds the promise of supplying government revenue to address poverty in the world's richest country as well as to tackle the moral crisis of severe income inequality. Imposing income caps in the private sector is not practical across industries, and legislation mandating equalized family income is unpopular: a 1969 survey found that 80 percent of the U.S. public opposed the concept of every U.S. family receiving the same income.[96] Yet raising taxes on the wealthy allows for income differentials while protecting against poverty and harnessing our spiraling income inequality. It is also consistent with growing public sentiment to tackle income inequality, reflected in a study finding that most Americans (52 percent) now agree it is government's responsibility to reduce income differentials between rich and poor (up from just 39 percent in 1985).[97] Relatedly, another study found that 92 percent of Americans preferred to live in a society with less income disparity; respondents chose the model of a country such as Sweden rather than perfect income equality.[98]

Back in 1942, President Franklin Roosevelt proposed raising taxes to 100 percent for U.S. residents earning what today would be equivalent to more than $345,000 a year, adjusted for inflation;[99] this amount is close to the income of today's top 1 percent of earners. Although U.S. tax rates on the wealthy were once quite substantial (at times in the twentieth century exceeding 90 percent), Reagan led the crusade to lower taxation for the rich. He accomplished a reduction in the tax rate for those in the highest earning bracket from 70 percent down to 28 percent during his presidency, thus helping launch the Great Divergence period. The highest tax bracket later jumped to 39.6 percent, where it stayed until 2003, when President George W. Bush succeeded in lowering it to 35 percent. After the American Taxpayer Relief Act of 2012, the highest rate returned to 39.6 percent for single filers earning more than $400,000 and married couples earning more than $450,000. Yet the reality of our taxation system for the rich is even more favorable, with low tax rates on capital gains and dividends (mostly taxed at a low rate since 2003) making a huge contribution to income inequality, and a host of deductions, such as the mortgage-interest and real-estate-tax deductions, considerably lowering the effective rate paid by the wealthy. For example, mega-wealthy financier Warren Buffett paid only 17.4 percent of his 2010 income in taxes, leading him to propose higher tax brackets for the wealthy![100] Mitt Romney, who continues to urge lower taxes for the rich, paid only 13.9 percent in taxes on his household's 2010 income of about $22 million—far below the flat tax Buffett proposed in late 2012 for wealthy taxpayers: 30 percent for income between $1 and $10 million and 35 percent for income above that. Imagine the possibilities of obtaining revenue from a reformed tax structure. One commentator suggested that redistributing 42.5 percent of one year's increase in the net worth of just the four hundred richest Americans would have lifted thirty million U.S. residents above the poverty line.[101]

Obama was able to extinguish the Bush tax cuts for high-income earners as an initial baby step toward reducing economic inequality. Overall, though, the grassroots Occupy movement fizzled after briefly galvanizing U.S. residents against the economic piracy of the super-rich. I am not contending here that distributive measures targeting the wealthy have political viability—although the passage by voters in 2012 of Proposition 30, California's temporary high-earner tax increase for education, suggests the allure of temporary increases tied to funding popular causes such as schools or public safety. Rather, I am suggesting how we would treat our workers and the poor generally if we felt compassion toward them as fellow human beings, and I am suggesting as well that society eventually will regret our present policies, which leave many residents in the world's richest country uncertain where their next meal will come from.

6

Sexuality and Dehumanization

Homophobia in U.S. Law and Life

Homosexual conduct is, and has been, considered abhorrent, immoral, detestable, a crime against nature, and a violation of the laws of nature and of nature's god. . . . It is an
inherent evil against which children must be protected.
—Alabama Supreme Court Chief Justice Roy Moore

God Hates Fags.
—Westboro Baptist Church (Topeka, Kansas)

Hate Fags? The answer's "yes."
—Eminem, "Criminal"

No Homo.
—Professional basketball star Roy Hibbert in a 2013
postgame interview that drew a $75,000 fine

Despite considerable progress in their legal and societal treatment since
the 1960s, for the most part the U.S. homosexual population remains
constructed in subhuman terms. Pejorative terms abound such as *fag,
faggot, fairy, queer, fruit, sissy, dyke,* and *homo,* as well as the dismissive
retort of "no homo" in today's hip-hop culture. Despite the Supreme
Court's invalidation in 2003 of criminal antisodomy laws, which were
previously enforced against LGBT populations, opportunities remain for
constructing the U.S. sexual minority population in criminal, and thus
subhuman, terms. Singer Anita Bryant, a staunch critic of gay equality,
famously galvanized voters in Florida against gay rights by suggesting
homosexuals prey on children, warning in a full-page *Miami Herald*
ad in 1977 that "recruitment of our children is absolutely necessary for
the survival and growth of homosexuality. Since homosexuals cannot

reproduce, they must recruit, must freshen their ranks."[1] She claimed further that giving rights to homosexuals would next mean equal rights for "people who sleep with St. Bernards."[2] Writing in 2003 to dissent from the Court's invalidation of antisodomy laws enforced against U.S. gays, Supreme Court Justice Antonin Scalia essentially compared homosexuality to bestiality in stating the impossibility of distinguishing homosexuality from this traditional morals offense.[3] Similarly, in denouncing same-sex marriage in 2003, politician Rick Santorum compared homosexuality to "man on child, man on dog, or whatever the case may be."[4]

Gays have been variously constructed as public health threats, both mentally and physically. Until release of the 1973–1974 diagnostic manual by the American Psychiatric Association, medical authorities viewed homosexuality as a mental disease—an abnormality;[5] this diagnosis justified brutal, involuntary medical "treatments" encompassing removal of sex organs, lobotomies, and electric-shock treatment.[6] That view of abnormality persists among some. In 1986, U.S. Senator Strom Thurmond asked the director of the National Gay and Lesbian Task Force whether his organization advocates "any kind of treatment for gays and lesbians to see if they can change them and make them normal like other people?"[7] In 2012, however, California sided against what Governor Jerry Brown called the "dustbin of quackery"—that sexual orientation can be altered through treatment—by outlawing therapy aimed to convert gay youth (under age eighteen) to a straight sexual orientation.[8] And, in 2012, the American Psychiatric Association removed its mental-illness classification of "gender-identity disorder," under which a man, for example, believing himself more properly identified as a woman, was seen as mentally ill. Yet in 2013, a representative of the Family Research Council testified against including gender identity in Maryland's antidiscrimination laws, arguing that transgender people have a "disconnect with reality" requiring psychological treatment.[9]

Antigay attacks readily invoke imagery of disease and filth and particularly exploit the fear of AIDS transmission. For example, the influential head of the Family Research Institute (once called the Institute for the Scientific Investigation of Sexuality) has written: "The typical sexual practices of homosexuals are a medical horror story—imagine exchanging saliva, feces, semen and/or blood with dozens of different men each year. Imagine drinking urine, ingesting feces and experiencing rectal trauma on a regular basis. . . . Each year, a quarter or more of homosexuals visit another country. Fresh American germs get taken to Europe, Africa, and Asia. And fresh pathogens from these continents come here."[10] Socialite Paris Hilton channeled this fear in a secretly recorded taxi-cab conversation in 2012, when she deemed gay men "disgusting" and opined "most of them probably have AIDS."[11]

In sum, these images and constructions suggest that homosexuals and transgender people are somehow less than human. Some make this connection even more explicit. A college student who later became an aide to a Republican state senator in Maryland was disciplined for violating his school's conduct code by his Facebook posting opposing a gay-rights campus group: "Why do we have to tolerate the sub-human actions of people like this on campus?"[12] ESPN sports-radio announcers in 2012 described a transgender college basketball player, Gabrielle Ludwig, as "he/she" and "it."[13] Marcus Bachmann, husband of 2012 presidential candidate Congresswoman Michele Bachmann, referred to gays as "barbarians" who need to be educated and "disciplined."[14] Pope Benedict XVI (Joseph Ratzinger) implied that gay people are not fully developed humans in his 2012 remarks against gay marriage, in which he called for the Catholic Church to continue promoting values "that permit the full development of the human person."[15] Ratzinger had earlier called homosexuality "an objective disorder" and an "intrinsic moral evil."[16]

The subhuman construction of gay people underlies their ill treatment in U.S. law and also encourages outrageous threats to their well-being. For example, in 2012, North Carolina Baptist pastor Charles Worley advocated mass murder akin to practices in Nazi Germany by proposing airlifting all "lesbians" and "queers and homosexuals" into electric-fenced pens where they would eventually die off.[17] Indeed, the Nazis had targeted gays as well as Jews, sending thousands of arrested homosexuals to concentration camps, where many died. Fear of AIDS has also led some to suggest isolating individuals infected with HIV, akin to sending people to leper colonies and also to the pastor's abhorrent idea for electric fences; such isolation would disproportionately affect gay populations.

LGBT residents are frequent victims of gay-bashing and hate crimes, with gay children as special targets, even inside schools.[18] In one study,

97 percent of public school students reported hearing homophobic remarks from their peers.[19] Prompted by society's foul attitudes, gay youth disproportionately commit suicide. To cite just one case, Jadin Bell, a 15-year-old in Eastern Oregon who complained of bullying and name-calling, hung himself in early 2013 at a school playground. Many homophobes seek out gays to inflict physical violence. Heartbreaking examples of murderous rage include the much-discussed killing in Wyoming of Matthew Shepard, who was tortured and tied to a fence by two men who allegedly murdered him out of hatred toward gays but who later claimed their motive was robbery. Another killing, in Maine, involved three teenagers who threw a gay man off a bridge; they bragged afterward that they "jumped a fag and beat the shit out of him then threw him into a stream."[20]

Gay persons, like today's undocumented immigrants branded "illegals" for their immigration offenses, were once defined as criminals through state antisodomy laws. Before the Supreme Court in 2003 invalidated a Texas law criminalizing sodomy, police applied these laws, then operative in over a dozen states, to prosecute gay sex. Sodomy arrests, particularly against same-sex couples, reached historic highs in the mid-1900s,[21] as gay sex became a priority of U.S. law enforcement. Police regularly raided gay bathhouses and bars in aggressive intrusions. In 1979, San Francisco police stormed a gay bar wielding riot sticks and yelling "motherfucking faggots" at the patrons.[22] Led by J. Edgar Hoover, the FBI had homosexuals and their advocacy organizations routinely under surveillance.[23] As late as 1986 the Supreme Court upheld the discriminatory application of criminal sodomy laws, with Chief Justice Warren Burger concurring in that result by citing English authority calling consensual homosexual relations a "deeper malignity" than rape and a "disgrace to human nature."[24] Yet just seventeen years later the Supreme Court reversed course in striking down a Texas sodomy law operative only against same-sex partners; the Court concluded that the U.S. Constitution's due process guarantee of liberty protected the sexual privacy of consenting adults.[25] In so ruling, the Court relied in part on the actions of other nations, particularly in Europe, that affirmed the ability of gay adults to engage in consensual sexual conduct without being branded as criminals. But despite the Supreme Court's decision, which defanged state antisodomy statutes outlawing consensual adult sex, police continued to harass gay persons through lewd-conduct laws that invite discriminatory treatment against gay sex undertaken in semi-public settings such as cars and public restrooms.[26]

Given the general absence of federal protection, discrimination remains widespread against LGBT persons in private venues from the workplace to housing; as of 2013 the U.S. House refused to consider legislation protecting gay employees from workplace discrimination. Organizations such as the Boy Scouts of America exclude gays from membership with impunity,[27] and some hospitals may deny them the right to visit their hospitalized same-sex partner, although in 2010 Obama mandated regulations that outlawed such discrimination in hospitals receiving federal aid. One organization investigating workplace discrimination nationwide concluded that between 16 and 44 percent of gays suffered discrimination in hiring, firing, or otherwise.[28] Employers in more than half the states face no legal impediment to firing workers (or refusing to hire them) based on sexual orientation. Ninety percent of transgender workers have experienced mistreatment or harassment in the workplace.[29] Evidencing disdain for gay teachers, who have been fired over the years throughout the United States for "immorality" such as bisexuality or "known homosexual[ity],"[30] Oklahoma enacted an outright prohibition against homosexual teachers; it was effective from 1978 until the Supreme Court struck it down in 1985.[31] Tapping the prevailing discriminatory sentiment, voters in Colorado approved a ballot measure in 1992 excluding any "homosexual, lesbian, or bisexual" from benefitting from any state or local antidiscrimination law, but the Supreme Court invalidated this expansive measure.[32] The U.S. military once discriminated against gays, who after 1993 were allowed to serve if they remained quiet about their homosexuality (the policy known as Don't Ask, Don't Tell). But some progress is evident on the antidiscrimination front. Congress finally removed the ban on openly gay service members, effective in 2011, consistent with a U.S. public-opinion poll in which 77 percent supported military service by openly gay individuals.[33] In 2011, the United States supported a U.N. declaration that expressed "grave concern at acts of violence and discrimination, in all regions of the world, committed against individuals because of their sexual orientation and gender identity."[34]

Until recently the United States barred or impeded the immigration of homosexuals—as reflected in the Immigration Act of 1917, which excluded "persons of constitutional psychopathic inferiority," intended by Congress to prevent "homosexuals and sex perverts" from immigrating.[35] The act was modified in 1952 to exclude those with a "psychopathic personality"; Congress eventually repealed the exclusion of homosexuals as inconsistent with contemporary psychiatric theories by enacting the Immigration Act of 1990.[36] Yet until 2013 same-sex partners were denied the benefits of family reunification under narrow immigration-law allowances because Congress, under the Defense of Marriage Act, discussed below, did not recognize their marriage or their union.

Gay couples long faced inequality in their efforts to secure the approximately fourteen hundred federal and state legal benefits associated with marriage, encompassing everything from Social Security rights to immigration allowances.[37] Despite considerable progress in recent years, during which some states gave same-sex couples the right to marry, or to obtain some legal benefits of marriage through the subordinate recognitions of civil unions or domestic partnerships, widespread state restrictions remain.[38] Most states explicitly ban same-sex marriage, many through state constitutional provisions (including thirteen states that outlawed same-sex marriage during the single year of 2004).[39] The federal government joined the anti-gay-marriage ranks by enacting the Defense of Marriage Act (DOMA) in 1996, signed by Clinton, which defined marriage to exclude same-sex couples from obtaining more than one thousand federal benefits and empowered states to refuse to recognize same-sex marriages performed in the states that allow them. But the Supreme Court struck down DOMA's denial of federal benefits as unconstitutional in 2013, finding that "no legitimate purpose overcomes the purpose and effect to disparage and to injure those whom the State, by its marriage laws, sought to protect in personhood and dignity."[40]

Although progress toward humanization has been made on the family-law front too, LGBT men and women still face restrictions in parenting. In the contentious context of child custody after divorce, homosexuals once had little or no chance of obtaining custody and sometimes even visitation.[41] Once antisodomy laws were repealed by many states and then held unconstitutional by the Supreme Court, the underlying justification for refusing to place a child with a parent who might face criminal prosecution disappeared. Now, most courts either treat sexual orientation as irrelevant in custody battles or apply a nexus test that demands some evidence of actual harm to the child based on the parent's sexual orientation and lifestyle.[42] Yet some courts still regard homosexuality as "invariably detrimental to a child's best interest."[43] A Virginia court even went as far as to award custody to a child's maternal grandmother based on the mother's felonious (before the Supreme Court's 2003 privacy ruling) lesbian relationship.[44] In the context of adoptions, almost every state now allows same-sex adoption, with Florida one of the last hold-outs. Florida's law, flatly prohibiting adoption by any "homosexual," was held unconstitutional in 2010,[45] and the state Department of Children and Families removed the question of sexual orientation from its adoption forms. But harsh rhetoric continues to plague LGBT parents despite these advances: in 2012 Bryan Fischer, an official of the American Family Association, called for an "Underground Railroad" (akin to the nineteenth-century escape network for black slaves) to abduct children from same-sex households in the interest of their safety.

*   *   *

Despite the encouraging signs of humane treatment of our significant LGBT population, it is evident we are far from the equality that would accompany a humanized vision of this group. Same-sex marriage has become the lightning rod for discussion of gay rights in the United States and remains the policy area with the most to gain from voters and legislators who view our gay population with compassion and humanity. As actor Sean Penn opined while accepting the 2008 Best Actor Oscar for his portrayal of slain gay politician Harvey Milk, "I think it is a good time for those who voted for the [California] ban against gay marriage to sit and reflect and anticipate their great shame . . . . We've got to have equal rights for everyone."[46] Young Americans solidly support same-sex marriage, with 57 percent of those under forty years old approving it, compared with only 31 percent of older Americans.[47] Washington state embraced marriage equality in 2012, allowing my colleague at Seattle University, Lisa Brodoff, to marry Lynn Grotsky, her life partner of almost thirty-two years. Grotsky described her elation in receiving one of the first marriage licenses for same-sex couples under the newfound equality: "Now it's like we're regular people."[48]

Aside from the provision of same-sex marriage and accompanying benefits, discrimination against LGBT persons needs to be erased in their employment, housing, healthcare, and more, and sexual orientation and gender identity need to be included in the antidiscrimination laws and enforcement priorities of federal, state, and local government. Meanwhile, violence and discrimination escalate against transgender people, and LGBT youth face widespread homelessness. Still today, no federal law protects gay people from discrimination in employment, education, access to public accommodations, or housing, all of which routinely occurs. As many have reminded us, these aren't special rights demanded by gay and transgender people but the right of all of humanity to equality.

Dehumanizing Criminals

The Monsters of Death Row

In striking down capital punishment . . . we achieve a "major
milestone in the long road up from barbarism" and join the
. . . other jurisdictions in the world which celebrate their
regard for civilization and humanity by shunning capital
punishment.
—Justice Thurgood Marshall

When examined by the principles applicable under the
Cruel and Unusual Punishment Clause, death stands con-
demned as fatally offensive to human dignity.
—Justice William Brennan

My father once offered me his views on the death penalty; they made
sense to me, especially when I had my own son years later. He declared
his opposition to capital punishment, unless of course one of his
children was murdered. As a parent I could understand his need for
retributive justice and repeated it often as my own position. On further
reflection, however, his reasoning raised many questions. What if the
victim's parents were deceased? What if the killer was the parent? Or
the child killed a sibling? What if the killer had his or her own children,
who would experience the same wrenching loss? My views on death
sentences evolved eventually to employ a constitutional trope approving
of capital punishment on its face but rejecting it as applied. In other
words, given the racial and class disparities of those sentenced to death
and the evidentiary and procedural flaws inherent in so many capital
prosecutions, while I might support the death penalty in principle, I
could not support it in practice given its flawed application. This,
in essence, was the position the American Law Institute took when I
attended my first meeting of that organization in 2009. In a decision

I supported, it withdrew its Model Penal Code provision dealing with the appropriate uses and procedures for capital punishment, effectively neutralizing the position of that influential legal organization on this contentious subject. Opponents of the death penalty were able to secure language that explained the repeal "in light of the current intractable institutional and structural obstacles to ensuring a minimally adequate system for administering capital punishment."[1] Since then, and especially while writing this book, I've challenged my belief in the legitimacy of capital punishment even if imposed in the fairest of circumstances against the perpetrator of the most heinous acts imaginable. Although as a father myself I have not fully accepted my conclusions below, I aspire to embrace them as my own, as our evolving compassionate society inevitably will.

Some of the subhuman constructions discussed previously have led to deadly consequences, albeit not state-administered. Although not intended by most government officials, the death of thousands of undocumented immigrants on their journey to the United States is tolerated as a consequence of our restrictive border-enforcement policies. Farmworkers die prematurely from cancers and other afflictions that result from their being routinely doused in pesticides. The impoverished sometimes die from inadequate healthcare and malnutrition. Hatemongers sometimes kill immigrants and gays, often emboldened by our complex network of anti-immigrant and antigay laws and practices. Pre-dating and later coexisting with state-administered capital punishment, mob lynchings in the United States were the precursors to some of today's hate crimes against immigrants and gays.[2] Directed at blacks in the South and Mexicans in the Southwest, these horrific killings for spectacle, mostly tolerated by law enforcement despite their lawlessness, eventually transformed into today's vigilante violence, while government executions captured some of their spirit of appeasing the frenzied community need for retribution. But none of these tragic outcomes carry the government imprint that marks capital punishment as a state (and federally) administered intentional taking of human life.

Justified by proponents in large part as a tool of retribution, capital punishment aims to exact revenge against so-called monsters of society, whose crimes are often so disgusting they are recounted in grisly detail in court opinions written by justices who permit rather than stay their execution. Echoing societal attitudes toward most murderers is the book *Monsters of Death Row: Dead Men and Women Walking*, which presents the stories of some of the thousands of prisoners awaiting execution in the United States. As described in the book's introduction, the "monsters on Death Row are not normal human beings." Rather, they are "fiends who have stabbed, hacked and even filleted their victims, some of whom were only a few months old."[3] Advocates for the death penalty freely invoke this subhuman characterization, describing their targets as monsters, fiends, scumbags, garbage, animals, and the like. Against the backdrop of the failed vote in 2012 on California's Proposition 34 to end capital punishment there, a mother described her son's serial killer as a "pure evil monster." Robert Rhoades was sentenced to death for murdering her eight-year-old son after kidnapping and torturing him, inflicting dozens of nonlethal stab wounds, all the while continuously raping the captured boy and ultimately killing him the next morning. The mother's website steadfastly urged preserving the death penalty "for California's worst killers."[4] As might be expected, comments posted on her site demonized Rhoades variously as a monster, an animal, a dog, and a "piece of shit." Emphasizing the subhumanity of accused or convicted murderers, in 2013 a Philadelphia district attorney yelled at an abortion doctor on trial for murder for performing abortions of late-term pregnancies where the mother's life was not at risk (abortions that were therefore illegal under state law), "Are you human?"[5]

The power of the subhuman characterizations that attach to perpetrators of awful crimes is reflected in the continued vitality of capital punishment in most U.S. jurisdictions. In contrast to the European Union, Canada, and Mexico, our federal government and most U.S. states continue to sentence the perpetrators of certain abominable crimes to death. As described below, although imposition of the death penalty has lessened considerably over time through evolving constitutional principles of dignity and fairness, capital punishment remains part of our nation's punishment arsenal.

Among the evolving legal constraints on capital punishment has been the nature of the crime committed. Offenses triggering execution once included horse stealing, forgery, burglary, aiding a runaway slave, and witchcraft, the latter resulting in the hanging deaths in the late 1600s of twenty suspected witches in Salem, Massachusetts.[6] Into the 1960s, some southern states still allowed capital punishment for robbery and rape, particularly if the defendant was black.[7] Similarly, during the days of lynching, blacks in the South might be killed for raping a white woman as well as for testifying against or even arguing with whites or for voting for the wrong political party.[8] In a 1977 decision, the Supreme Court applied the U.S. Constitution's proscription of cruel and unusual punishment to bar execution for kidnapping and raping an adult woman.[9] Later, in 2008, at a time when five states (Georgia, Louisiana, Montana, Oklahoma, and South Carolina) capitalized the crime of child rape, and fourteen states (and the federal government) authorized the death sentence for nonhomicide crimes, the Supreme Court effectively narrowed the constitutional allowance of execution so that the only crime it covered was murder (in the case of crimes against a person). In this decision, regarding the aggravated rape of an eight-year-old stepdaughter, the Court relied on "evolving standards of decency" to constrain capital punishment to first-degree murder.[10] The Court left open, however, the constitutionality of execution for crimes it characterized as those against the state, such as treason, espionage, terrorism, and drug trafficking. Previously, the Court had struck down the imposition of capital punishment against a getaway driver convicted for his role in a home-invasion robbery that ended with his accomplices murdering an elderly Florida couple, a killing he neither committed nor intended.[11]

The Supreme Court has also applied the Constitution to restrict capital punishment to certain individuals, thereby protecting the mentally deficient and minors. In 2002, the Court prevented execution of mentally deficient criminals, looking to the large number of states barring their execution as evidence that our society views the mentally deficient as "categorically less culpable than the average criminal."[12] Despite this decision, the Court failed to intervene in 2012, when Texas executed a black man with an IQ of just 61, as states have the discretion to specify their own standards of mental incapacity. In 2005, the Supreme Court denied the execution of those under age eighteen when they commit murder,[13] a decision bolstered in 2012 by the Court's striking down a mandatory sentence of life imprisonment without parole for those under eighteen at the time of their crimes.[14]

In addition to the courts narrowing the candidates and crimes for capital punishment, the method of execution has evolved over time at the behest of state legislators, and sometimes courts, as science has developed seemingly more humane and less painful ways to kill. Executions were once more of a spectacle and included the excruciating pain of being burned alive at the stake. Once the staple of executions in the nineteenth century, hangings (causing death by snapping the prisoner's neck) gave way to other methods of death, although a federal appeals court in 1994 upheld hangings by Washington state as a constitutional method of execution.[15] First used in 1890, the electric chair gradually replaced the noose—for example, in Florida in 1923.[16] The agony of electrocution is excruciating, but it can destroy the brain within seconds. Still, the electric chair could malfunction and in some cases the prisoner might live for as long as twenty minutes while being painfully electrocuted.[17] Electrocution burns the body's internal organs and can even cause flesh to catch fire, a fact that prompted the Georgia Supreme Court to rule in 2001 that electrocution, with "its certainty of cooked brains and blistered bodies" and its "excruciating pain," is cruel and unusual punishment under the Georgia state constitution.[18] Developed in the United States to execute prisoners and most horrifically employed by the Nazis to murder millions of Jews from 1941 to 1945, the U.S. gas chamber relied on hydrogen cyanide gas, which causes lack of consciousness and death.[19] Several states employing capital punishment embraced execution by gas. Before being replaced in turn largely by lethal injection, the gas chamber claimed 594 prisoners from 1924 to 1999,[20] despite upset over its cruelty.[21] A few states preferred firing squads, with Utah famously executing convicted murderer Gary Gilmore in 1977 by using five gunmen behind a curtain with five holes for their rifles. Eventually, death by lethal injection became the clear choice of states and the federal government for less painful executions; it was used first in Texas in 1982.[22] Concerns over the pain of a potentially slow-acting, one-size-fits-all lethal injection given different prisoner body weights, however, prompted outcry from death-penalty opponents. The Supreme Court nonetheless gave these executions the green light. Ruling on the method of execution for the first time since an 1878 decision upholding firing squads,[23] the Supreme Court in 2008 validated Kentucky's use of a three-drug death "cocktail" that induces unconsciousness, paralysis, and cardiac arrest: "Simply because an execution method may result in pain, either by accident or as an inescapable consequence of death, does not establish the sort of 'objectively intoler-able risk of harm' that qualifies as cruel and unusual."[24] Kentucky had switched from the electric chair to lethal injection in 1998, reflecting the shift toward lethal injection in the remaining capital-punishment states. Yet death cocktails remain an inexact science as states scramble to obtain and experiment with lethal drug combinations; an Ohio prisoner executed by injection in 2014 took more than twenty minutes to die while gasping for air, presumably validating warnings from his lawyers that the inmate, Dennis McGuire, would "suffocate to death in agony and terror."[25] Also in 2014, Oklahoma officials stopped their botched lethal injection execution of Clayton Lockett after the inmate's vein exploded and the sedatives failed to take hold, but he died of a heart attack on the gurney forty-three minutes later.[26]

Procedural flaws have dogged executions throughout their history. In a profound statement of the constitutional need for standards to guide the jury in imposing the death sentence, the Supreme Court effectively halted executions for a few years with a 1972 decision that sent states scrambling to repair their statutes.[27] States responded by, among other things, bifurcating trials into guilt and penalty phases, requiring the presence of certain aggravating circumstances as a condition for execution, requiring the judge or jury imposing the sentence to take account of the individual's character and record, and ensuring consistency and accuracy by a higher court reviewing the death sentence.[28] Despite these reforms, serious problems remain with capital punishment as applied. These include the reality that from its first imposition in colonial America, executions have targeted African Americans: for example, in the late eighteenth century in Connecticut, of those convicted of sexual assault blacks were the only ones executed (by hanging).[29] Similarly, in the southern states, the prosecution of rape as a capital offense (until prohibited by the Supreme Court) was reserved for blacks raping white women.[30] In the hundred years following the Civil War, every Mississippi execution for an offense other than homicide (that is, either rape or armed robbery) involved a black defendant and a white victim.[31] A Texas jury was even told in 1997 that being black increased the probability of future dangerousness, an aggravating factor that can support a death sentence.[32] The disproportionate application of the death penalty to black defendants evokes the days of lynchings; almost 85 percent of those lynched in the South from 1882 through 1951 were black.[33] Matching this disparity, almost four-fifths of prisoners lawfully executed in the South between the end of the Civil War and 1945 were black.[34]

Advances in science have exonerated many prisoners, including those on death row;[35] these exonerations raise questions of wider innocence and concern over the implementation of a punishment that effectively precludes meaningful exoneration. Realities of inadequate legal representation for poor defendants and widespread instances of prosecutorial misconduct further impugn capital punishment.[36] In deciding to strike the section on appropriate uses and procedures of execution from its Model Penal Code in 2009, the American Law Institute relied on a report stating that problems with the death penalty were intractable, including the following:

(a) the tension between clear statutory identification of which murders should command the death penalty and the constitutional requirement of individualized determination; (b) the difficulty of limiting the list of aggravating factors so that they do not cover (as they do in a number of state statutes now) a large percentage of murderers; (c) the near impossibility of addressing by legal rule the conscious or unconscious racial bias within the criminal-justice system that has resulted in statistical disparity in death sentences based on the race of the victim; (d) the enormous economic costs of administering a death-penalty regime, combined with studies showing that the legal representation provided to some criminal defendants is inadequate; (e) the likelihood, especially given the availability and reliability of DNA testing, that some persons sentenced to death will later, and perhaps too late, be shown to not have committed the crime for which they were sentenced; and (f) the politicization of judicial elections, where—even though nearly all state judges perform their tasks conscientiously—candidate statements of personal views on the death penalty and incumbent judges' actions in death-penalty cases become campaign issues.[37]

*   *   *

In 1994, North Carolina executed David Lawson, convicted years earlier of a double murder committed during a burglary, once the Supreme

Court rejected Lawson's petition for a stay of execution. Wearing only boxer briefs, a diaper, and socks, he allegedly shouted repeatedly "I'm human" as gas entered the death chamber. As the gas began taking effect he could only cry the word "human," and then several minutes later Lawson managed only to grunt until his body went still.[38] If we were to recognize the humanity of death-row inmates as Lawson pleaded, notwithstanding their awful crimes, the appropriate legal response would be swift and decisive: we would abandon the death penalty and replace it with some reasonable substitute, presumably life in prison without the possibility of parole. Eighteen U.S. states have already done this, with the most recent inclusions of New Jersey (2007), New Mexico (2009), Illinois (2011), Connecticut (2012), and Maryland (2013), and the early abolitions of Michigan in 1846 (except, until 1963, for treason) and Wisconsin in 1853. Washington and Oregon joined this group temporarily when their governors declared a moratorium on capital punishment. Oregon's governor, a physician, relied on the procedural and moral infirmities of capital punishment to impose a moratorium on executions during his term, which ends in 2015, explaining: "I refuse to be a part of this compromised and inequitable system any longer and I will not allow further executions while I am governor."[39] He was influenced too, as no doubt were those in some of the other states, by the staggering cost of the protracted appeals now required in order to help ensure procedural fairness. Likely some of these states were swayed further by the questionable and even fading justifications proffered for capital punishment—retribution and deterrence.[40] The importance of retribution decreased somewhat as executions shifted from being a public spectacle and from being carried out with the use of older, more painful methods. And the narrowing of eligible offenses, the outlawing of the execution of minors and the mentally deficient, and the introduction of procedural safeguards such as aggravating factors and lengthy appeals, all operate ironically to detract from the deterrence value of capital punishment. As some justices of the Supreme Court recognized, "The available evidence uniformly indicates, although it does not conclusively prove, that the threat of death has no greater deterrent effect than the threat of imprisonment."[41]

Globally, we are the only Western industrialized nation still administering the death penalty, with European countries, Canada, and Mexico having abolished the death penalty and all of them refusing to extradite accused murderers to the United States if they would face the death penalty here.[42] Most of these countries adopted the more humane approach of life without parole for abominable crimes. Mexico's Supreme Court even ruled in 2001 that the possibility of life without parole precluded extradition unless U.S. officials committed to a lesser sentence, although the court relented in 2005.[43] Norway lies at the opposite extreme from the U.S. embrace of capital punishment, employing a more compassionate and rehabilitative system; mass murderer Anders Breivik, who slaughtered seventy-seven people in a racially motivated 2011 rampage, was sentenced by a five-judge panel to a minimum ten-year, maximum twenty-one-year sentence, the latter being the longest sentence Norway permits. Still, the sentence can be extended indefinitely in five-year increments should Breivik be considered a danger to society at the time. This light sentence would likely outrage most U.S. residents; in 2001 the U.S. government executed by lethal injection domestic terrorist Timothy McVeigh, whose bombing claimed 168 victims. But there is much room in the spectrum of justice for punishment short of execution.

Despite the evident international and even the slight domestic trend toward repeal of the death penalty, thirty-two U.S. states still authorize execution, as does the U.S. government. In 2008, only China (with an estimated 1,718 killed), Iran (346), and Saudi Arabia (102) executed more persons than did the United States (37);[44] and this was a down year given that the United States averaged 70 executions annually from 1996 to 2005.[45] The U.S. numbers fail to reflect coercive use of the death penalty to prompt guilty pleas carrying life sentences rather than death, as when a Latino defendant, later proven innocent after twelve years in prison, pled guilty to murder after a Texas detective warned him, "Hispanics always get the needle."[46] Although largely dormant in some U.S. states due either to lack of jury imposition of capital punishment or to lengthy appeals, executions are alive and well in the southern states, which have accounted for 83 percent of executions since the Supreme Court gave the green light in 1976 to executions accompanied by sufficient procedural safeguards.[47] Texas leads the way with one-third of U.S. executions.[48] Moreover, public opinion widely appears to favor the death penalty, as evidenced most recently by the vote against the 2012 California proposition to eliminate the death penalty there and substitute life imprisonment without parole. As a nation, then, we are still far from willing to replace capital punishment with a more humane sentence.

Proponents of the death penalty have successfully framed its application as saving innocent lives despite the absence of proof of any deterrent effect. For example, as Texas governor, George W. Bush contended, "When the death penalty is administered in a . . . sure and fair way, it will save lives," and his brother Jeb Bush, while governor of Florida, concurred that "Floridians believe in the death penalty because they know it saves innocent lives."[49] Just as I have framed our subhuman construction of death-row inmates, proponents of capital punishment might rejoin that a murderer has likely treated his or her victim as subhuman or otherwise exhibited disdain for human life. Although this rejoinder would not explain our historical record of executing criminals for offenses not involving death or even bodily harm, the restriction of the death penalty today to murder raises this battle of subhuman constructions. The answer is that although a troubled individual might disregard the value of human life, our society has an obligation, enforceable by the potential for future regret, to honor the humanity of all its residents regardless of their offenses against our humanity. The only way to preserve a civilized society is to disallow any bad actors from swaying our resolve to treat everyone as human, even if their acts against humanity test that resolve. In thus far resisting calls to reinstate the death penalty during the bloody War on Drugs, which has killed thousands of innocent victims, some of them children, Mexico stands as a testament to the widely shared global view that capital punishment violates human rights. Although each subsequent U.S. murder may challenge our resolve, the predictive framework of subhumanity suggests we must side with ideals of rehabilitation and humanity rather than with the temptation of retribution by death.

*   *   *

Championed by the National Rifle Association (NRA), laws stretching the bounds of permissible self-defense have swept through many state legislatures. Known as Stand Your Ground laws, these allowances of potentially lethal force extend beyond the sanctity of so-called Castle laws, which permit self-defense within the home without an obligation to retreat and which almost all states recognize. In a Stand Your Ground jurisdiction, even outside the home, such as within the Florida gated community where George Zimmerman encountered and killed teenaged Trayvon Martin in 2012, a person can remain and employ deadly force despite having a clear path to safety. The NRA's advocacy of these laws reveals the likely weapon (and lethal outcome) in these encounters, as evidenced by Zimmerman's semi-automatic pistol.

Many commentators criticize Stand Your Ground laws in ways that resonate with subhuman constructions. Whereas traditional self-defense laws generally supply an affirmative defense that is difficult to rely on, Stand Your Ground laws better protect the shooter from prosecution.[50] In this respect, while traditional self-defense laws balance societal interests in self-preservation and recognition of the value of the assailant's own human life, Stand Your Ground laws are seen as creating incentives to kill.[51] Moreover, in a fundamental way they even exceed the disdain of death sentences for humanity, as Stand Your Ground laws allow private citizens to deliver their own death penalty, without a trial, and effectively to turn crimes carrying relatively short sentences, such as burglary and other property offenses, into a death sentence.[52] The strongest connection to death sentences, however, is the disproportionate racial impact of Stand Your Ground laws; for example, a Florida investigation found that under these laws a higher percentage (73 percent) of those killing a black person than of those killing a white victim (59 percent) faced no criminal penalty.[53]

The racial implications and applications of Stand Your Ground laws prompted the NAACP to complain to the U.N. Committee on Human Rights, citing a study that white-on-black killings were more likely to be found justifiable in Stand Your Ground jurisdictions and pointing to the spike in (justifiable) homicides in these states attributable to these "shoot-first" laws. Connecting Stand Your Ground laws to the scant regulation accompanying the sale of weapons, the complaint seeks an assault-weapons ban, improved weapons background checks, and repeal of Stand Your Ground laws.[54] Even U.S. Attorney General Eric Holder criticized these state self-defense laws, contending that "by allowing and perhaps encouraging violent situations to escalate in public, such laws undermine public safety." Exhibiting a different take on the human rights implications of these laws, an NRA spokesperson lashed back at Holder, calling self-defense a "fundamental human right."[55] These laws, however, occupy the landscape of regret as they continue to target criminals who somehow get what they deserve from a solo judge, jury, and executioner, and, more broadly and ominously, perhaps throw us into a Hobbesian war of every man against his neighbor.[56]

8

Flying While Muslim

"Ragheads" and Human Rights

I think your motto should be post-9-11, "raghead talks tough,
raghead faces consequences."
—Ann Coulter

Arabs aren't really human and most Americans would just
like to drop a nuclear bomb on them—any of them.
—Michael Savage, hate-radio talk show host

If I see someone come in [the airport] and he's got a diaper
on his head and a fan belt around that diaper on his head,
that guy needs to be pulled over and checked.
—U.S. Congressman John Cooksey (Louisiana)

[Remove] that rag.
—Mississippi judge to practicing Sikh arrested in 2013 for
failing to comply with police who stopped him for driving
with a flat tire and ridiculed him as "depraved" and a
"terrorist"

Even before September 11th, Arabs and Muslims were frequent targets of subhuman constructions, with Hollywood films describing them as "jackals," "towel-heads," "sons of dogs," "scum-buckets," "sons of unnamed goats," "pigs," "rats," and "camel-dicks."[1] Particularly vile characterizations included variations on familiar slurs of African Americans: "sand niggers" and "dune coons." After the September 11th attacks, the images became even more ominous, vicious, and urgent, as represented by a cartoon that depicted an evolutionary chart, with a bearded Middle Easterner positioned between apes and Uncle Sam plunging a knife into Uncle Sam's back.[2] Muslims in particular were constructed as terrorists—as cowardly subhuman savages who ruthlessly and without justification killed innocent people. One scholar described the prevailing image of the Muslim terrorist as "a violent monster" by nature, "dark and evil, part real and part phantom, part human and part animal, part man and part woman, part bearded and part veiled, [and] part strategic and part crazy."[3] Radio host Michael Savage has labeled War on Terror detainees as "subhuman" and has hypothesized that only through conversion to Christianity can they become "human beings."[4]

Because the September 11th hijackers were Muslim, those of the Islamic faith are at the core of these subhuman constructions, but by no means is the prevailing terrorist, subhuman image limited to Muslims. As evidenced by hostile characterizations in the media, politics, the U.S. workplace, and by hate crimes and racial profiling, the subhuman terrorist characterization also implicates those appearing to be Muslim (whether by their use of head wrappings, their physical appearance, or other cues), which encompasses Arabs, South Asians, and other groups, origins, and faiths. Among U.S. Muslims, a 2009 Gallup poll found great racial diversity, with 28 percent identifying as white, 35 percent as black, 18 percent as Asian, and 18 percent as other/mixed.[5] Muslims, then, are difficult to profile visually and specifically.

The resulting post–September 11th conflation of Muslim and Muslim-appearing individuals is consistent with the longstanding derogatory media images of Arabs described above. It encompasses Palestinians, who are predominantly Muslim and who are routinely subjected to a subhuman construction as fanatic, suicide bomber-terrorists attacking Israel. For example, pro-Israel advertisements in 2012 on New York transit buses read, "In any war between the civilized man and the [Muslim/Arab] savage, support the civilized man."[6] These advertisements invoke the same dichotomy used by a U.S. Commissioner of Indian Affairs in the late 1800s to justify Native removals within the United States: "Savage and civilized life cannot lie and prosper on the same ground."[7] The conflation of appearance and faith implicates Arabs generally; Sonny Landham, a U.S. Senate candidate from Kentucky, in suggesting the United States bomb Arabs "back into the sand," categorized terrorists broadly "The Arabs, the camel dung-shoveler, the camel jockeys, whichever you wanna call 'em, are terrorists."[8] It encompasses too the prophet of the Islamic religion, Muhammad, whom televange-list Pat Robertson labeled a "wild-eyed fanatic" and a former Southern Baptist president called a "demon-possessed pedophile."[9]

Two groups most vividly experience the consequences of these demeaning images—the broader group of Muslims and Muslim-appearing populations, who are subjected to undue scrutiny given these prevailing suspicions, and, on a more individualized basis, suspected terrorists held within the criminal and military justice systems, who suf-fer dehumanizing consequences for their crimes and suspected crimes. Both groups are discussed below, with the prediction that we will regret the overbroad categories of potential terrorists and the unduly harsh consequences applied to them and to suspected terrorists when the hys-teria over the September 11th terrorist attacks subsides.

In contrast to the Oklahoma City bombing orchestrated by Timo-thy McVeigh, an Anglo terrorist who raised no suspicions of any ter-rorist tendencies inherent in all Anglo Americans, the September 11th bombing immediately implicated all adherents to Islam and those seen as Arab or Muslim. Backlash was swift from both private and govern-ment actors. On the private front, hate crimes ensued. Illustrating the difficult time the public had in deciding which individuals or groups deserved condemnation, victims included Muslims, Arabs, and South Asians. Those beaten included a Muslim woman in Virginia, stabbed in the back while being called a "terrorist pig," a Hindu pizza delivery man from India brutally beaten in Massachusetts,[10] and an Iranian American salon owner in New York savagely beaten by assailants who called her a "terrorist." Among those murdered in the United States as scapegoats was an Indian Sikh (a South Asian religion), Balbir Singh Sodhi, who was shot wearing his Sikh turban while planting flowers outside his Ari-zona gas station by a gunman aiming to kill "ragheads." While on his rampage, the gunman fired into the house of an Afghan family and shot at a Lebanese American clerk at another gas station.[11] A Texas gunman went on a similar spree seeking out "local Arab-Americans, or whatever you want to call them"; he killed a Pakistani store clerk who was cook-ing hamburgers, blinded a Bangladeshi clerk with metal fragments, and murdered an Indian Hindu, Vasudev Patel, a convenience-store owner and father of two; none of the victims were Arab.[12] In a similar backlash, mosques across the United States were singled out for arson, vandalism, and hate threats. Evidencing a similar inability to focus collective anger on any particularized target, U.S. teenagers set fire to a Sikh temple in late 2001 apparently in the mistaken belief that the temple was a place of worship for, or otherwise related to, the Islam religion.[13] Developers of new mosques faced community opposition, such as from a group of private citizens who sued a Tennessee county that issued permits for a mosque expansion; they claimed that Islam is not a religion but rather a political ideology.[14] Most notably, proponents of an Islamic cultural center in the vicinity of Ground Zero, which was opposed as constituting a sacrilegious mosque on that turf, faced strident resistance to the project.[15]

Complementing these hate crimes is rampant workplace discrimination against Muslims and, through the conflation of religious identities, those seen as Muslims. For example, Abraham Yasin, an Illinois correctional officer, was awarded damages by a federal jury in 2009 for facing a hostile work environment in which he was called a "terrorist," "sand nigger," "bin Laden," a "shoe bomber," and a "camel jockey."[16] A Muslim Texas A&M professor sued the university alleging religious persecution by colleagues who tormented him by desecrating his prayer rug with lab mice urine and feces, among other ways.[17] While a presidential candidate in 2012, Herman Cain flatly declared he would appoint Muslims neither to his cabinet nor to the federal judiciary.[18] During a 2011 presidential debate, candidate Newt Gingrich impugned the patriotism of U.S. Muslims by suggesting that loyalty oaths by Muslims as a condition for employment in his administration would be meaningless because Muslims, whom he compared to Nazis and Communists, would presumably lie.[19]

Following September 11th, many Muslim-appearing individuals were removed from airplanes, despite having passed airport security checks, under the discretion pilots can exercise to remove objectionable passengers from flights. As with hate crimes and employment discrimination, the net was thrown widely and implicated non-Muslims, and in any event encompassed several presumably innocent parties profiled on the basis of their perceived ethnic origin or religion. For example, a United Airlines pilot booted a passenger, a U.S. citizen of Egyptian origin, based primarily on his name—Mohammad. The phrase Flying While Muslim acquired the same familiarity among its victims as the similar profiling by government officials of those Driving While Black or Driving While Hispanic.

Although removals by flight crews do not implicate the government, the federal Transportation Security Administration, responsible for airport security, has been accused of racial profiling in singling out Muslim-appearing passengers for additional screenings. More generally, as a consequence of the September 11th attacks, fear of the terrorist Muslim almost singlehandedly changed U.S. public opinion on racial profiling, with 60 percent of U.S. respondents favoring profiling, especially when directed at Arabs, in contrast to a finding a few years earlier, in 1999, that 81 percent opposed racial profiling.[20]

Apart from airport security, the federal government implemented programs after September 11th that singled out Arabs and Muslims for heightened scrutiny. Among these was the Alien Absconder Initiative, an immigration-enforcement initiative from 2002 that aimed to locate noncitizens with unexecuted removal orders. Although most of the immigrants in this classification are Latino/a, the government focused instead on locating men of the Islamic faith or of Arab ethnicity. Earlier, in late 2001, the Department of Justice instituted a voluntary program "to interview aliens whose characteristics were similar to those responsible for the attacks," with the hope of gathering information on terrorist plots from the thousands of noncitizens the federal government interviewed.[21] A special registration program (the National Security Entry-Exit Registration System) required immigrant men over the age of sixteen from twenty-five countries (all except one, North Korea, regarded as Muslim countries) to register with and submit to interrogation by the U.S. government. Likely duplicated in other police departments, the Los Angeles and New York City police undertook extensive surveillance of Muslims. In New York City, police monitored both the daily routines of Muslims and the content of mosque sermons in an effort to map the city's Muslim "human terrain."[22] U.S. Muslims hoping to end this spying program based on religious faith filed suit against New York City in 2012.

Another example of the hysteria that followed the attacks is the assault on Islamic law, exemplified by the Save Our State constitutional amendment that Oklahoma voters approved in 2010 to prohibit state courts from considering any Islamic (Sharia) law in deciding cases. Despite the reality that no Oklahoma court had apparently ever invoked Islamic law, 70 percent of voters approved the measure. Federal courts blocked implementation of the discriminatory law as contrary to the constitutional protection against the governmental establishment of religion.[23]

In sum, the profiling of Muslims, and in many instances more generally of Arabs, Middle Easterners, and South Asians, does more than classify them as potential terrorists. It strips them of their prerogatives of citizenship within the United States and questions their loyalty. Perhaps the most powerful example of the delegitimizing consequences of identification with Islam occurred during Obama's 2008 presidential campaign, when he was dogged by accusations he was secretly a Muslim (and not even born within the United States). Presumably his accusers meant to imply Obama was disloyal to the United States and somehow would impede the ongoing War on Terror. A poll conducted shortly after September 11th confirmed fears of disloyalty generally associated with Muslims, with less than half those polled believing U.S. Muslims were loyal to the United States.[24]

Still, we have progressed some as a country since the distressing government internment of over a hundred thousand Japanese Americans in 1942, following the Pearl Harbor attack, although that attack was carried out by the Japanese government rather than, as in the case of the September 11th attacks, a group of individuals who claimed inspiration, rightly or wrongly, from Islamic teachings.[25] Despite a poll after September 11th revealing that one-third of respondents supported internment of Arab Americans, and a call by U.S. Senator Saxby Chambliss (a Republican from Georgia) that we allow local sheriffs to "arrest every Muslim that comes across the state line,"[26] the United States did not institute the mass imprisonment of all Muslim or Arab residents in the United States. Yet in the case of those individually accused of terrorist involvement, the United States engaged in tactics that ignored human rights and decency, as we have done in past regrettable responses to wartime hysteria.

Immediately after September 11th, the U.S. government launched a nationwide dragnet of secret arrests, detaining between twelve hundred and two thousand Muslims, Arabs, and South Asians without public disclosure of the nature of their charges or the names of individuals held.[27] Many were detained in high-security prisons within the United States, while others languished in Guantánamo, Cuba, and secret prisons around the world with little acknowledgment of human rights. One scholar summarized the widespread U.S. disregard for international norms of human rights in the months following September 11th, including our costly, deadly, and ultimately failed hunt for weapons of mass destruction in Iraq: "Soon, the [Bush] Administration was engaged in a questionable war in Iraq. . . . Ignoring prohibitions on extra-judicial killings, it began to murder suspected terrorists, even if they were U.S. citizens. Muslim prisons were set up in Iraq, Afghanistan, Guantánamo Bay, and at secret places where detainees were interrogated contrary to customary and treaty-based international law. Some detainees were rendered to friendly Muslim nations for interrogation by means of torture. . . . At home, hundreds of Muslim immigrants and citizens were detained without any legal process. Some were beaten in detention."[28] As this scholar summarizes, the United States conducted or arranged torture, beatings, and humiliation for suspected terrorists, if they weren't killed outright before capture.

Within the United States, the most publicized allegations of wrongdoing emerged from litigation against federal officials, including former Attorney General John Ashcroft, brought by Javaid Iqbal, a Pakistani Muslim who worked in New York City as a cable television installer. Swept up in the detention raids after September 11th, Iqbal was held for more than a year in a Brooklyn federal prison, the Metropolitan Detention Center, where he alleged he suffered "numerous instances of excessive force and verbal abuse, unlawful strip and body cavity-searches, the denial of medical treatment, the denial of adequate nutrition, extended detention in solitary confinement, the denial of adequate exercise, and deliberate interference with [his] rights to counsel and to exercise of [his] sincere religious beliefs."[29] A 2003 report on the Metropolitan Detention Center, where a majority of detainees were held, revealed allegations of physical abuse that included bending and twisting of arms and hands, lifting detainees off the ground by their arms, stepping on their leg-restraint chains, pushing their heads against a t-shirt emblazoned with the U.S. flag, excessively strip-searching them, banging on their cell doors during sleeping hours, and handling detainees in rough and inappropriate manners. Verbal abuse alleged by detainees included statements such as "Whatever you did at the World Trade Center, we will do to you."[30]

Established in 2002, the detention camp at the Guantánamo Bay Naval Base in Cuba offered the Bush administration a location removed from the United States where it could detain and torture War on Terror prisoners from Iraq, Afghanistan, and elsewhere. Taking the position that Guantánamo detainees were not entitled to the protections of international humanitarian law found in the Geneva Conventions of 1949 on the humane treatment of prisoners of war,[31] the Bush administration oversaw the torture of detainees in Guantánamo and other detention centers outside the United States.[32] John Yoo, a law professor at the University of California Berkeley and an appointee of the Bush administration, famously laid the legally untenable groundwork for torture at Guantánamo in the so-called Torture Memos. Exceeding legal credulity, Yoo contended that War on Terror detainees were "enemy combatants" somehow outside the reach of the Geneva Conventions and thus fair game for enhanced interrogation techniques such as waterboarding. Under Yoo's reasoning, the president held absolute power to ignore laws prohibiting torture as defined by international norms, despite the fact that credible scholars all rejected the idea that the Conventions somehow exclude certain detainees from protection. Exemplifying Yoo's defiant interpretation was his response to questioning on whether any law could prevent the president from "crushing the testicles of the [detainee's] child," to which Yoo replied no treaty forbade it and whether any other law prohibited this torture depended on "why the president thinks he needs to do that."[33]

Aside from this disgusting hypothetical, the reality of waterboarding in Guantánamo by U.S. operatives sparked national debate on the morality of torture. Long considered torture, waterboarding consists of simulating the sensation of drowning. The CIA subjected one terrorist suspect to waterboarding 183 times.[34] Because waterboarding causes the brain to believe it is drowning and will perish, yet doesn't cause permanent physical injury to the brain, it failed to meet Yoo's proffered redefinition of torture as only interrogation designed to cause organ failure, serious bodily injury, or death.[35] Waterboarding wasn't the only horror inflicted on terrorist suspects. Secretary of State Donald Rumsfeld approved tactics in the War on Terror that the United States had criticized as torture when employed by other countries, such as forced nudity, shackling detainees in painful positions, solitary confinement, threats of dog attacks, use of temperature extremes, forced standing, sleep deprivation, and deprivation of light.[36] Guantánamo detainees also alleged they were beaten by guards, fed food rations ten years expired, and given foul drinking water. Interrogators dehumanized their victims. Female interrogators forcibly squeezed their genitals and detainees were left to urinate and defecate on themselves while chained on the floor in fetal positions for twenty-four hours or longer.[37] As one suspected terrorist interrogator logged, "Began teaching detainee lessons such as stay, come and bark to elevate his social status to that of a dog."[38] Law professor Muneer Ahmad represented Omar Khadr, a young terror detainee held in Guantánamo, who U.S. officials treated as a human mop after he urinated on the floor while denied a bathroom break during his interrogation. The U.S. soldiers poured solvent on the sixteen-year-old Khadr, lifted him up, and used his body to clean the floor of urine. Additionally, they threatened Khadr with rendition to other countries where they told Khadr older men would rape him.[39] As described by Professor Ahmad, the Guantánamo detention center was a project of comprehensive dehumanization, accomplished by cultural erasure through construction of detainees as terrorists, by legal erasure through ignoring prisoner rights, and by physical erasure through torture.[40]

All these officially approved techniques paled in comparison with the horrors that emerged from the Abu Ghraib prison in Iraq, where U.S. military police committed unspeakable human rights violations against prisoners of the War on Terror. As depicted in photographs of the degradation, naked prisoners were piled on top of each other in sexual pyramids, led around on leashes as if they were dogs, and forced to masturbate. Credible evidence emerged that an inmate was forcibly sodomized "with a chemical light and perhaps a broom handle."[41] Defending such dehumanization, radio host Rush Limbaugh contended that the detainees "are the ones who are subhuman. They are the ones who are human debris, not the United States of America and not our soldiers and not our prison guards."[42]

By executive order, President Obama rejected cruel interrogation techniques such as waterboarding, later calling that practice "contrary to America's traditions." At the same time, his green light for drone kill-ings of suspected terrorists ensured that there were few opportunities for interrogation. Presidential candidate Mitt Romney's harsher inter-rogation position in 2012 suggests torture waits in the wings for the next Republican president, as Romney flatly declared he did not believe waterboarding was torture.[43]

Complementing the torture of terrorist detainees were new U.S. laws authorizing invasions of privacy through warrantless wiretaps (under the Uniting and Strengthening America by Providing Appropri-ate Tools Required to Intercept and Obstruct Terrorism Act of 2001—the PATRIOT Act) and indefinite executive detention without trial or charges (under the National Defense Authorization Act for Fiscal Year 2012, challenged unsuccessfully in federal court) of, as some interpreted it, even U.S. citizens engaged in hostilities against the United States or any members of al Qaeda or "an associated force." In sum, the United States overreacted as it often does in times of national crisis, but even more than ten years after September 11th some of the fundamental excesses of the War on Terror remain. Among these is the Guantánamo detention camp, which survived Obama's efforts to shutter this symbol of the dehumanization of the ongoing War on Terror.

*   *   *

What reforms and policies would follow from humanization of the hostile post–September 11th images? As with policies and practices that implicate the universe of Muslim and Muslim-appearing populations generally, and those governing suspected terrorist operatives more particularly, this discussion must proceed in two phases. First, consider the reforms attendant to a societal regard of Muslims as valued contributors to our diverse cultural fabric rather than as being potentially allied with rogue terrorist plots to destroy us. Properly respecting their humanity and their religious beliefs would entail terminating programs that subject them to profiling solely on groupwide suspicions of terrorist complicity, such as the longstanding profiling and human mapping of the Muslim community undertaken by the New York City police. Consistent with the International Covenant on Civil and Political Rights, article 20, we would protect against the advocacy of any religious hate that incites discrimination, hostility, or violence.[44] In accord with international human rights law, we would permit Muslims the same freedoms we allow practitioners of other religions.[45] Once Muslims are seen as valued members of the collective social community, U.S. residents might drop their opposition to mosques and Islamic cultural centers, and rally against hate crimes directed at Muslims as an affront to community values of inclusion.

Second, in the case of individuals suspected of terrorist involvement, reform is complicated by the specter of future terrorist attacks. Unlike the death penalty, which has been demonstrated to offer little in the way of general deterrence of future wrongful acts by others, oftentimes terrorist suspects are interrogated with the aim of procuring information about the planning of future attacks. In this manner, public officials have argued torture is justified to discover and prevent horrendous acts that would cause mass death—not through the general deterrence of that terrorism but through the information torture elicits. Considerable public support backs this moral reasoning, as a CNN poll determined that 45 percent of respondents would not object to torture should it provide information about terrorism.[46] Even if we were to view terrorist suspects individually as human, in the manner urged in Chapter 7 for death-row inmates, presumably the greater good of preventing additional murder, and thereby protecting the sanctity of human life, might prevail in this conundrum of clashing values. Still, the experience of U.S. interrogations and torture after September 11th suggests we in fact gained little information about future terrorist plots, and more important there is nothing to confirm we would have failed to procure that same information through treating detainees in a more humane manner. If anything, publicity of the horrors and degradations of Abu Ghraib bred more new vengeful terrorist operatives and plots around the world to punish the United States than any excessive interrogation techniques ever uncovered and prevented. Led by two former members of Congress, Republican Asa Hutchinson and Democrat James Jones, a nonpartisan task force on torture formed during the Bush administration released its findings in 2013; the report confirmed both that "it is indisputable that the United States engaged in the practice of torture" and that there was no "firm or persuasive evidence" that abusive interrogation produced information not obtainable by other means.[47]

As a further expression of humanity and human rights, we might willingly extend the same protections to suspected terrorists that we extend to other criminal suspects in our longstanding recognition of the presumption of innocence. Rather than indefinite and secret detentions and denials of rights to counsel,[48] we should allow suspected terrorists the same procedural protections that the most egregious murder suspects receive.

*   *   *

Prisoners are the new niggers, gooks, [and] kikes.
—Bo Lozoff, prisoner advocate[49]

The degradations of Abu Ghraib and the horrors of Guantánamo may seem remote from our own domestic criminal justice system, with its constitutional protections and seeming transparency, yet in recent years we have retreated from advances in human rights toward a privatized, more mean-spirited, and less rehabilitative punishment system that mirrors our disdain for suspected terrorists. Supermax prisons, which subject prisoners to extended isolation, are commonplace and in the opinion of some scholars and activists constitute a form of unlawful torture.[50] Supermax prisons came into use in the 1980s and 1990s to house the most violent prisoners, the so-called worst of the worst, but have been used routinely for ordinary prisoners who violate contraband rules or other prison rules and orders. Estimates peg the number of inmates in state and federal super-maximum security prisons as perhaps a whopping one hundred thousand.[51] The preferred technique of supermax imprisonment is solitary confinement, a strategy the United States abandoned in the late 1800s and later resurrected and institutionalized within the supermax prison.[52] Prisoners may spend twenty-three hours a day alone in a tiny windowless cell, constantly bathed in artificial light. At one California supermax alone, Pelican Bay, about five hundred of its prisoners have been held in solitary confinement for more than ten years, ninety of them for longer than twenty years.[53] Despite contentions that solitary confinement amounts to torture and causes mental illness, the Supreme Court has yet to declare it an unconstitutionally cruel and unusual punishment.

Countering the narrative of supermax confinement as reasonable and ordinary, an investigative reporter in 2011 detailed chilling abuses at the hands of prison guards in a Maine supermax cell. Undertaken in response to prisoner disobedience, such as protesting bad food, forceful cell extractions occurred throughout the day, using "five hollering guards wearing helmets and body armor [to] charge into the cell. The point man smashes a big shield into the prisoner. The others spray mace into his face, push him onto the bed, and twist his arms behind his back to handcuff him, connecting the cuffs by chain to leg irons. As they continue to mace him, the guards carry him screaming to an observation room, where they bind him to a special chair. He remains there for hours."[54]

Augmenting the horrors and degradations that occur deep within the thick walls of U.S. supermax prisons is the far more transparent and equally demeaning spectacle in the Arizona desert of Sheriff Joe Arpaio's tent-city prison. Housing prisoners, including undocumented immigrants his officers racially profiled in sweeps, the jail tents can reach temperatures of 138 degrees in the scorching summer heat.[55] When the inmates aren't sweltering in these makeshift prisons, they are degraded by being forced to wear pink underwear or even video-taped in their holding cells during strip searches or while using the toilet.[56] The U.S. criminal justice system aims to degrade and shame those within its grasp as less than human whether they are suspected Muslim terrorists or undocumented immigrants caught for petty theft or other crimes. As detailed in Chapter 9, our current system of mass incarceration completes the circularity of subhumanity, with vulnerable and disfavored groups profiled as criminally inclined and as requiring societal control and with the brutality of imprisonment and postconviction consequences further dehumanizing them by stripping them of both economic and personal liberties.

9

From Slavery to the New Jim Crow of Mass Incarceration

The Ongoing Dehumanization of African Americans

Why did Obama's great granddaddy cross the road? Because
my great granddaddy tugged his neckchain in that direction.
—Post-2012-election tweet of Chet Walken

I don't believe in calling him the first black president, I call
him the first monkey president.
—On-air remarks of Arizona radio host attacking President
Barack Obama

While conceptualizing this book I would ask friends and colleagues
to identify the most regrettable policy or practice in U.S. history. Not
surprisingly, slavery came up most often. As readily demonstrated in this
book and elsewhere, subhuman images of black slaves accompanied this
abominable practice. Yet despite the abolition of slavery as declared by
the Thirteenth Amendment to the U.S. Constitution in 1865, subhuman
constructions of African Americans abound today, accompanied by
policies and practices that continue their past subordination.

Here, I examine what it means for overcoming subhuman constructions that they persist even in the face of acknowledged regret of past
mistreatment of the same targeted group. Further, how do subhuman
constructions evolve? Does the image of the vulnerable group soften
over time in everyone's mind, or do just enough people reject a subhuman construction so that policy change is feasible even as others retain
and act on the most derogatory constructions? Relatedly, do some
members of the vulnerable group achieve an improvement of image
while others are left behind? Consider the potential gap in the American imagination between the image of comedian Bill Cosby, holder of a
doctorate, who played a physician on television's *The Cosby Show*, and
our perception of the black welfare queen discussed in Chapter 5 or the

black criminal addressed below. What does it mean for the advancement of the image of African Americans that President Obama, a highly educated former law professor and our first black president, can be dismissed publicly by some as a subhuman animal?

Clues to answering these queries come from the various landscapes of past and future regret examined in this book. As discussed below, it is evident that movement away from subhuman constructions and their consequences comes slowly, despite our attempts to distance ourselves from regrettable practices such as slavery by framing them as the product of past unenlightened generations. This persistence of perceived subhumanity and its consequences raises the compelling question of how we might accelerate the pursuit and evolution of humanity. Additionally, might the evolution of humane treatment for certain groups that are still subject to lingering oppression itself serve as a predictor of future regret for the current types of subordination? In other words, might admitted regret over past mistreatment flag current subordination of the same vulnerable groups (such as blacks) for eventual additional regret and prompt special diligence to eradicate the current oppression and ensure against taking steps backward in this progress toward humanity?

Below I address the evolution of the black image and the regrettable treatment of African Americans through the present day. Plainly, although the most egregious offense—the enslavement and sale of human beings under the rule of law—has long been prohibited in the United States, modern-day oppression continues to ravage the African American community. Our societal mistreatment of Mexicans and of homosexuals presents similar examples of the progression over time of vulnerable groups that, while having made some progress in status, are still buffeted by unrelenting subordination. After briefly sketching the progression of other vulnerable groups, I focus on the black experience and, in Chapter 10, on women.

For Mexicans, segregated schools and businesses impeded their everyday life in the early 1900s in the U.S. Southwest. Because many whites felt Mexican children were "intellectually inferior to Anglos," they were segregated in schools and pushed out of those schools toward the workplace at an early age.[1] Restaurants in Texas excluded "Spanish or Mexicans," funeral parlors denied burials to Mexicans, and courthouse restrooms relegated "Colored Men" and "Hombres Aqúi" (Mexican Men Here) to their own space.[2] Arizona restaurant signs read: "No Dogs or Mexicans Allowed." Movie theaters segregated their main floor and balconies; union leader César Chávez, a U.S.-born citizen who served in the U.S. Navy during World War II, was arrested for defying the "whites only" section of a Delano, California, movie theater.[3] Public swimming pools reserved the day before pool cleaning for "Mexican Day." A sign in a mid-1900s Texas public park instructed "Mexicans and Negroes" to "Stay Out," as "This Park Was Given for White People Only."[4] Ultimately, the Supreme Court's eradication of the schoolhouse segregation of blacks and federal and state government enactment of civil rights laws encompassing other segregated spaces benefitted Mexican Americans and other Latinos/as. Despite this advancement of humane treatment of Mexican Americans, is everyday life for Latinos/as markedly better today? Perhaps for some, but what about the undocumented Mexican immigrants hunted by Sheriff Joe and Arizona ranchers, as well as by Border Patrol agents and other federal immigration authorities deep within the United States? Relatedly, has the image of Mexican Americans and other Latinos/as, now intertwined with the image of undocumented immigrants, improved since the time when segregation was rampant? An AP poll finding 52 percent of U.S. residents in 2011 openly expressing anti-Latino/a sentiments suggests otherwise.[5]

Gay people have also enjoyed some progress in their legal and societal treatment. Within a ten-year span ending in 2012, the Supreme Court struck down laws criminalizing gay sex, voters in three states authorized same-sex marriage in 2012 (joined by three state legislatures in early 2013), and Congress repealed the policy that barred openly gay, lesbian, or bisexual personnel in the military. In 2013, the Supreme Court struck down the federal Defense of Marriage Act, which denied federal benefits to same-sex couples. Yet, as discussed in Chapter 6, numerous tools of oppression remain. As with other vulnerable groups, it is difficult to measure whether, in fact, the LGBT societal image has markedly improved coincident with these recent policy gains.

Mentally ill persons are an additional example of a group that, having advanced in legal and societal treatment through the repeal of involuntary sterilization, still endures subordination such as by institutionalization away from residential communities that fear their presence.[6] Moreover, mentally ill persons face increasing criminalization of their status by police officers ill trained to confront their mental issues when responding to minor calls, such as for disturbing the peace or harassment, or when merely encountering someone who fails to immediately comprehend and heed their orders; the result often is escalation to police brutality and tragedy. For example, police in Saginaw, Michigan, three of them later demoted or disciplined, killed a mentally ill, homeless man in 2012 when he failed to drop a small knife,[7] and Seattle paid a $1.5 million court settlement in 2011 to the family of a mentally challenged Native American artist killed by police while he crossed a downtown street carving a piece of wood.[8] As illustrated by tragic mass shootings in movie theaters, shopping malls, and schools, we also seem unable to detect and treat mental illness until someone enters the criminal justice system, and once that person is there we focus on punishment rather than treatment. Particularly when mental illness intersects with homelessness, our societal criminalization of the status and necessities of the homeless and our defunding of treatment programs for the mentally ill or safety nets for the homeless ensure regrettable tragedies.

Not every group discussed has made progress in image or treatment. For at least one of the vulnerable groups discussed in this book, Muslims, their image and the legal and societal consequences of that negative image have worsened, primarily as a result of the September 11th terrorist attacks (and the 2013 Boston Marathon bombing), which were wrongly attributed by many to religious beliefs. Other groups have perhaps stagnated in their societal image: arguably death-row inmates are seen as similarly monstrous today as in years past, although, as explained in Chapter 7, over time we have narrowed our most negative views of and our harshest punishments for just those adults who kill. The detailed focus below, however, is on those groups whose image or treatment has evolved toward humanity in some perceptible way.

This chapter, along with Chapter 10, considers the above questions using the models of the African American racial experience and the history of gender inequity for women. Both groups battled longstanding subhuman or, at least in the case of women, subordinate constructions. Both have suffered fundamental mistreatment, such as the slavery of blacks and the denial of the vote to women, that U.S. law has since corrected. Despite these advancements, African Americans and women (albeit to a lesser degree) still face subordinating images and deleterious legal and social consequences. In light of this mistreatment, it seems hypocritical for our generation to look back with horror at the institution of slavery, for example, and ask of earlier generations, "How could they?" Rather, we may simply be a few steps forward on the long road to humanity that runs through our nation's history, or, even less optimistically, perhaps that road leads nowhere transformative at all and merely demarcates the permanence of racism, as some scholars have warned, despite the allure and façade of forward motion.[9] Even if real progress toward antisubordination goals is underway, a later generation might, and as I posit likely will, look back at our time and view these current methods of subordination as connected with and no less virulent than the past practices we find so abhorrent. Particularly as subhuman constructions remain evident, might later generations view our current campaign to imprison Black America as little different from slavery's denial of their freedom? Rather than ultimately sharing historical blame for past travesties, we should ask how we might recognize these marches toward humanization, such as racial and gender equality, and not only speed them up but make a clean break from past (and current) injustice. That is the aim of these chapters.

Relatedly, even as we apologize for past regrettable practices, we tend to reuse those techniques against new vulnerable groups. For example, were the mass post–September 11th interrogations, secret arrests, and detentions of U.S. Muslims much removed from the group suspicion against and internment of Japanese Americans during World War II? Were the legal exclusions of Chinese immigrants under the Chinese Exclusion Act markedly different from the physical and symbolic exclusion of Mexican and Central American immigrants accomplished by the border fortifications of the Secure Fence Act of 2006 and prior border-armoring? Was the testing of experimental AIDS drugs on vulnerable foster children, particularly in the 1990s, reminiscent of the infamous and regrettable Tuskegee Syphilis Experiment?[10] As the subordination of some groups remains longstanding, although carried out by evolving techniques, such as with African Americans, other groups more rapidly advance in their societal constructions, as with the Irish,

Italians, and other European immigrant groups who were vilified until their migrations slowed. At the same time, new groups succumb to oppression and dehumanization. For example, in the case of dehumanization on religious grounds, although Jews have moved beyond the days of blatant "No Jews Allowed" signs and Catholics are less discriminated against, we now vilify Muslims as anti-American and as potential terrorist threats. Is the blueprint for group dehumanization and oppression so apparent and adaptable that even as some groups make progress, others are prone to remain behind or fall victim to dehumanization in a moment? Moreover, the permanence yet fluidity of dehumanizing constructions may ominously suggest that some greater force exists in human nature toward dehumanizing groups or that embedded economic and power structures compel these outcomes. Despite the apparent long road to humanity, the remaining discussions are grounded in optimism along the way, as well as faith in the power of the human spirit and compassion to evolve, with the safety net of our own self-interest in generational reputation should those "better angels" fail us.[11]

*   *   *

Despite the eradication of slavery in 1865 and the rejection of racially segregated schools and businesses in the 1950s and 1960s, Black America remains in a state of crisis in image, economic condition, and legal treatment. Despite the invalidation of de jure segregation and the institution of slavery, African Americans face laws and practices that disproportionately affect and endanger their well-being. On the socioeconomic front, Africans Americans experience the dismal reality of high unemployment (14.1 percent in 2012 while the overall U.S. rate was 8.1), low incomes (a median household income of only $32,068), high poverty (27.6 percent in 2011), and mass incarceration, which affects their economic opportunities (up to 80 percent of young black men in some cities have criminal records).[12] In the late 1990s and early 2000s, blacks were targeted by abusive subprime lenders in the prelude to the foreclosure crisis that stripped many black homeowners of their equity and residences, often the only modicum of wealth they possessed.[13] Their societal image remains distressingly poor, with 51 percent of U.S. residents polled in a 2012 AP study expressing explicit antiblack sentiments.[14]

Indeed, rather than stagnating, the image of African Americans appears to be worsening of late, perhaps consistent with our tendency in times of economic downturn to scapegoat vulnerable groups. For example, a 2008 survey of explicit antiblack attitudes found a lesser number (48 percent) than in 2012 expressing these negative sentiments.[15] Obama's ascendancy to the presidency in 2008, rather than ushering in some postracial nirvana where color lines fade, drew vitriolic taunts from observers such as the Arizona radio host quoted in the epigraph to this chapter who called him a "monkey." Later, in decrying his 2012 reelection, racist tweets called Obama a nigger and other slurs.[16] Conservative rocker Ted Nugent even called President Obama a "subhuman mongrel" before joining a Texas Republican gubernatorial candidate on the campaign trail.[17] As a writer for an African-American news service opined in 2012: "We're in a racist renaissance. It's a rebirth of the oldest forms of racism. It's not new, not different. It's like the 1800s, the most archaic abusive terms are applied to black people every single day."[18]

Even if the so-called racist renaissance is temporary and coincident with the economic downturn, it is clear that the progress of African Americans, as measured by their image and their social and legal treatment, has barely crept forward. Despite our willingness as an enlightened society to distance ourselves from the past horrors of slavery and segregation, we are little removed from these appalling practices. Moreover, as argued by some, we have simply replaced oppressions of the past with new practices that accomplish the same purpose of subordinating and controlling an entire people. Arguably, then, the practices of slavery, segregation, and today's mass-incarceration campaign and other injustices might simply meld together into a seamless history of oppression of Black America that causes later generations to wonder, "How could they?"

The similarities among these three phases of oppression, as linked by the common thread of subhuman images, lend themselves to an interpretation that implicates our generation in past (and current) oppression. Starting with the "peculiar institution" of slavery, which brought enslaved Africans to the United States for sale to white men, our legacy of mistreatment of African Americans is steeped in a subhuman construction. Examples of this sentiment abound in the U.S. experience. Published in 1900, the book *The Negro a Beast* purported to detail the biblical and scientific basis for excluding blacks from the human family, contending "the negro is . . . one of the lower animals."[19] Similarly, a South Carolina law once called Africans "barbarous, wild, and savage" in legislating a fine, but no jail time, for murdering a black slave.[20] In its 1857 decision in *Dred Scott v. Sandford*, no less an authority than the U.S. Supreme Court declared that African Americans were "a subordinate and inferior class of beings" who could not be U.S. citizens.[21] Relying on this decision, the Mississippi Supreme Court in 1859 refused to give effect to the emancipation by the state of Ohio of a Mississippi-born slave. Painting a staggering portrait of this African American woman as less than human, the Mississippi justices described her as belonging to "an inferior caste . . . occupying, in the order of nature, an intermediate state between the irrational animal and the white man." In rejecting the notion that Ohio's enlightened view of the civilization and citizenship of Africans might somehow bind Mississippi, a bedrock state of slavery, Mississippi's court equated conferring citizenship on African slaves with treating monkeys as human:

> But when I am told that Ohio has not only the right thus to degrade and disgrace herself, and wrong us, but also, that she has the right to force her new associates into the Mississippi branch of the American family, to claim and exercise rights *here,* which our laws have always denied to this inferior race, and that Mississippi is bound to yield obedience to such demand, I am at a loss to understand upon what *principle* of law or reason, of courtesy or justice, such a claim can be founded.
>
> Suppose that Ohio, still further afflicted with her peculiar philanthropy, should determine to descend another grade in the scale of *her peculiar* humanity, and claim to confer citizenship on the chimpanzee or the ourang-outang (the most respectable of the monkey tribe), are we to be told that "comity" will require of the States not thus demented, to forget their own policy and self-respect, and lower their own citizens and institutions in the scale of being, to meet the necessities of the mongrel race thus attempted to be introduced into the family of sisters in this confederacy?[22]

Renowned as a great scientist of his day, Harvard professor of zoology Louis Agassiz made an even closer connection between Africans and monkeys in claiming a black child's intellectual growth is stunted because his brain "bears a striking resemblance . . . to the brain of an ourang-outang."[23] These vile comparisons of blacks to animals outlived slavery, as illustrated by the slurs targeting President Obama and, earlier, the sad odyssey of Ota Benga, a four-foot, eleven-inch-tall African from the Congo actually housed in the Bronx Zoo during the early 1900s. Initially sharing a cage with an orangutan, Benga was allowed later to wander the zoo to the delight of patrons who chased and harassed him.[24] While he was at the zoo, the New York Times described him as a pygmy who was "very low in the human scale."[25] Benga eventually committed suicide, demonstrating the toll exacted on a human by a subhuman construction.

Characterizing African slaves as subhuman was the gateway to enslaving them, stripping them of their birth names and culture, selling them separately from their family members, and denying them the right to acquire property and legally marry. White masters and their families similarly could viciously beat their nonperson slaves with impunity and, in the case of black women, rape them to increase profitability through offspring, fulfilling the economic vision of Thomas Jefferson, who opined, "I consider a [slave] woman who brings a child every two years as more profitable than the best man on the farm."[26] Only with the ratification of the Thirteenth Amendment to the Constitution in 1865, abolishing slavery, and the Fourteenth Amendment in 1868, guaranteeing citizenship to all persons born in the United States, did African Americans gain some measure of legal humanity. Attempting to demarcate our generation as distinct and distant from the inhumanity of slavery, the House of Representatives in 2008 and the U.S. Senate in 2009 apologized for slavery. Private businesses joined the apology bandwagon in this presumably more enlightened age, with banking giant JPMorgan Chase apologizing in 2005 for its predecessor bank, which accepted slaves as loan collateral, as did Wachovia Bank the same year.

We can't distance ourselves from the inhumanity of slavery so readily, however, as slavery simply mutated into new strains of oppression that, along with the subhuman image of African Americans, survive today. Slavery's first mutation was through the Black Codes, which southern states passed soon after the Civil War to limit the freedom of newly freed slaves. Among their provisions, these laws aimed to keep black workers on their former plantations. South Carolina, for example, required blacks to pay a substantial fee to work in jobs outside of agriculture or domestic service. Some laws prevented blacks from owning or renting their own farmland. To obtain work, former slaves signed labor contracts with plantation owners that controlled their every move, such as by requiring permission to leave the plantation. Most egregiously, blacks without employment were arrested under vaguely worded vagrancy laws in these Black Codes that effectively criminalized blacks without plantation work. Consequently, black prisoners, if unable to pay a fine, were hired out to a white plantation owner or other employer—essentially, as reflected in the title of a 2008 book, *Slavery by Another Name*.[27] Crimes triggering this consignment might include the offense of miscegenation, leveled against black men who had sex with white women, or the crime of leaving the employ of a plantation farmer before harvest end or other trivial offenses targeting blacks including using profane language and petty theft, such as riding a train without a ticket. Some employers might pay the prisoner's modest fine directly in return for labor, while other states leased convicts to private employers offering dangerous work. In Alabama, for example, nearly 45 percent of its leased prisoners died in one of the early years of the convict-leasing program.[28] Dangerous jobsites in the South that survived into the 1900s included coal mines where convicts worked while bound by ankle shackles; and, at one prison work camp, inmates slept nights in rat-ridden bunks stacked three high with 150 convicts sharing three barrel tubs for washing.[29] Local labor demand might dictate police vagrancy sweeps to supply plantations with needed convict labor. Eventually, rather than leasing prisoners to private employers, some state prisoners were deployed in chain gangs. These practices survived into the middle of the twentieth century, when the federal government moved to outlaw involuntary servitude;[30] this change coincided with the beginning of the civil rights era, launched by the Supreme Court in *Brown v. Board of Education* to eliminate another vestige of slavery—segregation.

Segregation contributed to the second, postslavery, phase of black oppression. With the blessing of the Supreme Court, which permitted segregated railcars in its 1896 decision of *Plessy v. Ferguson*,[31] states, local governments, and private businesses advanced their goal of separating blacks from white residents in all aspects of everyday life. Segregation was in place in schools, parks, hospitals, restaurants, restrooms, and even telephone booths.[32] Despite the provision of separate but ostensibly "equal" schools, in many realms segregation meant black residents needed to find their own facilities from nondiscriminatory providers. For example, black travelers and patrons needed to locate hotels and restaurants that would serve them and needed to hunt for neighborhoods free from restrictive private covenants preventing sales to or leases by black residents.[33] Judicial and legislative pronouncements roughly from 1948, when the Supreme Court struck down racially restrictive housing covenants, through the federal civil rights laws of the mid-1960s, eventually ended our legal tolerance of outright segregation.[34]

Some antiblack laws and practices were slower to fall, such as state bans on interracial marriage, which survived until the Supreme Court's 1967 decision in *Loving v. Virginia*, which relied on the equal-protection guarantee and the due process liberty interest to choose one's spouse to vacate the criminal conviction of a married interracial couple (a white man and black woman) arrested in their marital bedroom.[35] The trial judge had invoked his religious beliefs to punish the Lovings, stating that because God "separated the races [onto separate continents] . . . he did not intend for the races to mix."[36] Strong sentiments in favor of antimiscegenation laws remain,[37] particularly in the South, as Supreme Court decisions alone often fail to squelch racist preferences; a 2011 poll of Republican voters in Mississippi found that a 46 percent plurality believed interracial marriage should still be illegal![38]

Most evident in this racial history is the resilience of subordination and the foul images that drive it. For example, although the Fifteenth Amendment to the Constitution (passed by the antislavery party, the Republicans, over the objection of every Congressional Democrat), ratified in 1870, ostensibly prevented states from denying the right to vote on the basis of race or status as a former slave, states readily circumvented its mandate by imposing poll taxes many blacks could not afford, disenfranchising voters convicted of certain crimes (a restriction still operative today in many states, having been validated by the Supreme Court[39]), and requiring so-called literacy tests as a condition for voting. These literacy tests included difficult civics questions, but white voters could be passed in the test giver's race-savvy discretion or grandfathered if their ancestors had voted. Sometimes voting was conditioned on ridiculous tests that rivaled rigged carnival games in their difficulty, as when prospective voters needed to correctly determine the number of jelly beans in a jar; again, the registrar might simply pass all white applicants and fail even a black applicant who somehow guessed correctly.[40] Illustrating the racial animus behind state impediments to democracy that reached all blacks, James Vardaman, governor of and later a U.S. Senator for Mississippi, explained in 1904 that he was "just as opposed to [civil rights leader] Booker Washington as a voter" as he was "to the coconut-headed, chocolate-colored, typical little coon" who shined his shoes daily, as "neither is fit to perform the supreme function of citizenship."[41] Although some of the most blatant racial restrictions on voting are now outlawed, new impediments have taken their place, such as intimidation of African American voters in Florida during the 2000 presidential election and similar attempts nationally to suppress nonwhite voting in the 2012 election by a variety of means including reduced voting hours and citizenship identification laws.[42]

Methods of eluding both civil rights laws and judicial decisions aimed at eradicating segregated facilities were varied but similarly effective. They ranged from official action, such as when Jackson, Mississippi, closed its public swimming pools rather than desegregate them, a strategy the Supreme Court upheld against constitutional challenge in 1971,[43] to white flight from racialized urban neighborhoods to the suburbs or to private schools in order to flee integrated schools. Overall, although de jure segregation and discrimination may have been outlawed, it is otherwise business as usual given the variety of lawful strategies available to maintain the prevailing social order.

In the third and current phase of oppression, the most pronounced strategy evident today to subordinate blacks and to define their apparent place in the social order is their mass incarceration. With roots in the private-public mechanism of racialized lynchings, the Black Codes, and legal segregation, which constrained black freedom, and even in slavery, which supplied the ultimate restriction on liberty, mass incarceration is today's application of the law to the maintenance of the prevailing social order.

Although the roots of mass incarceration extend to slavery and the Black Codes, I view the mid- to late-1960s and, later, the 1980 Reagan years, as crucial periods in the institution of current practices that imprison blacks (and Latinos/as) disproportionately. The Civil Rights Act of 1964 seemingly, among its broad mandates on segregation, ended lunch-counter discrimination, presumably signaling a shift in societal and legal treatment of African Americans. But negative attitudes toward blacks remained bubbling under the surface. Although moral equality in law was achieved through these antisegregation and antidiscrimination laws, a pronounced backlash occurred when African Americans began clamoring for economic equality. Cities were burning in the mid-1960s as black residents expressed their disgust with the dismal economic prospects in urban ghettos; the 1965 Watts riot in Los Angeles and riots in the summer of 1967 in Newark and Detroit frightened white voters who assumed they had appeased black communities with racial equality at lunch counters and in voting booths. Richard Nixon was able to seize this political opportunity in 1968 by running a successful "law-and-order" campaign for the presidency that appealed to white voters alarmed by urban unrest. Nixon's successful "southern strategy" manipulated disaffected white voters by stirring up fears of minority groups and championed "states' rights" to deflect federal civil rights initiatives. Reagan and other candidates later followed that same blueprint. As described in Chapter 5, concurrent with urban unrest, the emergence of the welfare queen in the 1980s as code for African Americans abusing the welfare safety net signaled the end of the mid-1960s' War on Poverty, which never took flight.[44] The double whammy of economic despair sparking urban violence and perceived dependence on and abuses of social welfare programs prompted additional emphasis on law and order through aggressive policing of communities of color. When the War on Drugs entered these urban landscapes at the same time, the perfect storm for today's mass incarceration was set in motion.

Nixon is credited with first invoking the rallying cry of a War on Drugs and naming drug use "public enemy number one" in a 1971 press conference.[45] But it was Reagan, having already vilified welfare queens, who ramped up drug-enforcement efforts, announcing he was "running up a battle flag" on illicit drugs.[46] U.S. drug laws were always connected to racial control. As I documented in my book on U.S.-Mexico border policy, *Run for the Border*, opium laws originated in racist fears that predominately male Chinese immigrants living in Chinatowns were seducing white women with opium. Cocaine was seen in the early 1900s as a catalyst for violence by black men. Allegations spread that cocaine gave blacks superhuman strength and that black "cocaine 'fiends'" were raping white women or going on murderous sprees while high on the drug."[47] Regulation came swiftly under the 1914 federal Harrison Act, which also regulated opiates. Marijuana regulation followed a similar racialized path that linked marijuana smoking by blacks in the South and by Mexican Americans in the Southwest to "murder, rape, and mayhem threatening Anglo residents."[48] Congress regulated marijuana in 1937, on the heels of the movie *Reefer Madness* (1936), which called marijuana a "ghastly menace," an "unspeakable scourge," more "vicious" and "deadly" than heroin, and a drug that was "destroying the youth of America" and causing "acts of shocking violence."[49] Bolstering this claim with flimsy evidence, the film warned that one marijuana smoker killed his family with an axe. Ironically, subhuman constructions, predominantly of racial minorities, prompted the drug laws that today consign some of these groups to the dehumanization of mass imprisonment and accompanying economic despair.

The introduction of crack cocaine in the mid-1980s, during Reagan's tenure, played perhaps the largest role in boosting the modern drug war and the practice of mass incarceration. Made by simply dissolving cocaine with baking soda and boiling and drying the mixture into hard "rocks" for smoking or inhaling vapors (freebasing), crack cocaine offers users a shorter, more intense high than powder cocaine; crack cocaine became popular among the urban poor, particularly black users, in contrast to the affinity among Hollywood and suburban users in the 1980s for snorting powder cocaine. Fears of crack as some supercharged catalyst of violence among black men merged with stereotypical images of the lazy black welfare queen to birth the pejorative reference to crack babies, presumably surviving on public assistance. Enhanced enforcement arrived under the federal Anti-Drug Abuse Act, which Reagan signed in 1986. Authorizing increased spending on drug enforcement and mandating minimum drug sentences, this law also introduced a 100:1 sentencing disparity between powder and crack cocaine, which survived until Obama, who otherwise championed the drug war, signed the Fair Sentencing Act of 2010, which reduced the sentencing disparity to 18:1. Before the reduction, defendants with five grams (a gram is about the weight of a paper clip) of crack cocaine were sentenced to a mandatory minimum five-year prison term, while a possessor of powder cocaine would need five hundred grams (over one pound) to draw the same minimum sentence. Demonstrating the racial significance of the sentencing disparity, in 2008, 80 percent of those sentenced under the federal crack-cocaine law were African American.[50]

The War on Drugs invites the dehumanization of users, denigrated as junkies and addicts, and justifies the consequences of incarceration. Indeed, notable figures have even urged the murder of drug users, akin to the fate suggested by some for other vilified and dehumanized groups, such as undocumented immigrants. Former Los Angeles police chief Daryl Gates testified before the U.S. Senate in 1990 that casual drug users should be "taken out and shot" for their offense, and television personality Judge Judy reportedly urged the distribution of dirty needles to remedy heroin addiction by death.[51]

Our War on Drugs is the centerpiece of the third historical phase of African American oppression, mass incarceration—what one legal scholar called "the new Jim Crow" facing Black America.[52] Moreover, that incarceration campaign negatively affects Latinos/as and U.S.-Mexico border policy as well. By deploying racial profiling and expanded enforcement budgets in neighborhoods of color and the borderlands, the drug war results in a staggeringly racialized prison population. As I have written elsewhere, despite studies that Anglo youth use marijuana at higher rates than blacks or Latinos/as, youth of color are disproportionately targeted and arrested for drug possession.[53] Police concentrate drug-enforcement resources within black and Latino/a neighborhoods, ignoring more flagrant drug use on college campuses. When Anglo rocker Jon Bon Jovi's daughter was arrested in 2012 for heroin possession, it was only after she was found overdosed in her dorm room at exclusive Hamilton College in New York, not because police were patrolling and searching the campus for drug users (and even those charges were dropped because of New York's Good Samaritan 911 law encouraging emergency treatment of overdoses). Black communities face an entirely different level of scrutiny. Here traffic stops for "Driving

While Black" are well known. The Louisiana Police Department even used a training film that exhorted officers to rely on a driver's skin color as a basis for making traffic stops in pursuit of drug violations.[54]

Racial profiling, now less overtly sanctioned, nonetheless is readily employed in the detection of many crimes and is particularly favored for drug offenses. Although police officials may claim color-blindness in enforcing laws, feigning compliance with the supposed postracial ideals of our country, the reality is that with the Supreme Court's blessing police officers may racially profile with virtual impunity. All the officers need do is rely on some minor traffic offense, which is inevitable if the police follow any car long enough, and the hunt is on. Not surprisingly, the court decision announcing this flexibility involved two African Americans arrested for crack cocaine. Officers patrolling a known "high drug area" in Washington, D.C., focused their sights on a Nissan Path-finder with two black occupants waiting at a stop sign for an unusually long time. When the unmarked police car made a U-turn back toward the vehicle, it turned without signaling and traveled at an "unreasonable speed." When they stopped the Pathfinder at a traffic light down the road, the pursuing officers told the driver to put the vehicle in park and approached on foot, observing two large plastic bags, containing crack cocaine, in the passenger's hands (knowing this plain-view scenario sounds fishy, I try to keep a straight face when discussing this case in the classroom while watching the inevitable student reactions). Alternatively, the officers might have asked for consent to search the vehicle (knowing most drivers fail to understand their right to object to a search without a warrant) or called for back-up with a drug-dog to sniff around the vehicle, which can ordinarily be accomplished during the normal duration of a traffic stop without any warrant or even particularized suspicion.[55] The two occupants challenged as racially motivated the targeting of their car by the Washington, D.C., police because the police did not offer sufficient probable cause for the stop. Rejecting their argument, the Supreme Court "effectively condoned racial profiling,"[56] ruling that because the driver had violated traffic laws, an officer's motive in stopping him, even if attributable to race, would not invalidate the traffic stop.[57] Although an officer's impermissible motive for pulling over a traffic suspect would not run afoul of the Fourth Amendment's bar of unreasonable search and seizure, singling out black drivers for traffic stops presumably would violate the Constitution's Equal Protection Clause, assuming the officers would admit their racialized motive. Still, the prospect of a civil action for damages brought by a criminal defendant for a violation of his constitutional rights means little in the reality of criminal prosecutions, where the ability to exclude evidence obtained in violation of the Fourth Amendment matters most.[58] The two black defendants caught with crack cocaine ended up serving almost a decade in prison.

With the green light from the Supreme Court for pretext traffic stops and with an officer's ability to engage in so-called stop-and-frisk searches for weapons of persons reasonably suspected of criminal involvement (a standard short of probable cause),[59] police have the tools they need to racially target blacks and Latinos/as and to discover any illicit drugs. Moreover, police sometimes resort to outright fraud against and untruths about racial minorities, as in 1999 when a narcotics officer in Texas racially framed more than 20 percent of the black adult residents of the town of Tulia for cocaine dealing; the arrests led to sentences as long as ninety-nine years that were later undone when the deception came to light.[60]

As discussed in Chapter 8, the terrorist acts of September 11th fostered public acceptance of racial profiling, and, despite official denials, it remains at the core of most policing, especially for the enforcement of drug and immigration laws. Racial profiling underlies other types of subordination described in this book, particularly the mass internment of Japanese Americans on the group suspicion of their disloyalty rather than on individualized determinations and proof of any treasonous intent. As well, immigration authorities rely on profiling to capture and deport Mexican-appearing migrants, resulting in deportations that are overwhelmingly of Mexicans.[61] Local authorities also readily profile Mexican-appearing drivers for traffic stops. With the possibility of being charged with criminal offenses because of undocumented status, such as driving without a license or without insurance, which requires a lawful driver's license, Mexican-appearing drivers can find profiled traffic stops turning into extensive searches and even deportations through the federal Secure Communities program. With the aid of misunderstandings caused by language barriers, the different cultural experience of Mexicans in their dealings with Mexican police, and the ready impounding of cars, U.S. police may also be able to find the mother lode of their profiled stop—illicit drugs.

No matter how they are arranged, the statistics on drug imprisonments, imprisonments of blacks and Latinos/as (largely due to the War on Drugs), and our overall prison population are staggeringly grim. As Professor Michelle Alexander lamented in 2010, the U.S. prison population jumped from three hundred thousand to more than two million in less than thirty years, with much of that increase coming from drug convictions. Increasingly privatized, prisons are emerging as profit centers for entrepreneurs. At the end of 2007, more than seven million U.S. residents were jailed, were on probation, or were parolees.[62] The upshot is that the United States incarcerates at the world's highest rate—750 imprisoned for each 100,000 population—surpassing prison-happy regimes such as Russia, China, and Iran.[63] The United States is home to 25 percent of the world's prisoners but only 5 percent of its population.[64] Blacks and Latinos/as represent 58 percent of U.S. prisoners despite constituting only one-third of the U.S. population.[65]

The War on Drugs plays a decisive role. Drug convictions accounted for two-thirds of the increase in federal prisoners and more than half the state-prison increase between 1985 and 2000.[66] Alexander reports that about a half million U.S. residents are imprisoned today for drug offenses, an increase of 1,100 percent over those imprisoned for drug offenses in 1980; overall, more than thirty-one million have been arrested since the War on Drugs was launched. Alexander dispels the myth that most of those arrested are dealer kingpins—in 2005, four out of five U.S. drug arrests were for possession rather than for selling; and as for the myth that arrests are for possession or sale of the more dangerous drugs, marijuana possession accounted for almost 80 percent of the growth in 1990s' drug arrests.[67]

Blacks and Latinos/as are targeted for these drug arrests. African Americans constituted 80 to 90 percent of drug offenders imprisoned in seven states, as Human Rights Watch reported in 2000;[68] and, in ten states, black men were imprisoned on drug charges at rates from twenty to fifty-seven times greater than those for white men.[69] In 2008, 87 percent of the 40,000 arrests in New York City for marijuana possession were of blacks and Latinos/as, although they constituted only about half the city's population, and marijuana alone accounts nationally for

750,000 annual arrests.[70] With drug arrests leading the way, an estimated three of four young black men in Washington, D.C., are expected
to spend time in prison, and in some major cities 80 percent of young
black men have criminal records.[71]

Alexander's labeling of the drug war and its consequent mass incarceration as the New Jim Crow comes mostly from the severe postconviction consequences for African Americans. Not only do those on
parole or probation face imprisonment for subsequent minor infractions, such as failing to keep an appointment with a parole officer, but
convicted criminals are subject to lawful discrimination in virtually
every aspect of their lives. As Alexander states powerfully, "The 'whites
only' signs may [be] gone, but new signs have gone up—notices placed
in job applications, rental agreements, loan applications, forms for
welfare benefits, school applications, and petitions for [occupational]
licenses, informing the general public that 'felons' are not wanted here.
A criminal record today authorizes precisely the forms of discrimination we supposedly left behind—discrimination in employment, housing, education, public benefits, and jury service. Those labeled criminals can even be denied the right to vote."[72] As she details, felons are
rejected by employers and are barred from public housing for at least
five years, and some states permanently deny felons the right to vote.[73]
Thirty-two states ban food stamps to convicted drug felons (but not to
other criminals, such as murderers), jeopardizing countless families
with children.[74] The bulk of drug felons are drug users, not dealers. Possessing even relatively small amounts of marijuana is a felony in many
states, with a few states elevating a second minor offense of any amount
possessed to a felony. For example, Alabama prosecutors applied its
second-strike law to an African American Vietnam veteran in Mont-
gomery who was arrested on a second offense of possessing about $10
worth of marijuana (a few joints) and who was ultimately imprisoned
on a plea bargain for five years for that offense; his imprisonment then
launched the litany of oppressive life consequences detailed above.[75]

As in prior chapters, one should ask what policies and reform would
we implement if we truly valued black residents. Would we continue
to exert control through mass criminalization within black communities and tolerate the harsh discriminatory consequences of these
criminal convictions? Foremost in any compassionate reform agenda is

consideration of a 2011 report from the NAACP that appropriately conjoins the dismal funding of public education and the outrageous cost of financing the War on Drugs. As the report reveals, we spend more than seventy billion dollars annually on prisons, with many of those dollars going to incarcerate drug users, as well as many billions more spent on policing drug laws.[76] Much of this funding, particularly at the state level, comes at the expense of funding schools. The NAACP called, therefore, "for the downsizing of prisons and the shifting of financial resources from secure corrections budgets to [more vulnerable and variable] education budgets."[77] Educational success positively correlates with both economic prosperity and lower crime rates, yet educational funding remains in crisis in many states as rising prison and police costs deplete general funds.[78] Rather than continuing policies and practices that result in prisons doing a much better job of admitting racial minorities than colleges, we must redirect resources toward affordable higher education as well.

In addition to bleeding education and social-services budgets and diverting those funds to law enforcement and prisons, the War on Drugs has taken shape as a war on families. Playing the U.S. drug czar in the 2000 film *Traffic*, actor Michael Douglas appropriately asked, "If there is a war on drugs, then many of our family members are the enemy. And I don't know how you wage war on your own family." At the same time that many conservative commentators decry the disunity of black families and blame the parents, they fail to account for the role of the drug war and mass incarceration in tearing black families apart. As Alexander reminds us, "The mass incarceration of people of color is a big part of the reason that a black child born today is less likely to be raised by both parents than a black child born during slavery. . . . Thousands of black men have disappeared into prisons and jails, locked away for drug crimes that are largely ignored when committed by whites."[79] She notes compellingly that more black men are imprisoned today or on probation or parole than were enslaved in 1850.

The NAACP report also urges reforms in drug laws—including the complete elimination of sentencing disparities between crack and powder cocaine, the elimination of mandatory minimum drug sentencing, and the more frequent use of diversion to treatment instead of imprisonment, a far less expensive option.[80] In *Run for the Border: Vice and*

Virtue in U.S.-Mexico Border Crossings, I pointed to the ghastly bloody consequences of the drug war for Mexico (more than fifty thousand Mexicans killed from 2006 through 2012) to call for selectively decriminalizing and taxing drugs that compare to alcohol on the measures of user and external societal harm. Here, compassion for the humanity of those most often victimized by drug laws and their consequences reinforces that call for reform. By any measure, marijuana would be first on the decriminalization/legalization list;[81] the result would be vast savings to state and federal budgets, not to mention the potential for obtaining revenue through taxation. Ballot measures authorizing the recreational use of marijuana, passed in Colorado and Washington in 2012, could be the first steps in reversing costly drug-enforcement policies that have racialized roots and racialized consequences. Experiences from other countries that have decriminalized drugs, notably a 2009 study of Portugal's 2001 reform, found deaths from drug overdoses (not including marijuana, for which overdosing is not possible from recreational use) were down, while drug use failed to increase;[82] these results suggest that reform would not launch a spree among drug users. Presumably, monies saved from reduced enforcement would be spent equally on education budgets and on treatment for those addicted to drugs. For drugs sufficiently harmful to society, such as methamphetamine, which is particularly popular among poor whites, mandatory drug treatment, rather than imprisonment, would be warranted for first-time and even repeat offenders. For marijuana and other decriminalized drugs, possession by minors would be criminalized to the same degree that possession of alcohol is, thus dampening rampant racial profiling of juveniles of color. Schools, in turn, should reconsider zero-tolerance policies for controlled substances, as these suspension and expulsion policies supply a pipeline of offenders to the adult prison system.

Racial profiling reaches beyond drug crimes to ensnare African Americans and Latinos/as for other offenses, ranging from traffic violations to vague crimes such as loitering and disturbing the peace. Despite the post–September 11th support for racial profiling in the War on Terror, it has no place in a country that aspires to judge its citizenry by the content of their individual character and not their skin color or appearance. Recognizing the racialized origins and enforcement of drug laws and shifting from an emphasis on imprisonment to treating addiction will eliminate racial profiling's primary turf and embolden community attack against racial profiling's other uses. Community outcry must also uproot and expose private racial profiling as equally offensive, as when stores profile black customers as potential shoplifters or credit frauds. Such profiling most notably was alleged in a 2013 incident in which a black student purchasing an expensive belt at the upscale Barneys New York was falsely accused and arrested apparently solely on the assumption that a young black man could not possibly afford the item.

Police violence is often unchecked in communities of color. As Alexander observes, "Lynch mobs may be long gone, but the threat of police violence [against black suspects] is ever present. A wrong move or sudden gesture could mean massive retaliation by the police."[83] As community members express to local police their belief that racial profiling should have no place in their community, local outcry can equally prompt accountability and training to prevent police brutality against vulnerable groups, whether in Ferguson, Missouri, or Anytown, U.S.A.

Finally, states must revisit the consequences of criminal records to ensure we rehabilitate rather than further punish these individuals. There is no cause for denying the voting franchise to felons, whether released or still imprisoned. Decent housing is a human right, and given the dismal employment opportunities for ex-convicts, transitional public housing should not be denied them absent some clear and present threat to the property or to other tenants.

*   *   *

We should ask ourselves how future generations may judge our current treatment of African Americans. Will they view our racial profiling and consequent mass incarceration as simply the latest mode of black control and subordination once carried out by slavery and Jim Crow laws? Have we just found seemingly more justifiable and ostensibly compassionate ways to kill the black spirit, as we have done for capital punishment, which has progressed from hangings to supposedly less cruel death-cocktail injections? Was slavery, apart from the ludicrous revisionist history portraying that institution as somehow compassionate toward black families, any worse than being stripped of freedoms and sent to prison?

Might we somehow elude the negative characterization of today's mass incarceration by attacking the individual character of those arrested? In other words, can the oppression of blacks through slavery and Jim Crow laws be distinguished from mass incarceration by arguing that slavery, in the slave states and territories, and Jim Crow laws affected all resident blacks? In contrast, it might be argued that some blacks, particularly the affluent and well educated and well dressed, may escape the police scrutiny and fate of other blacks today. This situation offers the opportunity, at least, for some to pronounce the advancement of our societal treatment of African Americans, with defects of individuals to blame for those ensnared in the criminal justice system. Yet the criminal justice system and the negative societal images of African Americans aren't necessarily constrained by class. President Obama, Harvard educated, is nonetheless the subject of vile comparisons to monkeys. Henry Louis Gates Jr., a distinguished Harvard professor, who was arrested at his home in 2009 for disorderly conduct after police interrogated him for breaking into his own residence, was later called a "banana-eating jungle monkey" by a Boston police officer.[84] If anything, Anglos are threatened by the economic and political success or aspirations of some blacks, and they construct these individuals as perhaps even more threatening than the rest of the black population. Of this mind, consider Mississippi governor Theodore Bilbo, a Ku Klux Klan member, who claimed in 1920 that Mississippi was happy to receive "niggers" who understood their subordinate place to white men but had no desire for the entry of blacks "contaminated with Northern social and political dreams of equality."[85] In our color-conscious society, no African American (even Bill Cosby's fictional Doctor Huxtable) is immune from scrutiny. When future and, one hopes, more enlightened generations examine the full record of today's racialized oppression, I submit we won't be able to hide behind the law-and-order defense to justify mass incarceration. Instead, later generations will question why we used law and the criminal justice system to inflict more damage on the African American community and its families than illicit drug use alone ever did.

10

You've Come a Long Way, Baby?

Gender and Dehumanization

Wives, submit yourselves unto your own husbands, as unto
the Lord. For the husband is the head of the wife, even as
Christ is the head of the church: and he is the saviour of the
body. Therefore as the church is subject unto Christ, so let
the wives be to their own husbands in every thing.
—Ephesians 5:22–24

No doubt women in the United States have advanced considerably
toward equality since the nineteenth century, when they were denied
the right to vote and excluded from higher education and certain
professions. Nevertheless, women suffer ongoing subordination that
questions their decision making about their bodies and the value of
their contributions in the workplace. They also routinely experience
the violence of gender hatred in the form of rape, domestic abuse,
and other attacks. Before discussing this continuing oppression it
is important to recognize the unique dynamics that surround the
subordination of women. As discussed below, the image of women was
rarely one of disgust akin to the image of the monstrous death-row
inmate or the vile comparison of black slaves to monkeys. Rather than
hostility, the dominant image was (and perhaps still is) one of fragility,
both physically and emotionally, and unsuitability for the rigors of
the workplace. But hate did (and does) exist in the mind of those who
terrorize women through rape and domestic abuse. Moreover, the
conception of women as not mentally suited for higher education or
certain professions is closely connected to similar conceptions of the
lack of intelligence of subordinated groups such as Latinos/as and
African Americans. Perhaps while not virulently subhuman, then, the
societal construction of women is nonetheless subhuman in its sense
that a woman is something less than a man.

Given that there are slightly more women in the United States than men (although men slightly outnumbered women until about 1950), a fair question is whether a subhuman construction can burden a majority group. It does not take a majority to design, propagate, and implement subhuman constructions, however, as evidenced by the mistreatment of blacks under South African apartheid, which was dictated by the white minority that controlled its government. What matters most for subhuman constructions is the ability to act on them to the detriment of the target group. The question throughout much of history, particularly U.S. history, then, is which group controls government, the judiciary, the military, and the acquisition of wealth—in essence, power. With women once denied the right to vote and husbands controlling their marital property, it was evident that men controlled the power to implement subordinating policy, a power that to a large extent they still retain.

Easily the most contentious dynamic surrounding the subordinate construction of women and its legal and societal consequences is the question of reproductive rights. Many right-to-life advocates contend that we in fact dehumanize the fetus and therefore tolerate abortions we would outlaw if we valued life from the moment of conception (or perhaps even before). At the same time, many of these pro-life advocates tend to view women as unsuited to make reproductive choices for their own bodies, thus setting up a situation in which women seeking abortions and abortion doctors are dehumanized by some as monsters, akin to death-row inmates, for failing to value the human life they allegedly took (or will take). This chapter confronts this challenging dynamic in examining which group is on the right side of history.

*   *   *

Probably the most dominant subordinating image of women throughout U.S. history has been their construction as delicate and in need of male protection. Supreme Court Justice Joseph Bradley invoked this paternalistic construction when he concurred with the Court's decision in 1872 that the constitutional protection against states abridging the privileges or immunities of U.S. citizens did not encompass the right to practice law. The Court thus let stand the Illinois

Supreme Court's refusal to issue a married woman a license to practice law. The Illinois judges rejected her application reasoning that, under the then-prevailing subordinate treatment of married women, she could not effectively enter into contracts, such as the contract between an attorney and a client. Justice Bradley, however, went beyond the federal constitutional question, however poorly decided, and added his views on civil law and the law of nature as preserving different destinies for men and women.[1] As Bradley and two other justices saw it:

> Man is, or should be, woman's protector and defender. The natural and proper timidity and delicacy which belongs to the female sex evidently unfits it for many of the occupations of civil life. The constitution of the family organization, which is found in the divine ordinance, as well as in the nature of things, indicates the domestic sphere as that which properly belongs to the domain and functions of womanhood. The harmony, not to say identity, of interest and views which belong, or should belong, to the family institution is repugnant to the idea of a woman adopting a distinct and independent career from that of her husband. . . . It is true that many woman are unmarried and not affected by the duties, complications, and incapacities arising out of the married state, but these are exceptions to the general rule. The paramount destiny and mission of wom[e]n are to fulfil the noble and benign offices of wife and mother. This is the law of the Creator.[2]

As Justice Bradley suggested, the roots for this subordinate construction of women date to the Bible, which implores, "Wives, submit yourselves unto your own husbands, as unto the Lord."[3] Essentially, this is the view that women more properly belong in the kitchen, "barefoot and pregnant," than in the workplace. It also suggests women are untrustworthy decision makers, whether in the home, the voting booth, or public office. Although one might argue that this paternalism nonetheless honored women by ensuring their protection from the harsh rigors of the workplace and government, similar romanticized notions surrounded slavery—that somehow the despicable institution of slavery benefitted black slaves by providing them food and shelter and therefore was better than the conditions they left behind in Africa.

But Supreme Court Justice William Douglas powerfully rebutted the romanticism of the so-called gentler sex in a 1973 decision invalidating a discriminatory policy:

> There can be no doubt that our Nation has had a long and unfortunate history of sex discrimination. Traditionally, such discrimination was rationalized by an attitude of "romantic paternalism" which, in practical effect, put women, not on a pedestal, but in a cage. Indeed, this paternalistic attitude became so firmly rooted in our national consciousness that, 100 years ago, a distinguished Member of this Court [Justice Bradley] was able to proclaim [that women belonged within the domestic realm, as excerpted above].[4]

No doubt our subordinating views of women carried severe consequences that, as Justice Douglas put it, effectively caged them. Douglas went on to compare the legal experience of women to that of black slaves:

> As a result of [subordinate] notions such as these, our statute books gradually became laden with gross, stereotyped distinctions between the sexes and, indeed, throughout much of the 19th century the position of women in our society was, in many respects, comparable to that of blacks under the pre-Civil War slave codes. Neither slaves nor women could hold office, serve on juries, or bring suit in their own names, and married women traditionally were denied the legal capacity to hold or convey property or to serve as legal guardians of their own children.[5]

Importing the British common law tradition of marriage, which suspended a woman's legal existence and gave control over the marriage unit to her husband, many U.S. states once prohibited women from entering into contracts without their husband's consent, and they could not own property independent of their husband's control.[6] Husbands even controlled any wages their wives earned. Married women gained the right to contract and own property with the passage by states of Married Women's Property Acts in the second half of the nineteenth century.[7] Yet fundamental change was slow in coming, if at all. The Supreme Court upheld the exclusion of women from the practice of law in 1872, as previously noted, and similarly refused to strike down a Missouri law in 1874 that denied women the right to vote;[8] both these exclusions were common in the states.

Progress came in the 1900s, as women were constitutionally guaranteed the right to vote when the Nineteenth Amendment was ratified in 1920; yet a Mississippi Tea Party leader suggested in 2012 that the country would be better off with only men voting, claiming women are too "diabolical" to vote.[9] But political clout did not accompany the ballot. Women still lag well behind men in elected positions; as of early 2014, after several 2012 election successes, a record number of only twenty women serve in the hundred-member U.S. Senate; they constitute almost half of the forty-four women who have ever served as senators during the more than two-hundred-year history of the institution.

Progress was slow on other fronts of humanity and equality. The Massachusetts Supreme Court decided in 1931 that because women were not persons under state law, they were ineligible to serve on juries.[10] Not until 1950 did Harvard law school admit its first woman, and women lawyers still lag far behind men in ownership and governance positions in major law firms. In the 1800s, Harvard resisted the entry of women to all its schools, with its then president, Charles William Eliot, questioning how one might police so many men and women of marriageable age and more disturbingly calling into question the "natural mental capacities" of women.[11] Apart from the stereotype that women were somehow less innately intelligent than men, denying women access to higher education played into the hands of employers who might contend women were less educated than men. Despite their eventual admission to colleges (Oberlin College was the first to admit women, in 1833), employers freely discriminated against women, finally prompting Congress to enact the Equal Pay Act of 1963 and the Civil Rights Act of 1964, which prohibited sex discrimination in employment. Yet employers continue to subject female employees to sexual harassment and discrimination in hiring and pay despite legal prohibitions, thus forcing women to protect their rights in court. The National Women's Law Center contends, for example, that today "American women who work full-time, year-round are paid only 77 cents for every dollar paid to their male counterparts."[12]

Much of today's subjugation of U.S. women imposes control over their bodies, presumably on the notion, akin to the arguments for former denials of voting and even jury service, that men are somehow better decision makers. Relatedly, grounded in many historic laws and the Bible, the perception still exists among some that women are the property of their husbands or perhaps whoever chooses to exercise dominion over them. This subhuman conception of women as vessels or personal property facilitates sexual harassment, stalking, sexual trafficking, and even rape and murder, as well as domestic abuse. For example, until recently U.S. states failed to criminalize marital rape, potentially allowing a legally separated man to rape his wife with impunity.[13] The prevailing subhuman construct of women is evident too in the overwhelming popularity of brutal pornography—googling "brutal porn" yields more than twenty million sites. Journalist Chris Hedges has documented how the U.S. porn industry eventually came to reflect "the endemic cruelty of our society" through its obsession with multiple penetrations, gagging, and physical and psychological degradation of women akin to the torture of prisoners.[14]

The battle for control over a woman's body and decision making is most contentious on the question of reproductive rights. Here, pro-life advocates decry the supposed dehumanization of the fetus as facilitating its destruction, while in turn those advocates often view women as mere objects or vessels for procreation and even as murderers for obtaining an abortion, thereby invoking the subhuman characterizations that surround death-row inmates who disregarded the sanctity of human life. A Saint Louis University professor of social work, William Brennan, wrote of various kinds of dehumanization in the past and present, focusing on domestic constructions of Native Americans and African Americans, international subordination of Soviet enemies and European Jews, and domestic dehumanization of women and of what he calls the unwanted unborn. While at the same time decrying the subordination of women through the denial of rights, such as the right to vote, and by violence against them through rape and other assaults, as well as visually through brutal pornography, Brennan advocates for the personhood of the fetus and therefore for legal and moral protection against abortion.[15] In another book, *The Abortion Holocaust: Today's Final Solution*, Brennan goes so far as to conjoin abortions and the Nazi efforts to eradicate Jews and others they found undesirable in their pursuit of the master race.[16] Brennan particularly singles out a 1990 magazine article written by Dr. Carl Sagan and his wife, Ann Druyan, who compared a woman's fetus in its early phases of development to a segmented worm, progressing to a newt or tadpole, a reptile, and finally a lower mammal—"mammalian but somewhat piglike" at the end of its seventh week.[17] Most abortions are performed before the eighth week of pregnancy, when the fetus has grown to about the size of a raspberry. In particular, Brennan scolds the Supreme Court for dehumanizing the fetus in its 1973 decision in *Roe v. Wade*, in which it recognized a woman's right to choose as a constitutional prerogative. As that decision states, "The fetus, at most, represents only the potentiality of life," and the "unborn have never been recognized in the law as persons in the whole sense."[18] Relying on the constitutional right to privacy as encompassing a woman's right to make her own reproductive choices, the Court in *Roe* struck down a Texas criminal abortion statute, similar to those then prevailing in a majority of states, that outlawed all abortions unless necessary to save the mother's life. As construed and narrowed by subsequent Supreme Court decisions, the touchstone for constitutional protection of a woman's right to choose turns on the viability of the fetus—its ability to survive outside the womb, using artificial aid if necessary. After viability, the states can go as far as to proscribe abortion, unless necessary for the mother's life or health. Before viability, the state may permissibly burden the woman's right to choose an abortion, as long as the regulation does not unduly burden her choice. In adopting this "undue-burden" standard in a plurality opinion, the Supreme Court in 1992 upheld provisions of a Pennsylvania law that imposed a twenty-four-hour waiting period for abortions, required parental consent for a minor daughter's abortion, and specified an informed-consent procedure requiring doctors to warn the recipient of the health risks of an abortion. However, the Court invalidated a spousal-notice provision directing the woman to notify her husband before obtaining an abortion, reasoning that such a notification might exacerbate or prompt spousal abuse.[19]

In the ensuing decades, a woman's right to choose has come under attack in many states. Although the Supreme Court in *Roe* suggested that viability usually occurs about seven months (twenty-eight weeks) into the pregnancy, while perhaps occurring as early as twenty-four weeks, conservative states are testing the limits of viability. The statutory ban on abortions after twenty weeks in Arizona, one of about a dozen states as of 2013 with this early a prohibition, was struck down in federal court that year.[20] States are also pushing the boundaries of the undue-burden requirement, with an emerging trend to require an ultrasound as a condition for an abortion; Kentucky's legislature has considered whether to require a woman seeking an abortion to be shown the ultrasound screen while the technician describes the fetus to her, with the hope, presumably, that the woman will forge a bond with her fetus and cancel the procedure. Some states and Congress have proposed life-at-conception bills that would define the start of human life at the moment of fertilization and aim to establish the fetus as a person for constitutional and criminal law purposes. Should these bills be enacted and the Supreme Court, with its more conservative composition than in 1973, rule as hoped by these proponents, abortions might be unlawful even in the case of rape or incest, and some recent methods of birth control might be threatened as well. Previously, in 1965, the Supreme Court had struck down, as contrary to a marital couple's constitutional right to privacy, a Connecticut law that unbelievably criminalized using any drug (primarily birth-control pills) or device to prevent conception.[21]

Despite existing Supreme Court rulings grounded in the Constitution, conservative politicians of late are attacking contraception and abortion regardless of even compelling circumstances such as rape and the mother's own survival. The 2012 election brought outrageous statements from conservative candidates, such as U.S. Senate candidate Todd Akin from Missouri, who contended abortion laws should not countenance a rape exception because when a rape is "legitimate" the female body has natural ways "to shut that whole thing down."[22] On a somewhat different but equally ludicrous note, Richard Mourdock, an Indiana candidate for U.S. Senate, remarked, "Even when life begins in that horrible situation of rape [and presumably is not "shut down"], that is something that God intended to happen" and therefore is a gift from God to the rape victim that cannot be rejected.[23] Republican congressman Joe Walsh, defeated in the 2012 elections along with Akin and Mourdock, even decried abortions where the mother's life was at risk, maintaining such seemingly compelling circumstances were just a rhetorical tool used by pro-choice activists who ignore medical advances that eliminate this risk.[24] Birth control also came under frequent attack. In contrast to the United Nations declaring for the first time in 2012 that family planning is a universal human right, Republican presidential candidate Rick Santorum warned in 2011 of the dangers of contraception when he stated, contrary to the Supreme Court, that states must deny contraceptives, as their use is "a license to do things in a sexual realm that is counter to how things are supposed to be."[25]

*   *   *

As with African Americans and the onslaught of crippling mass incarceration, the antiwomen rhetoric of conservatives seems to be sending women's progress backward of late. Centered on reproductive rights, as noted above, the current battle pits the alleged humanity of the early-stage fetus against the history of the subordination and negative constructions of women. The moral compass of subhumanity doesn't supply clear answers here as it does for the other kinds of subordination addressed in this book, aside from suggesting that both perspectives should be honored where possible. Although there seems to be no definitive reconciliation, perhaps common ground can be found on subjects such as economic rights, access to contraception, and protection against sexual violence. Ensuring the access of low-income women to contraceptives (both financially and geographically) will help address the statistic that these women are four times more likely to face unintended pregnancies and to receive abortions than their higher-income counterparts.[26] Abortions have held steady or declined in recent years, dropping as much as 5 percent in 2012, with the credit due to increased use of contraceptives, particularly by minors. The Supreme Court's protection of abortion no doubt was of most critical importance to low-income women, who lack the ready ability to finance effective birth control or to travel to U.S. states or to countries with more liberal abortion allowances.[27] Reforms in the workplace, from Congress enacting proposals to better enforce equal pay and mandating maternity leave, to employers on their own initiative offering work schedules and environments more suitable for working mothers, can address a number of ills for women whether they desire children or not. Despite these potential strategies to reduce unwanted pregnancies, conservative politicians have seemingly turned back the clock on women by attacking access to contraceptives by low-income women and even equal-pay initiatives. Seemingly, we are now at a crossroads: Will women continue their march toward economic and social equality or have those goals derailed in the singular interest of controlling their bodies?

Another potential for common ground exists in protecting women from attack through the savagery of rape and domestic abuse, which too many U.S. women suffer. Yet conservative politicians seem more interested in protecting a fetus conceived in rape than the rape victim, even suggesting as noted above that rape claims often are questionable rather than "legitimate." Regardless, government is better used to protect women's bodies from physical attack in the first instance than to regulate the privacy of family planning.[28] Instead of attempting to regulate abortion clinics, legislators ought to be funding domestic-violence shelters and meaningful policing against sexual abuse and sexual trafficking, which violate the bodies and dreams of U.S. women. The Center for Reproductive Rights launched an online petition, backed by prominent entertainers, that sets the tone for reform by declaring the following fundamental human rights of women, which no government may deny and rather should safeguard:

1. The right to make our own decisions about our reproductive health and future, free from intrusion or coercion by any government, group, or individual.
2. The right to a full range of safe, affordable, and readily accessible reproductive health care—including pregnancy care, preventive services, contraception, abortion, and fertility treatment—and accurate information about all of the above.
3. The right to be free from discrimination in access to reproductive health care or on the basis of our reproductive decisions.[29]

On the broader subject of gender discrimination, the United States is the world's only industrialized democracy that has failed to ratify the international human rights ideals of the Convention on the Elimination of All Forms of Discrimination against Women. Indeed, the only other countries left to ratify this U.N. General Assembly–approved agreement are Iran, Somalia, Sudan, South Sudan, and the small Pacific island countries of Palau and Tonga. The Convention comprehensively confronts gender inequality in all its reaches, including sex trafficking, laws that discriminate against women, and more generally societal discrimination that prevents the equality of women in the "political, economic, social, cultural, civic, or any other field." Notably, the Convention attacks the root of gender inequality by calling for the elimination of prejudices "based on the idea of the inferiority or the superiority of either of the sexes."[30] Only through full humanization of the female mind and body in societal perception will true equality in legal and societal treatment follow.

11

International Dehumanization

By slighting death, by acting, we pretended it was not the
terrible thing it was. . . . If it isn't human, it doesn't matter much if it's dead. And so a [Viet Cong] nurse, fried by
napalm, was a crispy critter. A Vietnamese baby, which lay
nearby, was a roasted peanut.
—Tim O'Brien

As mentioned in the Introduction, although my focus is on domestic
regret, much of the landscape of regret detailed above has international
dimensions. Most evidently, our vilification of Muslims and Muslim-
appearing individuals in prosecuting the War on Terror encompasses
fronts both domestic (such as the interrogative profiling of these
groups and antimosque and anti-Sharia law efforts) and international
(the torture of suspected terrorists at locations abroad and U.S.
military interventions in Iraq and elsewhere). Immigration is another
domestic policy with an international impact. In addition to drawing
Mexican laborers, the incessant lure by U.S. employers dependent
on cheap immigrant labor pulls many undocumented Central (and
South) American migrants north through Mexico on their journey to
U.S. jobs. As undocumented Mexican immigrants have suffered and
perished on their journey to and within the United States, so too have
Central American immigrants in their harrowing journey through
Mexico's drug-cartel ravaged regions. In the heyday of undocumented
immigration in the early- to mid-2000s, annually some three hundred
thousand to four hundred thousand immigrants from Guatemala, El
Salvador, Nicaragua, and the rest of Central America entered Mexico,
many headed north to cross the U.S.-Mexico border as undocumented
immigrants.[1] By 2012, a slight majority of the U.S. Border Patrol's
apprehensions in South Texas were of undocumented Central
American migrants.[2] Most poignantly, the 2010 massacre within
Mexico of seventy-two mostly Central and South American migrants

headed north is thought to have been prompted by their refusal to assist a Mexican cartel in smuggling drugs into the United States.[3]

Our mistreatment of farmworkers reflects the reality that most are vulnerable undocumented immigrants from Mexico. More broadly, the ready ability of U.S. manufacturers and even service providers to relocate jobs globally to the cheapest labor sources helps ensure the vulnerability of many U.S. workers, who constantly face the threat of job removal abroad when they demand a living wage. Even our imposition of the death penalty occasionally reverberates internationally, as when the United States flouts its treaty with Mexico that constrains extradition of Mexican nationals or any fugitive charged with an offense punishable in the United States by death. In 1989, for example, Texas police officers simply kidnapped two Mexican nationals within Mexico, bringing them to Texas to face capital murder charges, a tactic federal drug-enforcement officers have also employed.[4] Another international connection to domestic subordination was the journey, before the decision in *Roe v. Wade*, of many U.S. women who visited Mexican "abortion emporiums" in Tijuana and nearby Ensenada to obtain a surreptitious abortion there.[5]

Given these international connections, we can profit from examining how the moral compass of subhumanity works in foreign terrain. I do this using war and war-related campaigns as the most obvious site both of potential regret and of subhuman constructions that foster or at least accompany those interventions. Although it seems evident that we tend to construct military enemies as subhuman threats, causation is less clear. I address this tension in the Conclusion, where I suggest that capitalism may require or encourage exploitation of the vulnerable and thus there may be an incentive to dehumanize certain groups in order to justify their plunder. This potential is even more evident in wartime. Might we conveniently dehumanize the enemy to insulate our troops from the horrors of warfare, as a means to a military end, rather than as a catalyst for warfare in the first instance? Although I do not answer this question and realize that the answer may differ for the various military engagements in our history, it is clear that images of subhumanity accompany warfare. Moreover, although the focus below is on the U.S. military experience, dehumanization is evident in the military history of other countries and their conflicts.

One of the first instances of dehumanization by the U.S. military was domestic, as we succeeded in characterizing indigenous peoples as savages and subhuman threats to be exterminated. For example, a U.S. Army private chronicling the 1832 Black Hawk War in the Midwest called Native Americans more "like the wild beasts than man," and Francis Parkman, a famous historian of the nineteenth century, explained that because we look upon Natives as an "alien" and a "dangerous species of wild beast," we can "shoot them with . . . little compunction."[6] Because soldiers equated Natives with animals, such as wolves, military expeditions to exterminate them became "hunts," as reflected in an 1867 U.S. Secretary of War report calling the U.S. fight with Apache Indians "more like hunting wild animals than any regular kind of warfare."[7]

Later, our World War II conflict with Japan combined subhuman constructions with arguably the most wrenching foreign consequences. Depicted in subhuman animalistic terms as "monkeys, baboons, dogs, rats, vipers, cockroaches, or vermin,"[8] and in a 1942 New York City float, titled "Tokyo, We Are Coming," as yellow rats with U.S. bombs raining down,[9] the Japanese were poised for extermination. Indeed, a December 1944 opinion poll found 13 percent of U.S. residents answering "kill all Japanese" in response to a query about what should be done with Japan after the war.[10] In reality we came close to that goal during World War II, as we dropped an array of bombs on dozens of Japanese cities as fast as those weapons were made; the bombing killed hundreds of thousands of children and other civilians,[11] and it ultimately resulted in the only two wartime uses of nuclear weapons in history, both by the United States. Supported by 85 percent of U.S. residents at the time,[12] atomic bombs murdered Japanese civilians en masse in Hiroshima and Nagasaki. Ultimately condemned by a Tokyo court as "an illegal act of hostilities according to the rules of international law" for its targeting of undefended cities,[13] this mass murder went without apology for decades until Obama apparently intended to formally apologize during a 2009 visit to Japan.[14] Rejected by the Japanese government, as revealed in leaked documents, perhaps to avoid further encouraging the burgeoning antinuclear sentiment in a country that relies significantly on nuclear energy, our apology was never delivered. At the same time, our participation in ongoing nuclear disarmament may signal regret for having resorted to such arbitrary and merciless weapons of mass destruction, which now threaten our own security in the hands of others, such as Russia.

Although the United States rarely apologizes for its military interventions and foreign policy, as addressed in Chapter 1 we did formally apologize to domestic Japanese Americans swept into the subhuman construction and interned in U.S. detention camps. Also, Clinton apologized in 1999 for U.S. support of Guatemalan right-wing governments during a thirty-six-year civil war; our intervention there had led to the torture and murder of thousands of Mayan civilians. The apology called our training and other support of the Guatemalan military "wrong" but did not mention similar U.S. support of other oppressive Latin regimes.[15] We have not apologized for the massive acquisition of Southwest territory in the U.S.-Mexican War, for our problematic intervention in Vietnam (in 2000, Clinton flatly denied the need for any such apology), or for our role in orchestrating the 1990s' imposition of economic sanctions on Iraq; these sanctions were so oppressive, resulting in the deaths of more than one million Iraqis, that one legal scholar called them criminal genocide under the U.N. Convention on the Prevention and Punishment of Genocide of 1948.[16]

Applying the framework of subhuman constructions as predicting future regret, one could ask what current global subordination carried out by the United States fits this model. Foremost, of course, would be the War on Terror, as discussed in Chapter 8, with its torture of suspected terrorists as well as its destructive foreign intervention in locations such as Afghanistan. Ironically, given the dominant early-twentieth-century construction of Jews as subhuman in the United States and abroad, the foreign situs of future regret may be our military and economic support of Israel in its conflict with Palestine. We have successfully constructed Palestine's substantially Muslim population as one of subhuman suicide bomber–terrorists threatening Israel, as illustrated by the 2012 pro-Israel advertisements on New York transit buses mentioned in Chapter 8: "In any war between the civilized man and the [Muslim/Arab] savage, support the civilized man." Proponents of our financial support of Israel would be quick to point out that many Palestinians equally hate and demonize Jews; the prospects for regional resolution and stability are thus dismal.

Another candidate for regret may be our multifaceted role in Mexico's drug war, which has claimed thousands of innocent lives. As I documented in my book *Run for the Border*, Mexican drug cartels exist to serve U.S. users of their illicit cargo. Secretary of State Hillary Clinton acknowledged the obvious in admitting that "our insatiable demand for illegal drugs fuels the [Mexican] drug trade."[17] Over the years, the United States has cajoled Mexico into fighting narcotics trafficking aggressively on its own turf to complement U.S. domestic attempts to curb the intractable demand for illicit drugs. Through the Mérida Initiative, we funneled hundreds of millions of dollars to finance the Mexican military's current campaign against entrenched drug cartels, outfitting its military with helicopters and surveillance planes. As I observed in *Run for the Border*, that federal military initiative launched a bloody firefight with the cartels. They responded by terrorizing the Mexican people through the mass murder of children and other innocent victims in the hopes that the Mexican people would pressure their government to relent and return to the former system of government corruption, in which cartels acted more like U.S. alcohol suppliers than thugs. U.S. legalization of drugs, starting with marijuana, would squeeze the cartels better than any firefight, but the deaths of Mexican youth have little resonance north of the border to help prompt reform or even moral abstinence from drugs by users. Almost no U.S. residents heard about the Mexican cartel gunmen who in January 2010 murdered sixteen people, mostly teenagers, celebrating a birthday at a Mexico residence or the similar mass killing of seventeen young people attending a Mexico birthday party in July 2010.[18] In contrast, the tragedy of the 2012 Connecticut school shooting of twenty U.S. children was the story of the year and elicited mass public grief. Given our longstanding dehumanization of the Mexican people, these south-of-the-border deaths matter little to our policymakers and even less to U.S. drug users, who fail to acknowledge any connection between the deaths of innocent Mexicans and their own supply chain.

*   *   *

Lessons can be drawn from the international experience to augment the discussion in the Conclusion, which aims to humanize the groups we vilify. Wartime experience suggests we might soften our views when the exigency of the moment passes. As legal scholar Richard Delgado has remarked, "During war, we demonize our enemies, and thereafter actually see them as grotesque, evil and crafty monsters deserving of their fate on the battlefield. Later, during peacetime, they may become our staunch allies once again."[19] When these enemies are people of color, however, animosities and old war wounds may linger; in 1982 two white Michigan autoworkers beat a Chinese man, Vincent Chin, to death with a baseball bat. Thinking Chin was Japanese and upset over the economic competition from Japanese cars, the autoworkers called him a "Jap" in the language of World War II subordination and then murdered him.[20]

Technological developments in warfare suggest challenges ahead for the cultivation of compassion and for policy reform even if images of vulnerable groups soften. The airmen dropping atomic bombs on Japanese cities from high overhead had little sense of the humanity they destroyed on the ground below. As we move further from hand-to-hand combat to warfare through ground-combat robots and pilotless drones,[21] these technologies may render warfare more of a dispassionate video game than a traumatic human experience, with the result of further dehumanizing the enemy. Domestic applications of robot and drone technology (drones are already in use in U.S.-Mexico border enforcement) offer the potential to blunt any compassionate thoughts for the enemy. Rather, in the vein of the sci-fi thriller *RoboCop* (1987), undocumented immigrants crossing the U.S.-Mexico border and suspected criminals of color on U.S. streets could be dehumanized and hunted as we would search for and destroy international terrorist targets.

Our culture of violence abroad creates a complex circularity that imperils compassion. Having disrupted cultures and nations in Asia, the Middle East, and Central America through our military interventions in recent decades, we now find that that violence increasingly returns to our own streets. Whether through the terrorist acts of those enraged by our foreign policy or through mass murder by violent and mentally ill U.S. residents numbed to the human experience by their exposure to war's brutality and the increasing commodification of warlike aggression in U.S. cinema and video games, with both groups—terrorists and mass murderers—seen as subhuman, in the years ahead we can expect the arc of societal violence to compete with the encouragement of compassion. As long as war remains a ready and celebrated option for settling international disputes, compassion and humanization will be challenged domestically and abroad.

Additional lessons and strategies come from the international experience. As standards of humanity emerge from the development of international human rights, at the same time our oppression in other countries of subordinated groups suggests we might develop compassion by seeing and rejecting despicable treatment abroad. After all, we intervened in Nazi Germany despite prevalent anti-Jewish animus within the United States. Backlash against subhumanity, and thus a chance for humanization, might result when extremists abroad or domestically go too far in demonizing their targets. For example, the efforts in Uganda to impose increasingly harsh penalties for homosexual acts, even the death penalty[22] (as already exists in a few countries such as Nigeria and Iran), and the ongoing oppression of women in some countries through "honor killings," genital mutilation, and other types of brutalization might cause some to recoil in disdain from that mistreatment and to embrace efforts in the United States to institute compassionate policies for those demonized groups here. The Conclusion supplies additional ideas for establishing the United States and demarcating its identity as a proponent and incubator of broad-scale humanity and a promoter of ideals toward its attainment.

Conclusion

A Blueprint for Humanization through Compassion

Fleeing from situations of extreme poverty or persecution in the hope of a better future . . . millions of persons choose to migrate. Despite their hopes and expectations, they often encounter mistrust, rejection and exclusion, to say nothing of tragedies and disasters which offend their human dignity. . . . A change of attitude towards migrants and refugees is needed on the part of everyone, moving away from the attitudes of defensiveness and fear, indifference and marginalization . . . towards attitudes based on a culture of encounter, the only culture capable of building a better, more just and fraternal world. . . . We ourselves need to see, and then to enable others to see, that migrants and refugees do not only represent a problem to be solved, but are brothers and sisters to be welcomed, respected and loved.
—English translation of remarks by Pope Francis for the World Day of Migrants and Refugees

Having examined the absence of humanity for a number of U.S. groups and individuals throughout this book and the connection of subhuman images to regrettable U.S. policies, in this final chapter I question whether we can reshape those subhuman constructions to restore humanity and help establish and ensure our legacy as a generation of vision and compassion. The pessimists among us can point to at least two nagging shortfalls in the task of imagining and restoring a fully human image. First, as detailed in Chapters 9 and 10 and below, the process of humanization might take generations to accomplish, and, tending to be impatient, some among us may not wish to expend the energy on the initiatives suggested below that may not bear harvestable fruit within our lifetimes. Politicians, for example, rarely take a long view and focus instead on short-term imperatives to boost their reelection prospects. Second, a gloomy causation issue remains for some of the kinds of subordination raised in this book—namely, whether the subhuman images connected to injustice cause oppression or whether some more fundamental need for injustice prompts subhuman images to feed and justify that need, a process that signals the permanence of oppression. For example, consider the prevailing disdain for most low-paid workers, many of them from communities of color and immigrants, who populate jobs necessary for our economy. Does our system of capitalism require low-paid/underpaid workers for its success? If so, does our system necessarily mandate the creation of a subhuman working class, one that fails to garner sympathy from policymakers who might otherwise enact reforms that imperil the capitalist enterprise? Although total economic equality is unlikely, Chapter 5 nonetheless mapped out how the basic imperatives of capitalism might coexist with more humane treatment and opportunities for vulnerable workers and those unable to work. For some other groups, it is simply not true that an underlying engrained system requires their oppression. In the case of criminals, for example, no tenet of our culture or economic system or any of our survivalist needs hinges on whether we execute or merely imprison offenders, at least when executions are being conducted on racially neutral terms. Although some human rights advocates have called into question our imprisonment culture, which captures the labor of prisoners and supplies enormous profits to the increasingly privatized prison system, killing our prisoners runs counter to that profiteering.

A threshold question in sketching a framework for humanizing the images of vulnerable groups concerns the target audience. Are initiatives for humanization best directed at the hearts and minds of judges, legislators (state or federal), other policymakers, law enforcement, farmers (or, more appropriately, agribusiness), farm-labor contractors, corporate executives, the wealthy class, or the public generally? Explained below, my emphasis is on the general public, although I am mindful that positive change can originate from narrower sources.

Having highlighted throughout this book the pivotal role of judges in fostering regrettable policies and practices in the past, I think it is evident that judges have a particular incentive to question and improve their legacies and their decision making in light of past transgressions, lest (to borrow the phrasing of Supreme Court Justice Oliver Wendell Holmes) we suffer more generations of imbecile judges! Some of the canvas of regret examined above is well suited for judicial intervention, particularly eliminating the death penalty, which hinges on the constitutional cruel-and-unusual standard and is ripe for a ruling that aligns with the trajectory of international human rights and the growing state rejection of capital punishment. Although stare decisis typically compels honoring past precedent, our history of regrettable policies demonstrates that the Supreme Court occasionally breaks from the past, as it did in *Brown v. Board of Education*, abandoning the separate-but-equal ruling in *Plessy v. Ferguson*, and in *Lawrence v. Texas*, invalidating the antisodomy laws upheld just seventeen years before in *Bowers v. Hardwick*.[1] Still, judges are constrained in implementing social change. On the subject of immigration, for example, the plenary-power doctrine allows Congress and the executive to hold sway over U.S. immigration policy, although the courts have weighed in to negate state and local rules that frustrate Congressional intent, at least as long as Congress does not affirmatively invite local enforcement efforts. Elected judges are also vulnerable to hysteria and the prejudices of the moment. Moreover, many observers believe compassion is incompatible with the proper role of judges to apply the law, as was evident in the controversy over Obama's invocation of empathy and compassion as relevant standards in selecting a Supreme Court nominee, in that instance Sonia Sotomayor.[2]

Surveying the areas of acknowledged regret identified at the outset of this project reveals an array of political and judicial actors involved in eliminating those regrettable practices through transformative social policy. Although the Supreme Court played a role in ending official segregation, Congress more comprehensively outlawed segregation in a variety of venues from housing to employment to public accommodations by means of civil rights laws. Earlier, abolishing slavery involved war, an executive order (the Emancipation Proclamation), and a constitutional amendment approved by Congress and three-quarters of the states (although a few states rejected ratification of the amendment and Mississippi was the last state to finally approve it in 1995, preceded by Kentucky in 1976). Through its plenary power over immigration, Congress eventually rectified another policy of regret, its own Chinese

Exclusion Act. Implemented by an executive order signed by President Roosevelt in 1942, the internment of Japanese Americans terminated in 1945 through issuance of a military proclamation, and Congress authorized reparations to surviving internees in 1988. But Native American removals and land thefts, the subject of official apology by Congress in 2009, were never addressed in the form of Congressional compensation or restoration of lands.

From another direction, consider the various policymaking actors necessary for the reforms urged in this study. Some reforms call for federal policymaking. Compassionate immigration reform from Congress could supplant the hostile intrusion by states and local government into immigration policy. Federal law and federal actors set the tone for humanity, or its absence, in waging the War on Terror. Some reforms suggested above are amenable to either federal or state action. For example, the minimum wage in some states exceeds the federally specified amount, while in other states the federal salary is the wage floor. Other areas call for reform on both the federal and state level to undo past subordination. For example, drug laws, particularly those regulating marijuana, are mandated and enforced through a combination of federal and state efforts, as are laws taxing the wealthy and other income earners, and responsibility for financing and incentivizing public education and student financial aid. In the case of marijuana prohibition, however, the states and municipalities are beginning to lead the way toward enlightened reform that the federal government may choose to suppress, tolerate, or embrace.[3]

Finally, some reform, absent directives from the federal or state governments, could occur at the local level— through localized initiatives to squelch racial profiling in law enforcement, possibly through prosecutorial discretion not to seek the death penalty where otherwise allowed in a jurisdiction, or through local police departments, prosecutors, and judges not prioritizing or enforcing drug-possession laws, while preferring treatment options.

Most of the proposed reforms will emerge, if at all, from the will of the public, through votes or otherwise. Reform of drug laws and discriminatory marriage laws has begun to occur through the direct democracy of ballot initiatives despite the history of ballot measures being deployed against vulnerable groups such as LGBT populations and immigrants.[4] Politicians often take their cues from the prerogatives of voters, and even judges are vulnerable to ouster when elected by popular vote, as when hostile Iowa voters ousted three state supreme court judges, running unopposed in 2010, who had sided with same-sex marriage.[5] In theory, voters in sufficient number could accomplish most every reform proposed above. But implementing the ideals of humanity for vulnerable groups must not end with simply convincing a voting majority, as much of the oppression against vulnerable groups comes from individual actors who target these groups. Every day, women are sexually harassed, raped, and assaulted, and other groups, such as LGBT populations, face assaults and abusive behavior. Despite the legal protections sometimes available against these crimes, the existence of remedies is little comfort to victims and thus demands a broader target audience in the goal of building compassion for these vulnerable groups. Thus, the suggestions below for providing a framework for compassion and humanity are aimed at a wide audience of policymakers, voters, and more generally all U.S. residents. Where possible they seek to engage the silent middle between those vilifying vulnerable groups and the tireless advocates defending them.

At the outset, we need to recognize that there is no magic formula or silver bullet for instilling compassion in the general public. Certainly there is no legitimacy in the global and our own historical approach of instilling humanity in and fostering our compassion for despised groups through their forced conversion to Christianity. Although we tend to cheer and root for underdogs on the athletic field, we fail to do so in the voting booth or on the legislative floor when vulnerable groups are at risk. Nor is love of the American family necessarily an effective rallying call. Despite our affection for children, in the case of U.S.-citizen children of noncitizen immigrants we dehumanize them as anchor babies and in the case of children born to "welfare queens" we both dehumanize and racialize them as "crack babies." Despite our regard for the American family, we routinely separate parents from their children in carrying out deportations under the current restrictive immigration system; we still legislate against same-sex couples desiring to form a legal familial bond; and we don't hesitate to imprison parents for minor drug offenses, regardless of the disruptive impact on their families.

Compassion and humanity, then, must come simultaneously from many directions and approaches in the hope that something will stick. As a starting point, it is important to examine how subhuman constructions are propagated. Elsewhere I have described the role that the media play in initiating or at least in sustaining negative images of Latinos/as,[6] and the media have played no less a role in the other negative constructions detailed here. Whether on talk radio or blogs or in seemingly less politicized productions such as motion pictures, music, and television shows, members of almost every vulnerable group examined here have been portrayed as villains. Popular rap music in particular subjugates women and gays; Muslim-appearing villains dominate cinema;[7] many Internet pornography sites feature the brutalizing of women; talk radio bashes immigrants, particularly those from Mexico; and television news programs emphasizing local crime leave the impression of a spiraling and racialized crime wave at a time when violent crime is declining in most areas. Even product advertisements tap into the prevailing vilification of vulnerable groups, as when a television commercial for Kellogg's Nut 'n Honey cereal suggested that gay advances should be met with deadly force in depicting several men pulling handguns on the wagon-train cook they thought called them "honey."[8] Some of these kinds of dehumanization are more subtle, as when on television shows and in the movies Latinos/as, whether immigrants or not, are invisible in or absent from most urban landscapes unless they are hotel maids or menacing criminals. Other media, particularly talk radio, are increasingly virulent and direct in attacking vulnerable groups, with their apparent license to call President Obama a monkey and in another breath to advocate for the murder of subhuman migrant border crossers for their crime of economic desperation.

Elsewhere, I have written of the scant opportunities for deploying lawyers and judicial challenges to silence derogatory and hateful characterizations in the media.[9] The constitutional protection of free speech typically ensures that most of these slurs will survive attack. Ironically, pundits spewing hate speech find even greater protection in law when they attack groups with vicious rhetoric ("I think all Mexicans should be shot before they shoot us") than when they demean a particular individual. Even when targeting individuals with wild hyperbolic claims, most speakers can escape legal attack.[10] For example, the courts likely would insulate a radio host who calls out an undocumented student and labels her an illegal subhuman monster who should be killed and hung at the border as a deterrent to undocumented entries. If lawyers and lawsuits challenging hate speech won't work, what will? If ratings drive these programs, then obviously the public feeds off the frenzy and froth of hate these media outlets so readily deliver. How can these messages be attacked if ratings remain high? One strategy with proven success is to galvanize the ranks of a large group with purchasing clout and to deploy them against a national media organization. This approach succeeded in the campaign of Presente.org, among other groups, to drive news anchor Lou Dobbs, who routinely called immigrants "invaders" and "illegals," from CNN,[11] although Dobbs found a new soapbox on the Fox Business Network. No doubt CNN, with its national presence, valued the Latino/a demographic that was so often the subject of Dobbs's vitriol. Presente.org also led the charge against the word *illegal*, which is routinely used by the media to describe immigrants without legal authorization; the campaign prompted the Associated Press in 2013 to stop using the derogatory moniker "illegal immigrants."[12] Don Imus, once host of a national CBS radio program simulcast on the cable news network MSNBC, was dropped in 2007 after he called the Rutgers University women's basketball team "nappy-headed hos."[13] Outcry from the African American community over his slur against the black women on the Rutgers team presumably prompted several show sponsors to pull or suspend their advertising, although Imus resurrected his program on the Fox Business Network and other outlets.

Following the Presente.org model, which rallied Latinos/as and other groups against Dobbs, vulnerable groups might prioritize the worst on-air offenders of human rights and seek their removal or cancellation, mindful that the Fox Network seems to be a shelter for the relocation of wayward pundits. The same strategy can be used even more effectively with entertainers, who should permanently lose their fifteen minutes of fame when they cross the line of decency, as did *Seinfeld*'s Kramer, comedian Michael Richards, who used the "n" word repeatedly in suggesting a black heckler should be lynched from a tree. And homophobic singer Chris Brown should have been consigned to the proverbial cutout bin after he battered his entertainer girlfriend, Rihanna. Overall, entertainers ought to be judged by whether they elevate the oppressed, in their professional and personal lives, rather than by how well they flaunt fame and wealth.

To complement efforts to silence the most vehement offenders, who consistently tell the "bad stories" of vulnerable groups such as immigrants, these targeted groups should pursue opportunities in the mainstream media to tell the "good stories" that emanate from their human experience. The barrage of negative depictions would carry less weight if balanced with more positive portrayals. Because of the pervasive invisibility of Mexican immigrants in mainstream media, for example, the decidedly negative images shown end up serving as a blueprint for the entire group's culture and societal value.[14]

Despite the potential benefits of portraying vulnerable groups sympathetically in the mainstream media, no doubt entering the media mainstream in a positive light is not alone key to transformative social change. African Americans have played a doctor and lawyer couple on the hit *Cosby* show and have won Academy Awards as film stars, but still their public image remains poor among a majority of U.S. residents, as evidenced by the 2012 AP Poll discussed in Chapter 9. At best the positive portrayals, if sufficient in number, might neutralize the poison of other media content. Particularly challenging is the social-media, blogger, and Internet presence of so many hate-filled writers who lurk outside the mainstream in slinging mud at vulnerable groups. Obviously, then, the campaign to humanize the dehumanized must reach beyond a media strategy.

Although the media may be poorly suited to humanizing vulnerable groups themselves, the media can be a catalyst for changing and defining societal attitudes about critical issues and policies that harm these groups. For example, marijuana has decisively entered the mainstream of pop culture from rap music to television to cinema. Adult comedies today routinely depict recreational drug use by sympathetic characters who don't launch into a spree of murderous mayhem. At the same time, when drugs are portrayed on reality-television police shows in urban landscapes with users of color, the images are far less sympathetic. The ultimate message is consistent with current priorities in law enforcement—users of color in urban settings are vilified and profiled, while white users of recreational drugs are free to partake. But decriminalization of drugs will protect whites and users of color alike and help to hold the police state of mass incarceration at bay.

One humanization strategy I have adopted is an individual commitment to speak for vulnerable groups whenever possible. Having secured the national podium of a law professor, I have the privilege of access to a variety of audiences for speeches and presentations, whether on the radio, to members of community organizations, or to the general public, and of equal importance I am able to choose the issues I research and write about as a scholar. Almost two decades ago I made the decision to devote the bulk of my scholarly work, and my extensive public service, to securing dignity for vulnerable groups. In particular, I aimed to speak truth to the swirling falsehoods about Latinos/as and immigrants and to tell the "good stories" of the Latino/a experience, including my own family history, which can be traced deep into Mexico. Early on, I decided to write in the scholarly medium of books rather than exclusively in law reviews, which I feared only other law professors might read. I sought a wider audience for my legal writing, for example, by authoring a book on the friendship in the 1960s of Senator Robert Kennedy and labor leader César Chávez and its relevance for Latino/a politics and policies today.[15] My goal was realized years ago when I discovered from Internet searches that college students were reading my book debunking derogatory Latino/a stereotypes—*Greasers and Gringos: Latinos, Law, and the American Imagination.* I remain committed to countering those who promote the inferiority and subhumanity of vulnerable groups and challenge others with similar access to include the pursuit of dignity within their scholarly and speaking agendas.

In answering the question "Why should I care about a stranger . . . a person whose habits I find disgusting?," philosopher Richard Rorty suggests that appealing to our sentiments is more effective for generating compassion for disparate others than appealing to human rationality:

> A better sort of answer is the sort of long, sad, sentimental story that begins "Because this is what it is like to be in her situation—to be far from home, among strangers," or "Because she might become your daughter-in-law," or "Because her mother would grieve for her." Such stories, repeated and varied over the centuries, have induced us, the rich, safe, powerful people, to tolerate and even to cherish powerless

people—people whose appearance or habits or beliefs at first seemed an insult to our own moral identity, our sense of the limits of permissible human variation.[16]

The lesson for scholars is one critical race theorists have taken to heart in supplying personal narratives of their own struggles as well as those of other subordinated individuals and groups in an effort to appeal to the humanity, as well as the rationality, of readers. For example, in discussing the need for and content of compassionate immigration reform in Chapter 3, I asked readers to consider how they might reform our harsh immigration laws if they had family members in another country struggling to find work and unable to obtain a visa under current U.S. immigration policy. Assume further that work is available locally, and the distant family members have hungry children and are desperate for a solution that retains their dignity and protects their safety in migrating to the jobs.[17] At the same time I often appeal to rationality by debunking some of the circulating myths about immigrants' abuse of the system. The public often supplies the knee-jerk rule-of-law answer in explaining how undocumented immigrants harm our country, without realizing that channels for lawful entry are essentially closed except for certain high-skilled jobs and some family reunifications with long backlogs. Alternatively, the public falsely assumes that immigrants come for handouts rather than to take the hardest jobs imaginable for low pay. The lesson for scholars here is threefold: (1) those working in relevant fields— history, sociology, criminology, philosophy, psychology, law, ethnic studies, theology, and other areas—should devote their scholarly research and writing to projects that help dissolve hate toward vulnerable groups; (2) scholars should consider mediums for publication other than traditional research journals, aiming for broad dissemination of their ideas to the interested or curious public; and (3) scholars should just as often appeal to sentiment as to rationality and (especially post-tenure) should ignore those who claim that narratives and sentimental works are somehow not scholarly or are less scholarly than traditional research.

Historian Lynn Hunt suggests a related vehicle for encouraging empathy by her linking of the historical evolution of human rights, par-ticularly in Europe, to literature that appeals to our sympathies and tells the story that other groups are nonetheless like us because of their inner feelings.[18] Legal scholar Richard Delgado relies on Hunt's work to urge that vulnerable groups tell their stories "often and insistently." Delgado also observes that U.S. fiction has been ill-suited to spark these sympathies, as our fiction, "especially the popular sort, promoted solidarity and identification with the dominant group and emotional distance from [oppressed groups such as] minorities, Indians, and the poor."[19] I have often critiqued significant works of American fiction for their reliance on tired, derogatory stereotypes, such as John Steinbeck's classic, *Tortilla Flat*, which paints Latinos/as as shiftless drunkards and petty thieves who are too irresponsible to own homes.[20] Today's "literature" increasingly comes in the form not of books but of cinema and television shows that more often reinforce division than bridge it. Scholars interested in generating compassion toward oppressed groups might consider reaching well beyond their comfort zone and producing sympathetic works of fiction, whether through the medium of literature, film, television, or theater, or nonfiction in the form of documentary film or social-media videos.

Teachers and schools can play a critical role in confronting prejudice and instilling compassion. Arizona's legislature got it wrong in attempting to eradicate ethnic-studies programs it presumed were fostering contempt among Latino/a and other minority students by teaching their history of oppression. Better, Arizona should have mandated these same teachings in the mainstream curriculum for Anglo students, with the aim of generating ideas in the classroom for how, in light of this history, we might differently construct our vision of oppressed groups and reform how society treats them. The ultimate goal of this curriculum would be to acquaint students with the fundamental similarities in human experience and aspirations that can translate into meaningful social change when the students of today become the voters and decision makers of tomorrow. More generally, early childhood education that instills an ethos of compassion and that describes what it means to be a decent human being who sees value in everyone will help children, throughout their lives, to be alert to the societal mistreatment of vulnerable groups.

Another avenue exists to foster compassion among the general public for vulnerable and often misunderstood groups. The relationship-based expression "familiarity breeds contempt" may hold true for some couples but is inapposite in societal relations. In the context of immigration reform I have argued the value of building compassion through personal contact between the Mexican immigrants among us and the Anglo and other residents who share their communities. This idea came from my own experience in bridging political divides. Particularly during election seasons, I often found myself angrily questioning the politics of extremist Republicans, asking how they could espouse policies that I believed damaged the lives of vulnerable groups. Were they soulless? Subhuman themselves? To counter such thinking, I would draw on my personal relationships with my many Republican friends and family members, almost all of whom I valued as decent people and defenders of family. My familiarity with their humanity would lead me to conclude that we desired the same fundamental things and perhaps we could find common ground while respecting our different political views.

Many Anglos do not have close relationships with Latinos/as, as a 1990s' study confirmed.[21] To build compassion for (Mexican) immigrants, I imagine community, business, and religious leaders bringing immigrants and community residents together in summits to demonstrate the contributions of Mexicans and Mexican Americans to our cultural, economic, and political fabric. Immigrant residents would be able to tell narratives of their sometimes harrowing journey to the United States, what drew them, how their hard work helps the community, what keeps them here, and more generally their hopes, problems, and, increasingly, their American dreams. In short, they would be able to effectively display their humanity and the humane origins of their migrations, which were rooted in survival for themselves and their families. Engagements between dehumanized groups and other community members can prompt sympathy and reform for other groups as well. A study demonstrated that U.S. residents are more likely to support gay rights when they personally know a gay person: 73 percent of those who knew a gay person favored their equal rights.[22] In states now allowing same-sex weddings, for example, it would be hard to attend a gay marriage ceremony yet still envision the happy couple as somehow monstrous. In 2013, 57 percent of those surveyed in a CNN poll had a gay or lesbian family member or close friend, up twelve points from a 2007 survey. Nearly aligned with these numbers was national support for same-sex marriage, which jumped under the same poll from 40 percent in 2007 to 53 percent in 2013.[23] More directly linking personal relationships to support for same-sex marriage, in a 2013 Pew Research Center survey the reason most often given (32 percent) for a shift to support same-sex marriage was because the respondent knew a gay person.[24] Reversing his position on same-sex marriage in 2013, Ohio's Republican Senator Rob Portman credited his gay son for his newfound support.[25] Other groups are ripe for community summits of shared dialogue and understanding, particularly those of the Islamic faith and the homeless.

In examining subhuman constructions, philosophy professor David Livingstone Smith lamented in 2011 that we haven't adequately studied the mechanics or cognitive science of dehumanization. Toward this end, he urged prioritization of the study of dehumanization, suggesting that "universities, governments, and nongovernmental organizations need to put money, time, and talent into figuring out exactly how dehumanization works, and what can be done to prevent it."[26] My former law student John Shuford runs the Institute for Hate Studies at Gonzaga University, which studies similar questions at the core of building humanity:

What exactly is hate, and why do people hate?

How and why do we turn other humans, as well as non-human life, into objects for hatred and targets for violence?

How is hate experienced—by those who transmit or act upon it, by those who are its targets, and by bystanders?

Is there anything consistent or even predictable across social problems like racism, nativism, sexism, anti-Semitism, homophobia, misogyny, and religious intolerance?

What can be done to prevent hate before it takes root in action, or to address it effectively once it has become operative, even routinized and systemic?

Is it possible to create free, democratic communities where hatred does not manifest?[27]

While we await research into the generation of compassion across groups and social issues, below I offer specific suggestions for some of the vulnerable groups I have examined in this book. These suggestions reflect unique opportunities and dynamics that might exist for humanizing specific groups. Those groups whose images are transformed should remember their experience and help other groups achieve the same advancement.

For immigration, we can profitably study the experience of Anglo immigrants to the United States in the early twentieth century—Germans, Irish, Italians, among others—who were deemed to be of inferior racial stock, yet ultimately were "whitened" and today sometimes cite their own familial history of (they presume) lawful immigrants while railing against newcomers. Restrictive U.S. laws, particularly those outlawing the use of foreign languages in school instruction, and exclusionary social and business practices ("No Irish Allowed") accompanied the racialization of these groups before their image evolved and whitened to the point that U.S. residents now look affectionately at the Italian flag decorating an Italian restaurant (while viewing a display of the Mexican flag at rallies with disdain) and celebrate St. Patrick's Day and Oktoberfest with vigor. Grounds exist to be less optimistic about the evolution of our views toward Mexican immigrants, despite our equally festive celebration of Cinco de Mayo. Acceptance of these whitened groups came once their immigration slowed, but the proximity of Mexico, the history of U.S. economic reliance on Mexican workers, and our cross-familial and cultural connections all suggest a continuing and ongoing Mexican migration that may stave off any swell of compassion.

Those hoping to forge a compassionate image for today's immigrant groups have a manifesto to rely on for the contribution of immigrants to the United States—President Kennedy's *A Nation of Immigrants*. Detailing the value of immigrants in setting our national tone, Kennedy stated the case for liberalizing immigration policies by recognizing that the American dream "itself was in large part the product of millions of plain people beginning a new life in the conviction that life could indeed be better, and each new wave of immigration rekindled the dream."[28] Relatedly, Kennedy argued that immigrants are the "foundation of American inventiveness and ingenuity."[29] Although Kennedy focused on his Irish ancestors and other European immigrants, he recognized the shift in migration to Mexican immigrants, and his brothers Robert and Ted Kennedy fought to retain favorable legal treatment of Mexican immigrants under the so-called Western Hemisphere exemption, which gave way to restrictionist policies toward Mexico and Central American immigrants in the 1965 immigration reform.[30]

The Catholic Church can play a special role in fostering compassion for immigrants and in advocating for immigration reform. In 2005, a U.S. cardinal announced the launch of the Justice for Immigrants campaign to counter the prevailing anti-immigrant rhetoric with an educational initiative on the benefits of immigration and a policy initiative to gain reform for undocumented immigrants and their families. Notably, when the U.S. House passed a proposal in late 2005 that might have criminalized the provision of social services to undocumented immigrants by the Catholic Church and other providers, Cardinal Roger Mahony of Los Angeles contended the church would defy the law if necessary.[31] Given the lifeblood of membership that Latinos/as provide to the Catholic Church (71 percent of new U.S. Catholics since 1960 are Latinos/as[32]) and the consistency of immigrant rights with church teachings,[33] the church must continue these efforts toward humanization and reform, and at the same time it must question the legacy of its continued vilification of other vulnerable groups, such as gays. Pope Francis, thus far, has profoundly helped garner sympathy for many of today's vulnerable groups.

The media can aid the humanization of immigrants by acknowledging that routine use of pejorative references such as "illegals," "aliens," and "anchor babies" contributes to, or at least maintains, the dehumanized image of immigrants. The dichotomy in references is so pronounced that listeners can readily discern the immigration positions of speakers as enforcement-minded or compassionate merely by the terms they use to describe immigrants. Other vulnerable groups face the same societal array of pejorative and compassionate or at least neutral references, as illustrated by the examples given throughout this book. But although a mainstream news broadcaster today might, for example, avoid calling gay people "fags," that same speaker will readily label undocumented immigrants "illegal aliens." The media, then, must drop the "i" word, as the Associated Press did in 2013.

Because the mainstream media have done such a poor job of contributing to the humanization of undocumented immigrants, social media have risen to fill this void. After telling his story and "coming out" as an undocumented immigrant in the *New York Times*, Pulitzer

Prize-winning Filipino journalist Jose Antonio Vargas created a social-media website and campaign, Define American, to allow other undocumented immigrants to tell the story of their lives.[34] His own experience revealed the vulnerability and fragility of undocumented status when he was arrested in Minnesota in 2012 for driving without a license, a common offense of undocumented immigrants, who often are ineligible for licenses and insurance.

Given the Mexican background of most U.S. farmworkers, it is hard to separate farmworker rights from the immigration controversy. Although immigrant workers perform vital tasks, farmworkers have an advantage in that they can appeal to the public by emphasizing the critical importance of the nation's food supply. Nevertheless, farmworkers are relatively invisible in the food-production process. As the late Richard Chávez, César's brother, told me in a 2007 interview, "A lot of [Americans] think that fruits and vegetables grow right there on the supermarket shelf. They have no idea how the fruits and vegetables got there." This invisibility of production masks the inequities in the fields we never see or visit. Perhaps someday we will value and understand the hand that picks the wine grapes as much as we do the vintner's label. Briefly, in the 1960s, a good portion of the U.S. public cared about the farmworker cause for decent wages and safe working conditions. César Chávez, a humble family man of faith, tirelessly galvanized our better angels toward recognizing the humanity of farmworkers, who he alleged were being mistreated in the fields as "agricultural implements" and "beasts of burden to be used and discarded."[35] Co-founder of the UFW with Chávez, Dolores Huerta similarly drew public attention to the ongoing dehumanization of vulnerable field workers. Celebrities such as Senator Robert Kennedy and comedian Steve Allen embraced the union campaign to boycott grapes; the boycott helped bring revolutionary, albeit ultimately nominal, changes to the industry, but after it was over, wages proceeded to stagnate and even drop as farmworkers slipped from public consciousness. To counter this invisibility, farmworker advocates need to tell the stories of farmworkers better—the rigor of their work and the absence of financial reward. Consumers increasingly care about how the animals they eat are raised (for example, free-range or caged), where their food comes from, and whether it is grown organically without pesticides. A seafood market on the

Oregon coast, for example, informs customers of the name of the boat from which each fish was caught and the harvesting technique used. A brand (of wine, for example) might similarly distinguish itself by telling, on its label or in its advertising, the stories of the workers who supplied the product and their families and struggles and dreams. Some of our newfound attention to the production of food stems from growing imperatives for the fair and ethical treatment of farm animals and from the environmental ethos and consciousness that have emerged over the past few decades. We need to extend that attention and concern to the humans who bring food to our tables. An example of the type of publicity needed to both supply visibility to farmworkers and remind the public of the difficulty of their work is the UFW-initiated Take Our Jobs campaign, which was described in Chapter 4.

Suspected terrorists garner little sympathy. Muslims and Muslim-appearing U.S. residents have a chance to distinguish themselves from vilified terrorists by sharing stories of their often extensive civic engagement and by explaining how the basic tenets of Islam are inconsistent with any terrorist claim of religious inspiration. Despite efforts to tell these truths, such as in the TLC network reality show *All-American Muslim*, polls reveal that negative views of Islam by U.S. residents have increased, rather than decreased, since September 11th.[36] Although presumably another terrorist attack attributed by the public to Muslims will further dim the prospects for a compassionate image, regrettably it doesn't appear that the mere passage of time has quelled tensions. Despite the racial and ethnic identity of the 2013 Boston Marathon bombers as white Russian immigrants, their religious identity as Muslims helped racialize them and prompt retaliatory hate crimes against those perceived as Muslim. An encouraging sign (although perhaps ironic given the tensions between Muslims and Jews) is the history of overcoming widespread religious prejudice against Jews in the United States during World War II. In a short 1945 film starring Frank Sinatra, *The House I Live In*, a group of U.S. youths terrorizing a Jewish boy are told that "religion makes no difference, except maybe to a Nazi." Our record of religious tolerance must be reaffirmed against perhaps the steepest of challenges given the misdirected association between terrorism and religious faith.

Death-row inmates present formidable challenges to the nurturing of a sympathetic image. Although the methods of contemporary restorative justice for lesser offenses involve techniques such as victim-offender mediations, which may humanize the offender in the victim's eyes,[37] those transformations occur, if at all, in the context of face-to-face confrontations that do not translate well to the task of transforming broader societal perceptions.[38] Voters and policymakers might particularly resist humanizing a murderer by pointing to a perceived difference from some other dehumanized groups. Like suspected terrorists, death-row inmates are maligned for their conduct, often seen as mutable behavior, in contrast to their supposedly immutable characteristics such as race. Similarly, undocumented border entrants might be seen as voluntarily criminalizing themselves and therefore as different from immutable and more sympathetic actors. The mutable-immutable distinction, however, is a false one. Although some courts have relied on mutability in applying antidiscrimination laws,[39] the mutability distinction is a matter of perception and is inherently flawed. Undocumented immigrants, for example, although engaged in the conduct of entering or remaining in the United States without legal authorization, often are compelled by economic necessity. Similarly, circumstances such as poverty, childhood abuse, and stress often weigh into criminal behavior. Traits that once seemed mutable, such as sexuality, are increasingly seen as determined by immutable biological factors. And circumstances long thought immutable, especially race, are now more properly characterized as mutable social constructions, as revealed by the "whitening" over time of certain European immigrant groups, as discussed above. Even skin color is alterable with skin lightening or tanning techniques. Regardless of the mutability of the seemingly immutable, in the context of humanity it simply should not matter. Without regard to voluntariness, people, even murderers, deserve to be seen and treated (and in some instances punished) as humans.

Washington state's passage of a ballot referendum authorizing same-sex marriage offers insight into the advancement and humanization of gay equality issues, particularly those relating to the family unit. A coalition of business, faith (with the notable opposition of the Catholic Church[40]), and community leaders, among others, successfully cast the authorization of same-sex marriage as furthering the interest of community stability because it allows two people in love to form the cherished bond of marriage. The campaign also positioned the issue as one of tolerance for religious freedom and difference. One notable advertisement featuring a Seattle Methodist minister and his wife reflected these framings:

> *Rev. Lang:* We've been married 29 years.
> *Cathy:* And we have two sons.
> *Rev. Lang:* I struggled with the notion of same-sex marriage and it was compassion that, that broke in. My shift came when I realized that at the very core of my Christianity is the compassion that God has shown towards me.
> *Cathy:* For a couple to be able to take their vows in front of friends and family it means they're together, forever. And don't we want that for everybody?[41]

Protecting against hate crimes and discrimination of any kind against the LGBT community similarly ensures community stability and respect for the variety of human sexuality and gender identities.

Faith can also supply a bridge to humanizing the image and struggles of the impoverished. A 1998 published reflection of U.S. Catholic bishops highlighted the importance of antipoverty imperatives in urging that we put "the needs of the poor and vulnerable first," while respecting the basic human rights of workers to "productive work, to decent and fair wages, [and] to organize and join unions."[42] Fundamentally, rather than pursuing a race to the summit of income and power, we must respect the connectedness and humanity of those struggling for survival. A taxicab driver in Washington, D.C., aptly described to me the contrast between the greed he saw and the debilitating poverty on the streets; he simply couldn't enjoy working, eating, and living on the top levels of corporate and residential high-rises knowing there were people starving on the streets below.

*   *   *

Stalwart legal scholars such as Derrick Bell, Richard Delgado, and Mary Dudziak have developed and refined the theory of interest convergence, positing that fundamental social change, such as racial progress, tends to occur when it aligns with the self-interest of the powerful—in the United States, Anglos who control lawmaking and the judiciary.[43] Most compellingly, the theory helps explain the end of formal legal segregation of blacks from whites in schools and other settings by positing that the change was prompted by then-omnipresent Cold War concerns of vulnerability to the global spread of Communist alternatives if the United States couldn't get its racial house in order. It also explains the repeal during World War II of restrictive immigration laws barring Chinese entry as the result of China's becoming a U.S. ally at that time. Potential grounds for interest convergence support most, if not all, of the reforms suggested in this book. For example, promoting stability for Latino/a and other immigrants would boost the entry-level housing market, bolster the Social Security system, keep our economy competitive with that of India and of China,[44] and answer the question "Who will make all those beds, empty those bedpans, and clean the rooms of the aging [Anglo] crowd?"[45] Shifting from drug-war incarceration to addiction treatment would generate vast savings that the government could use for education, and, in turn, increased funding for education would reduce poverty and homelessness. More generally, abandoning our campaign of mass incarceration would make the streets safer (for example, most prisoners start by committing nonviolent crimes but entry into the penal system boosts their chance of committing violent offenses later), protect against a police state of declining civil liberties, and reduce racial unrest.[46] Treating LGBT populations with respect would spark global tourism to the benefit of U.S. destinations and promote community stability through marriage and the absence of hate crimes and discrimination. The list goes on.

As Delgado suggested in reviewing my book on the friendship of Senator Robert Kennedy and César Chávez, in addition to interest convergence, beleaguered groups need a favorable story or image to advance toward their fair treatment.[47] Although our hard-working farm laborers had that opportunity in the 1960s, when they were led by an articulate, religious, nonviolent family man who briefly captured national attention, they lost that moment, and a different narrative took hold consisting of Mexican immigrant workers taking U.S. jobs and being fortunate for whatever crumbs of the American Dream we toss their way. Windows for transformative change in narrative and policy accordingly may be narrow and fleeting, and proponents of humanity must be ready to seize daylight, particularly in times of economic prosperity and in the calm following periods of public hysteria such as global war or terrorist attacks. In this book I have suggested the challenges for our various vulnerable groups of forging the favorable narrative they may need to prompt our collective realization of and regret for how we have mistreated them in good times and bad, and I have outlined the opportunities they have for doing so.

My concluding aim here is to add an additional interest convergence that alone encompasses all of the injustices and attendant reforms identified and urged above. The selfish interest I identified in the Introduction rings true here. If we are confident of how society eventually will view the reforms I urge, then our generation has a chance to implement fundamental change that will define our time. Future generations may look back with admiration that we were the first enlightened society in U.S. history with both the blueprint and the resolve to set history and our future on a more compassionate path. We have the opportunity in this moment to determine what it means to be human and humane in this diverse country. Lives and souls hang in that balance. Selfishly, I hope we choose right.

NOTES

INTRODUCTION

Richard Delgado and Jean Stefancic, "Images of the Outsider in American Law and Culture: Can Free Expression Remedy Systemic Social Ills?," *Cornell Law Review* 77 (1992): 1258, 1277–1278.

1. Craig Steven Wilder, *Ebony and Ivory: Race, Slavery, and the Troubled History of America's Universities* (New York: Bloomsbury Press, 2013) (describing how slave labor was used by schools and even by students who brought slaves to campus as personal servants).

2. Sarah H. Ludington, "The Dogs That Did Not Bark: The Silence of the Legal Academy during World War II," *Journal of Legal Education* 60 (February 2011): 397.

3. See Elise Foley, "Immigrants to Wells Fargo: Stop Investing in For-Profit Detention," http://www.huffingtonpost.com/2011/10/17/immigrants-wells-fargo_n_1016339.html (posted October 17, 2011; last visited April 26, 2013).

4. Human Rights Campaign, "The Roman Catholic Hierarchy's Devotion to Fighting Marriage Equality," http://www.hrc.org/nomexposed/section/the-catholic-hierarchys-devotion-to-fighting-marriage-equality (last visited April 4, 2014).

5. Quoted in Joyce Murdoch and Deb Price, *Courting Justice: Gay Men and Lesbians v. the Supreme Court* (New York: Basic Books, 2001), 10.

6. *Bradwell v. Illinois*, 83 U.S. 130, 141 (1872).

7. *Buck v. Bell*, 274 U.S. 200, 207 (1927).

8. *Bowers v. Hardwick*, 478 U.S. 186 (1986); see generally Richard Delgado and Jean Stefancic, "Norms and Narratives: Can Judges Avoid Serious Moral Error?," *Texas Law Review* 69 (1991): 1929.

9. William O. Douglas, *The Court Years, 1939–1975: The Autobiography of William O. Douglas* (New York: Random House, 1980), 280.

10. *Plessy v. Ferguson*, 163 U.S. 537 (1896); *Brown v. Board of Education*, 347 U.S. 483 (1954). Ultimately, the Supreme Court let stand a lower court's invalidation of the California prohibition. Without ruling on the substantive merits of the case, the Court found legal standing absent after the named state-official defendants refused to defend the law and the ballot-initiative proponents took over the defense. *Hollingsworth v. Perry*, 133 S. Ct. 2652 (2013).

11. See generally Mary Midgley, *Animals and Why They Matter* (Athens: University of Georgia Press, 1983) (connecting the lack of societal regard for animal rights

to the disregard for human types of subordination involved in racism and sexism); David Farve, "Living Property: A New Status for Animals within the Legal System," *Marquette Law Review* 93 (2010): 1021.

12. Most climate scientists attribute global warming to human causes; for example, 84 percent did in a 2009 Pew Research Center poll: http://ossfoundation.us/projects/environment/global-warming/myths/31000-scientists-say-no-convincing-evidence (last visited March 19, 2013).

13. *Brown*, 347 U.S. 483 ("Whatever may have been the extent of psychological knowledge at the time of *Plessy v. Ferguson*, this finding is amply supported by modern [psychological] authority," citing authorities from the 1940s and 1950s). The social science studies Justice Earl Warren relied on were later criticized however; see generally Alexander Tsesis, *We Shall Overcome: A History of Civil Rights and Law* (New Haven, CT: Yale University Press, 2008), 255.

14. Cynthia D. Moe-Lobeda, *Resisting Structural Evil: Love as Ecological-Economic Vocation* (Minneapolis: Fortress Press, 2013) (documenting human suffering arising from environmental degradations caused by the U.S. culture of overconsumption).

CHAPTER 1. REGRET

1. David Livingstone Smith, *Less Than Human: Why We Demean, Enslave, and Exterminate Others* (New York: St. Martin's Press, 2011), 106 (presumably using the King James Bible, Cambridge edition); see generally Mark A. Noll, *The Civil War as a Theological Crisis* (Chapel Hill: University of North Carolina, 2006) (detailing disagreement over the position of the Bible on the institution of slavery), and Kenneth J. Zanca, *American Catholics and Slavery: 1789–1866* (Lanham: University of Maryland, 1994) (compiling contemporaneous materials on the relationship of the Catholic Church and slavery).

2. Rev. Jesse L. Jackson Sr., Rep. Jesse L. Jackson Jr., and Bruce Shapiro, *Legal Lynching: The Death Penalty and America's Future* (New York: New Press, 2001), 100.

3. Deuteronomy 22:23–24.

4. Leviticus 21:9.

5. Fred Galves, *Genesis Reloaded: Questioning a Literal Interpretation of the Bible* (Indianapolis: Dog Ear Publishing, 2012), 295 (citing Leviticus 20:13).

6. Jackson et al., *Legal Lynching*, 88.

7. The United States joined the so-called first-generation human rights conventions but generally failed to ratify such second- and third-generation conventions as the International Convention on the Protection of the Rights of All Migrant Workers and Members of Their Families. In late 2012, the Senate blocked ratification of the U.N. Convention on the Rights of Persons with Disabilities.

8. But see Berta E. Hernández-Truyol, "Querying *Lawrence*," *Ohio State Law Journal* 65 (2004): 1151 (describing the progressive stance on gay and lesbian rights taken by the Council of Europe, an organization of forty-seven nation-states, a body of which is the European Court of Human Rights). In 2011, the United States

co-sponsored a U.N. Human Rights Council resolution expressing concern about violence directed at sexual orientation and gender identity; this was the first adopted U.N. resolution to address human rights violations based on sexual orientation and gender identity.

9. Article 37 of the U.N. Convention on the Rights of the Child, for example, which the United States signed but has failed to ratify, prohibits capital punishment for crimes committed under the age of eighteen. Later, however, the U.N. Commission on Human Rights and the U.N. General Assembly called on nation-states to either abolish or place a moratorium on executions. See generally http://www.amnestyusa.org/our-work/issues/death-penalty/international-death-penalty/death-penalty-and-human-rights-standards (last visited December 6, 2012).

10. Universal Declaration of Human Rights, U.N. General Assembly Resolution 217A, December 10, 1948, art. 5 ("No one shall be subjected to torture or to cruel, inhuman, or degrading treatment or punishment.").

11. Patrick J. Buchanan, "A Brief for Whitey," http://buchanan.org/blog/pjb-a-brief-for-whitey-969 (posted March 21, 2008; last visited November 10, 2013).

12. "Bush: Slavery One of History's 'Greatest Crimes,'" http://www.cnn.com/2003/WORLD/africa/07/08/bush.africa/index.html?iref=mpstoryview (posted July 9, 2003; last visited April 4, 2014).

13. S. Con. Res. 26, 111th Cong. (2009). Slavery claimed other victims, including Native Americans. See generally Laurence Armand French, "Native American Reparations: Five Hundred Years and Counting," in *When Sorry Isn't Enough: The Controversy over Apologies and Reparations for Human Injustice*, ed. Roy L. Brooks (New York: New York University Press, 1999), 241.

14. Melissa Nobles, *The Politics of Official Apologies* (New York: Cambridge University Press, 2008), 91.

15. Avis Thomas-Lester, "A Senate Apology for History on Lynching," *Washington Post*, June 14, 2005.

16. Dorian Lynskey, "Strange Fruit: The First Great Protest Song," *the guardian*, http://www.theguardian.com/music/2011/feb/16/protest-songs-billie-holiday-strange-fruit (February 15, 2011; last visited April 4, 2014).

17. Thomas-Lester, "Senate Apology."

18. Pub. L. No. 111–118, H.R. 3326, sec. 8113 (2009).

19. See generally Elazar Barkan, *The Guilt of Nations: Restitution and Negotiating Historical Injustices* (New York: Norton, 2000), 216.

20. See generally Pedro A. Malavet, *America's Colony: The Political and Cultural Conflict between the United States and Puerto Rico* (New York: New York University Press, 2004).

21. Pub. L. No. 100-383, H.R. 442, 100th Cong. (1988). On the internment generally, see Martha Minow, *Between Vengeance and Forgiveness: Facing History after Genocide and Mass Violence* (Boston: Beacon Press, 1998).

22. See Chapter 11 for a brief discussion of leaked conversations with Japanese officials who rejected President Barack Obama's plans to deliver an apology.

23. The 112th Congress did so by means of Senate Resolution 201 and House Resolution 683.

24. Eric K. Yamamoto, Sandra Hye Yun Kim, and Abigail M. Holden, "American Reparations Theory and Practice at the Crossroads," *California Western Law Review* 44 (2007): 1, 75.

25. Ed Payne and Cristy Lenz, "Lawyers: U.S. Faces Suit on Syphilis Tests in Guatemala," http://articles.cnn.com/2011-03-09/world/guatemala.syphilis.lawsuit_1_reprehensible-research-syphilis-guise-of-public-health?_s=PM:WORLD (posted March 9, 2011; last visited October 26, 2012). The history of the abuse of vulnerable groups by U.S. doctors runs deeper, as it includes federally funded studies in the 1940s that exposed patients in mental institutions to hepatitis, government researchers who pumped gonorrhea bacteria into prisoner's urinary tracts, and mentally disabled children in Staten Island given hepatitis in experiments in the 1960s. Mike Stobbe, "Ugly US Medical Experiments Uncovered," http://www.washingtontimes.com/news/2011/feb/27/ap-impact-ugly-us-medical-experiments-uncovered/?page=all (posted February 27, 2011; last visited November 1, 2012).

26. Daniel J. Kevles, *In the Name of Eugenics: Genetics and the Uses of Human Heredity* (Berkeley: University of California Press, 1985), 116.

27. On women, Peter Schrag, *Not Fit for Our Society: Nativism and Immigration* (Berkeley: University of California Press, 2010), 93 (stating that some sixty thousand eugenic sterilizations were conducted in thirty-three states from the 1920s to the early 1970s). On Native American women, Barbara Perry, *Silent Victims: Hate Crimes against Native Americans* (Tucson: University of Arizona Press, 2008), 36–37. On Latinas in Puerto Rico, Steven W. Bender, *Greasers and Gringos: Latinos, Law, and the American Imagination* (New York: New York University Press, 2003), 141–142. See generally Kevles, *Name of Eugenics*, 169, 275 (stating sterilizations plummeted in the 1940s and were infrequent by 1950, with states beginning to repeal their laws in the 1960s).

28. Dave Reynolds, "South Carolina Governor Apologizes for State's Eugenics Past," http://mn.gov/mnddc/news/inclusion-daily/2003/01/010803sceugenics.htm (posted January 8, 2003; last visited April 11, 2014).

29. Valerie Bauerlein, "North Carolina to Compensate Sterilization Victims," *Wall Street Journal*, http://online.wsj.com/news/articles/SB100014241278873239712045786299432208819 14 (posted July 26, 2013; last visited April 4, 2014).

30. Paul Feist, "Davis Apologizes for State's Sterilization Program," *SFGate*, http://www.sfgate.com/bayarea/article/Davis-apologizes-for-state-s-sterilization-2663485.php (posted March 12, 2003; last visited April 4, 2014).

31. "Virginia Governor Apologizes for Eugenics Law," *USA Today*, http://usatoday30.usatoday.com/news/nation/2002/05/02/virginia-eugenics.htm (posted May 2, 2002; last visited April 4, 2014).

32. *Dred Scott v. Sandford*, 60 U.S. 393 (1857). For extensive commentary and background on the decision, see Earl M. Maltz, *Slavery and the Supreme Court, 1825–1861* (Lawrence: University Press of Kansas, 2009).

33. *Plessy v. Ferguson*, 163 U.S. 537 (1896).

34. *Johnson v. M'Intosh*, 21 U.S. 543 (1823).

35. Robert A. Williams Jr., *Like a Loaded Weapon: The Rehnquist Court, Indian Rights, and the Legal History of Racism in America* (Minneapolis: University of Minnesota Press, 2005), 56.

36. *Tee-Hit-Ton v. United States*, 348 U.S. 272 (1955).

37. *Korematsu v. United States*, 323 U.S. 215 (1944).

38. *Chae Chan Ping v. United States*, 130 U.S. 581, 606 (1889).

39. *Buck v. Bell*, 274 U.S. 200 (1927). Justice Pierce Butler, a Catholic, cast the lone dissenting vote. The Catholic Church rejected the precepts of eugenics. See Bill Piatt, *Catholic Legal Perspectives* (Durham, NC: Carolina Academic Press, 2012), 141; Kevles, *Name of Eugenics*, 119.

40. Kevles, *Name of Eugenics*, 110–111.

41. *Buck*, 274 U.S. at 207.

42. *Korematsu*, 323 U.S. at 218.

43. See generally William W. Fisher III, "Ideology and Imagery in the Law of Slavery," *Chicago-Kent Law Review* 68 (1993): 1051, 1068.

44. Quoted in Paul Finkelman, *Defending Slavery: Proslavery Thought in the Old South: A Brief History with Documents* (Boston: Bedford Books/St. Martin's Press, 2003), 22.

45. *Johnson v. M'Intosh*, 21 U.S. 543, 590 (1823).

46. See Williams, *Like a Loaded Weapon*, xx.

47. Quoted in Tsesis, *We Shall Overcome*, 166.

48. Keith Aoki, "'Foreign-ness' and Asian American Identities: Yellowface, World War II Propaganda, and Bifurcated Racial Stereotypes," *UCLA Asian Pacific Law Journal* 4 (1996): 1, 38, 39 (also describing the Japanese as devalued by the hara-kiri or kamikaze stereotype of the supposed lack of regard for human life that signaled their inhumanity).

49. Ibid., 29.

50. *Plessy v. Ferguson*, 163 U.S. 537, 561 (1896) (dissenting opinion nonetheless revealing anti-Chinese racism).

51. Malavet, *America's Colony*, 38–42 (construing the *insular* cases to include the decision in *Balzac v. People of Porto Rico*, 258 U.S. 298 (1922), holding that certain constitutional rights do not automatically extend to U.S. citizens living in unincorporated territories).

52. Bender, *Greasers and Gringos*, 23.

53. *Dred Scott v. Sandford*, 60 U.S. 393, 407 (1857).

54. Quoted in Finkelman, *Defending Slavery*, 20.

55. Quoted in ibid., 143, 149, 156.

56. Quoted in Daniel Jonah Goldhagen, *Worse Than War: Genocide, Eliminationism, and the Ongoing Assault on Humanity* (New York: Public Affairs, 2009), 323.

57. Quoted in ibid.

58. Quoted in William Brennan, *Dehumanizing the Vulnerable: When Word Games Take Lives* (Chicago: Loyola University Press, 1995), 82.

59. Quoted in Richard Lawrence Miller, *Nazi Justiz: Law of the Holocaust* (Westport, CT: Praeger, 1995), 35.

60. Christian B. Sundquist, "Science Fictions and Racial Fables: Navigating the Final Frontier of Genetic Interpretation," *Harvard Black Letter Law Journal* 25 (2009): 57, 64.

CHAPTER 2. WHAT DEHUMANIZATION PREDICTS

Liza Lugo, *How Do Hurricane Katrina's Winds Blow?: Racism in 21st-Century New Orleans* (Santa Barbara, CA: Praeger, 2014), 145.

1. Steven W. Bender, "Faces of Immigration Reform," *FIU Law Review* 6 (2011): 251, 258.

2. Samuel P. Huntington, *Who Are We? The Challenges to America's National Identity* (New York: Simon & Schuster, 2004).

3. See Lisa Marie Cacho, *Social Death: Racialized Rightlessness and the Criminalization of the Unprotected* (New York: New York University Press, 2012), 43–44 (describing the de facto status crime that attaches to the "illegal alien" label).

4. Finkelman, *Defending Slavery*, 3.

5. Alan Duke, "Paris Hilton Apologizes for Calling Gay Men 'Disgusting,'" http://www.cnn.com/2012/09/21/showbiz/paris-hilton-gays/ (posted September 21, 2012; last visited April 4, 2014).

6. Brennan, *Dehumanizing the Vulnerable*, 55.

7. Quoted in Miller, *Nazi Justiz*, 35.

8. Quoted in Smith, *Less Than Human*, 23.

9. *United States v. Windsor*, 133 S. Ct. 2675, 2696 (2013).

10. A federal district court struck down California's Proposition 8, outlawing same-sex marriage, as violating federal constitutional dictates of due process and equal protection; the Supreme Court let the ruling stand for want of standing after the named state official defendants refused to defend the law and the ballot-initiative proponents took over the defense, but the Court did not rule on the substantive merits of the case. *Hollingsworth v. Perry*, 133 S. Ct. 2652 (2013).

11. Frank Newport, "Americans, including Catholics, Say Birth Control Is Morally OK," http://www.gallup.com/poll/154799/americans-including-catholics-say-birth-control-morally.aspx (posted May 22, 2012; last visited November 1, 2012); the survey addresses birth control, the death penalty, and other "controversial issues."

12. Another contradiction of conservative values supporting regard for human life is opposition to funding prenatal care for low-income mothers, thereby contributing to our high infant-mortality rate. See George Lakoff, *Moral Politics: What Conservatives Know That Liberals Don't* (Chicago: University of Chicago Press, 1996), 25.

13. For example, consider the concurring opinion of conservative Supreme Court Justice Clarence Thomas in the 2013 decision addressing the University of Texas

affirmative-action admissions program, *Fisher v. University of Texas at Austin*, 133 S. Ct. 2411 (2013): "The University's professed good intentions cannot excuse its outright racial discrimination any more than such intentions justified the now denounced arguments of slaveholders and segregationists."

14. On race as a social construction see Ian Haney López, *White by Law: The Legal Construction of Race* (New York: New York University Press, 1996).

15. See generally Daniel Kanstroom, *Deportation Nation: Outsiders in American History* (Cambridge, MA: Harvard University Press, 2007), 63–70.

16. See the discussion of the history of restrictive immigration laws against homosexuals in Chapter 6; these laws culminated in the invalidation of the federal Defense of Marriage Act, which prevented recognition of same-sex marriages for immigration purposes.

CHAPTER 3. ALIENS, ILLEGALS, WETBACKS, AND ANCHOR BABIES

Howard Zinn, "No Human Being Is Illegal," http://www.truth-out.org/news/item/2663:no-human-being-is-illegal (posted August 15, 2011; last visited April 2, 2014).

1. Quoted in Otto Santa Ana, *Brown Tide Rising: Metaphors of Latinos in Contemporary American Public Discourse* (Austin: University of Texas Press, 2002), 86.

2. I was born in Beverly Hospital, in Montebello, a few miles from my mother's apartment in East Los Angeles.

3. "The Great Immigration Panic," *New York Times*, June 3, 2008.

4. Peter Schrag, "Immigration Hardliners Try to Unhinge America," *Nation*, December 29, 2007.

5. *All American Canal*, http://en.wikipedia.org/wiki/All-American_Canal (last visited April 11, 2014).

6. See Santa Ana, *Brown Tide Rising*, 72–74.

7. Patrick Buchanan, *State of Emergency: The Third World Invasion and Conquest of America* (New York: St. Martin's Press, 2006), 7–12. See also Lilian Jiménez, "America's Legacy of Xenophobia: The Curious Origins of Arizona Senate Bill 1070," *California Western Law Review* 48 (2012): 279, 305–306 (excerpting remarks of Maricopa County Republican Party Chairman Rob Haney, who, in advocating for Arizona's anti-immigrant law contended, "We are being invaded").

8. *United States v. Brignoni-Ponce*, 422 U.S. 899, 904 (1975) (concurring opinion of Chief Justice Warren E. Burger).

9. *City of Indianapolis v. Edmond*, 531 U.S. 32, 38 (2000) (opinion authored by Justice Sandra Day O'Connor). The enforcement focus on the U.S.-Mexico border and northerly "flows" and "tides" ignores the significant number of Canadian entrants who overstay their visas in their southerly journey to the United States.

10. Quoted in Steven W. Bender, *Run for the Border: Vice and Virtue in U.S.-Mexico Border Crossings* (New York: New York University Press, 2012), 143.

11. Quoted in ibid., 144.

12. Geraldo Rivera, *His Panic: Why Americans Fear Hispanics in the U.S.* (New York: Penguin Group, 2008), 131–133.

13. *United States v. Brignoni-Ponce*, 422 U.S. 899, 903 (1975) (concurring opinion of Chief Justice Burger). See generally Keith Cunningham-Parmeter, "Alien Language: Immigration Metaphors and the Jurisprudence of Otherness," *Fordham Law Review* 79 (2011): 1545 (discussing the Supreme Court rhetoric of immigration as criminality, floods, and attacks, and suggesting more humanized references and metaphors for migrants).

14. Bender, *Run for the Border*, 134.

15. Immigrants' Rights Project, American Civil Liberties Union, "Issue Brief: Criminalizing Undocumented Immigrants," February 2010, http://www.aclu.org/files/assets/FINAL_criminalizing_undocumented_immigrants_issue_brief_PUBLIC_VERSION.pdf (last visited December 3, 2012).

16. Quoted in Bender, *Greasers and Gringos*, 77.

17. Paul Davenport and Amanda Lee Myers, "Jan Brewer Admits She Was Wrong about Beheadings," http://www.huffingtonpost.com/2010/09/04/jan-brewer-admits-she-was_0_n_705722.html (posted September 4, 2010; last visited December 7, 2012) (discussing how Brewer later recanted and suggested she was referring to drug-war murders within Mexico).

18. See Ediberto Román, *Those Damned Immigrants: America's Hysteria over Undocumented Immigration* (New York: New York University Press, 2013).

19. Quoted in Bender, *Greasers and Gringos*, 73.

20. Quoted in ibid., 114.

21. Ibid., 116.

22. George A. Martínez, "Bobbitt, the Rise of the Market State, and Race," *American University Journal of Gender, Social Policy, & Law* 18 (2009): 587, 601 (discussing Huntington, *Who Are We?*); Bender, *Greasers and Gringos*, 86–87 (debunking the anti-assimilation claims).

23. See Zinn, "No Human" (detailing anti-immigrant legislation such as 1798 legislation directed at "dangerous foreigners": the Irish and French).

24. See Bill Ong Hing, "Immigration Policy: Thinking Beyond the (Big) Box," *Connecticut Law Review* 39 (2007): 1401, 1421.

25. Compare David G. Gutiérrez, *Walls and Mirrors: Mexican Americans, Mexican Immigrants, and the Politics of Ethnicity* (Berkeley: University of California Press, 1995), 72 (estimating the return of between 350,000 and 600,000 Mexicans and Mexican Americans) with "L.A. County Officials Apologize for Depression-Era Deportations," http://latimesblogs.latimes.com/lanow/2012/02/la-county-officials-apologize-for-depression-era-deportations.html (February 21, 2012; last visited June 20, 2012) (more than two million, most of them U.S. citizens).

26. Bender, *Run for the Border*, 125.

27. Gilbert Paul Carrasco, "Latinos in the United States: Invitation and Exile," in *Immigrants Out! The New Nativism and the Anti-Immigrant Impulse in the United States*, ed. Juan F. Perea (New York: New York University Press, 1997), 190.

28. California Senate Bill 670 (2005).

29. Christina Villacorte, "L.A. County Board of Supervisors to Issue Formal Apology over Mexican Repatriation," *Los Angeles Daily News*, http://www.dailynews.com/20120221/la-county-board-of-supervisors-to-issue-formal-apology-over-mexican-repatriation (posted February 20, 2012; last visited April 4, 2014).

30. Steven W. Bender, *Tierra y Libertad: Land, Liberty, and Latino Housing* (New York: New York University Press, 2010), ch. 2.

31. See Bender, *Greasers and Gringos*, 28–29 (discussing the negative shift in view toward Cuban immigrants in the 1980s as the Mariel boat lift brought darker-skinned and impoverished immigrants to the United States in contrast to the light-skinned and middle- to upper-class Cuban professionals who came before).

32. Kevin R. Johnson, "The End of 'Civil Rights' as We Know It? Immigration and Civil Rights in the New Millennium," *UCLA Law Review* 49 (2002): 1481, 1486; Daniel J. Tichenor, *Dividing Lines: The Politics of Immigration Control in America* (Princeton, NJ: Princeton University Press, 2002), 131 (discussing the conclusion of the influential *Dictionary of Races*, cited frequently in Congressional immigration debates, that "all these peoples from eastern and southern Europe . . . are different in temperament and civilization than ourselves.").

33. Quoted in John Higham, *Strangers in the Land: Patterns of American Nativism 1860–1925* (New Brunswick, NJ: Rutgers University Press, 1988), 55.

34. Schrag, *Not Fit for Society*, 8.

35. Bender, *Greasers and Gringos*, 230, and Bender, *Run for the Border*, 119.

36. *People v. Hall*, 4 Cal. 399 (1854) (concluding that Chinese were non-white for purposes of a state law prohibiting black and Indian legal testimony against whites), discussed in Aoki, "'Foreign-ness,'" 19–20.

37. Quoted in Aoki, "'Foreign-ness,'" 29–30.

38. Ibid.

39. Ibid., 31.

40. See Lucy E. Salyer, *Laws Harsh as Tigers: Chinese Immigrants and the Shaping of Modern Immigration Law* (Chapel Hill: University of North Carolina Press, 1995), 11–12.

41. Quoted in Alan M. Kraut, *Silent Travelers: Germs, Genes, and the "Immigrant Menace"* (New York: Basic Books, 1994), 81.

42. Quoted in ibid., 83.

43. Ibid., 15–16.

44. Quoted in Tichenor, *Dividing Lines*, 102 (testimony before the Joint Special Committee to Investigate Chinese Immigration).

45. Merchants, teachers, students, and travelers were exempt from the Chinese Exclusion Act by means of an 1880 treaty. On state and local laws, see Aoki, "'Foreign-ness,'" 20; Bender, *Tierra y Libertad*, 78; see also Salyer, *Laws Harsh*, 12 (detailing anti-Chinese provisions in California's 1879 constitution). On federal laws, see Tichenor, *Dividing Lines*, 107–108.

46. Bender, *Run for the Border*, 118.

47. Gabriel J. Chin, "Segregation's Last Stronghold: Race Discrimination and the Constitutional Law of Immigration," *UCLA Law Review* 46 (1988): 1, 13–14 (explaining that under these laws most Asians could not immigrate and most who were here could not naturalize).

48. For example, *Chae Chan Ping v. United States*, 130 U.S. 581 (1889) (upholding Congressional power to enact the Chinese Exclusion Act as amended, stating that "if . . . the government of the United States, through its legislative department, considers the presence of foreigners of a different race in this country, who will not assimilate with us, to be dangerous to its peace and security . . . its determination is conclusive upon the judiciary"); *Fong Yue Ting v. United States*, 149 U.S. 698 (1893) (aliens could be deported if Congress determined their race was undesirable); *Takao Ozawa v. United States*, 260 U.S. 178 (1922); *United States v. Bhagat Singh Thind*, 261 U.S. 204 (1923) (the latter two cases deferring to the Congressional determination that Japanese and Indians were racially ineligible for citizenship).

49. Quoted in Daniel Kanstroom, "Dangerous Undertows of the New Nativism: Peter Brimelow and the Decline of the West," in *Immigrants Out! The New Nativism and the Anti-Immigrant Impulse in the United States*, ed. Juan F. Perea (New York: New York University Press, 1997): 300, 310.

50. Without the immigration law (the Luce-Celler Act of 1946), the independence of the Philippines from the United States that same year would have precluded immigration.

51. Kanstroom, "Dangerous Undertows," 14–15 (noting that only 105 Chinese were permitted to immigrate annually).

52. Lynn Herrmann, "Kansas Lawmaker Compares Shooting Wild Hogs to Immigrants," http://digitaljournal.com/article/304685 (posted March 15, 2011; last visited June 26, 2012).

53. Andrea Nill Sanchez, "On Immigration, Alabama State Senator Advises Politicians to 'Empty the Clip' to Stop Undocumented Immigrants," http://thinkprogress.org/politics/2011/02/08/142922/scott-beason-immigration/ (posted February 8, 2011; last visited April 5, 2014).

54. Nia-Malika Henderson, "Herman Cain Meets with Sheriff Joe Arpaio, Stands By Electric Border Fence Comments," http://www.washingtonpost.com/blogs/election-2012/post/herman-cain-meets-with- sherriff-joe-arpaio-stands-by-electric-border-fence/2011/10/18/gIQAju5luL_blog.html (posted October 18, 2011; last visited April 2, 2014).

55. Stephen C. Webster, "GOP Lawmaker: Illegal Immigrants Are Like Hitler, Should Be Shot," http://www.rawstory.com/rs/2010/10/18/gop-lawmaker-compares-illegal-immigrants-hitler-shoot-kill/ (posted October 18, 2010; last visited June 26, 2012).

56. Elias Isquith, "Texas Tea Party Candidate Chris Mapp Won't Apologize for Anti-Immigrant Racial Slur," http://www.salon.com/2014/02/25/texas_tea_party_candidate_chris_mapp_won't_apologize_for_anti_immigrant_racial_slur/ (posted February 25, 2014; last visited April 2, 2014).

57. See Román, *Those Damned Immigrants*.

58. "Tennessee Sheriff Ready to Stack Undocumented Immigrants in Jail 'Like Cordwood,'" http://www.huffingtonpost.com/2013/08/22/immigrants-cord-wood-jj-jones_n_3795634.html (posted August 22, 2013; last visited April 4, 2014).

59. Catherine A. Traywick, "Anti-Immigrant Hate Crimes Rise with Hateful Political Speech," http://www.alternet.org/rss/1/445518/anti-immigrant_hate_crimes_rise_with_hateful_political_speech/ (posted January 21, 2011; last visited June 20, 2012).

60. Bender, *Greasers and Gringos*, 131–133.

61. Bender, *Tierra y Libertad*.

62. See Román, *Those Damned Immigrants*, 36.

63. Marisa Treviño, "A Just Verdict for a Hateful Crime," http://latinalista.com/2010/10/hate (posted October 28, 2010; last visited June 19, 2012).

64. "Alleged Hate Killer Had Been Committed," http://www.upi.com/Top_News/US/2010/08/23/Alleged-hate-killer-had-been-committed/UPI-32821282582387/ (posted August 23, 2010; last visited April 4, 2014).

65. Dean Schabner and Devin Dwyer, "'Minutemen' Vigilante Shawna Forde Guilty in Deadly Arizona Home Invasion," http://abcnews.go.com/US/minutemen-vigilante-shawna-forde-guilty-deadly-arizona-home/story?id=12916893 (posted February 14, 2011; last visited April 4, 2014).

66. American Civil Liberties Union, "U.S.-Mexico Border Crossing Deaths Are a Humanitarian Crisis, According to Report from the ACLU and CNDH," https://www.aclu.org/immigrants-rights/us-mexico-border-crossing-deaths-are-human-itarian-crisis-according-report-aclu-and (posted September 30, 2009; last visited April 4, 2014).

67. Proposition 187 was ultimately gutted by a federal court. *League of United Latin Am. Citizens v. Wilson*, 908 F. Supp. 755 (C.D. Cal. 1995) (striking down the refusal to educate undocumented children); *League of United Latin Am. Citizens v. Wilson*, 997 F. Supp. 1244 (C.D. Cal. 1997) (invalidating the other benefit-denial provisions as preempted by the federal Personal Responsibility and Work Opportunity Reconciliation Act of 1996).

68. All these examples are from Bender, *Run for the Border*, 131.

69. "A Culture of Cruelty: Abuse and Impunity in Short-Term U.S. Border Patrol Custody (2011)," http://www.nomoredeathsvolunteers.org/Print%20Resources/Abuse%20Doc%20Reports/Culture%20of%20Cruelty/CultureofCrueltyFinal.pdf (last visited July 18, 2011).

70. Bender, *Run for the Border*, 132–133.

71. See ibid., 136 (discussing how the border-traffic slowdown during the recession that started in 2008 is evidence that Mexican immigrants come for employment opportunities, not government benefits).

72. *National Geographic* (September 2007) (letters in response to article "Our Wall," May 2007).

73. Bender, *Run for the Border*, 131.

74. "Thirteen Killed as Van Hits Big Rig," *Los Angeles Times*, http://articles.latimes.com/1999/dec/05/news/mn-40766 (posted December 5, 1999; last visited April 4, 2014).

75. Bender, *Run for the Border*, 76–77 (describing the stark realities of U.S. sexual slavery, whose victims are often trafficked through Mexico and include under-age girls, as well as the trafficking to provide forced labor in U.S. agriculture and industrial sweatshops).

76. The Pew Hispanic Center estimated in 2006 that some 57 percent of the then twelve million undocumented immigrants in the United States were Mexican, with 24 percent from other parts of Latin America and 9 percent from Asia. Bill Ong Hing, *Deporting Our Souls: Values, Morality, and Immigration Policy* (New York: Cambridge University Press, 2006), 12.

77. Erik Camayd-Freixas, "Raids, Rights and Reform: The Postville Case and the Immigration Crisis," *DePaul Journal for Social Justice* 2 (2008): 1.

78. Roxanne Lynn Doty, *The Law into Their Own Hands: Immigration and the Politics of Exceptionalism* (Tucson: University of Arizona Press, 2009), 86–87. In 2013, a federal judge halted Sheriff Joe's tactic of charging immigrants with conspiring to smuggle themselves across the border. *We Are America v. Maricopa County Bd. of Supervisors*, 2013 WL 5434158 (D. Ariz. 2013).

79. Sioban Albiol, R. Linus Chan, and Sarah J. Diaz, "Re-Interpreting Postville: A Legal Perspective," *DePaul Journal for Social Justice* 2 (2008): 31, 36.

80. Steven W. Bender, "Compassionate Immigration Reform," *Fordham Urban Law Journal* 38 (2010): 107, 118.

81. American Immigration Council, "Falling Through the Cracks," http://www.immigrationpolicy.org/just-facts/falling-through-cracks#.UMjFY6gq61U.facebook (posted December 12, 2012; last visited December 12, 2012).

82. *United States v. Wong Kim Ark*, 169 U.S. 649 (1898) (holding that a child born to Chinese parents in U.S. territory is a U.S. citizen); see generally Ernesto Hernández-López, "Global Migrations and Imagined Citizenship: Examples from Slavery, Chinese Exclusion, and When Questioning Birthright Citizenship," *Texas Wesleyan Law Review* 14 (2008): 255.

83. Garrett Epps, "Denying Citizenship Un-American," http://www.azcentral.com/arizonarepublic/opinions/articles/2011/01/08/20110108epps08.html (posted January 8, 2011; last visited June 20, 2012).

84. Ian Haney-López, "What's the Matter with Anchor Babies, Anyway?," http://newamericamedia.org/2011/01/op-ed.php (posted January 8, 2011; last visited June 20, 2012).

85. Section 287(g) partnerships allow state and local law enforcement to assist federal officials with immigration enforcement.

86. Kevin R. Johnson, "Arizona Is Not the First State to Take Immigration Matters into Their Own Hands: Local Measures on the Rise with Twelve States Considering Similar Laws," http://www.immigrationpolicy.org/just-facts/

arizona-not-first-state-take-immigration-matters-their-own-hands (posted May 6, 2010; last visited June 20, 2012).

87. Arizona Proposition 102 (2006).

88. Arizona Proposition 200 (2004); but see *Arizona v. Inter Tribal Council of Arizona, Inc.*, 133 S. Ct. 2247 (2013) (invalidating a Proposition 200 requirement that prospective registering voters prove citizenship as contrary to the federal National Voter Registration Act).

89. *United States v. Arizona*, 132 S. Ct. 2492, 2512 (2012).

90. For all abuses except bread-and water diets, Mary Romero, "Are Your Papers in Order? Racial Profiling, Vigilantes, and 'America's Toughest Sheriff,'" *Harvard Latino Law Review* 14 (2011): 337, 347. For bread-and-water diets, Faith Karimi, "Sheriff Joe Arpaio: 38 Arizona Inmates Who Defaced Flag to Eat Only Bread, Water," http://www.cnn.com/2014/01/24/justice/arizona-inmates-bread-water/ (posted January 24, 2014; last visited April 4, 2014).

91. Jorge Rivas, "Department of Homeland Security and ICE End Sheriff Arpaio's 287(g) Contract," http://colorlines.com/archives/2011/12/department_of_homeland_security_and_ice_end_sheriff_arpaios_287g_contract.html (posted December 15, 2011; last visited June 20, 2012).

92. The federal lawsuit is described in Ian Millhiser, "Ten Most Disturbing Anti-Latino Practices Described by DOJ's Lawsuit against Sheriff Joe Arpaio," http://thinkprogress.org/justice/2012/05/10/482323/ten-most-disturbing-anti-latino-practices-described-by-dojs-lawsuit-against-sherriff-joe-arpaio/ (posted May 10, 2012; last visited April 4, 2014).

93. J. J. Hensley, "Judge: Sheriff Arpaio's Agency Engaged in Racial Profiling," http://www.azcentral.com/news/articles/20121109sheriff-arpaio-racial-profiling-lawsuit-ruling.html (posted May 24, 2013; last visited April 4, 2014).

94. Judd Legum, "Arizona Sheriff Joe Arpaio Arrests 6-Year-Old Undocumented Immigrant," http://thinkprogress.org/justice/2012/06/17/501097/arizona-sheriff-joe-arpaio-arrests-6-year-old-undocumented-immigrant/?mobile=nc (posted June 17, 2012; last visited April 4, 2014).

95. Declaration art. 30(e).

96. In 2013, a federal district court judge, while upholding the rest of the law, struck down as overbroad the provision prohibiting programs designed for students of a particular ethnic group. *Acosta v. Huppenthal*, 2013 WL 871892 (D. Ariz. 2013).

97. Jonathan J. Cooper, "Arizona Ethnic Studies Law Signed by Governor Brewer, Condemned by UN Human Rights Experts," http://www.huffingtonpost.com/2010/05/12/arizona-ethnic-studies-la_n_572864.html (posted May 12, 2010; last visited December 4, 2012).

98. *Plyler v. Doe*, 457 U.S. 202 (1982).

99. A federal appeals court struck this provision down as violating the Equal Protection Clause as interpreted in the *Plyler* decision. *Hispanic Interest Coalition of Alabama v. Governor of Alabama*, 691 F.3d 1236 (11th Cir. 2012).

100. Juan Crow, http://thedreamact.wikispaces.com/DREAM+Cartoons (last visited June 26, 2012).

101. Although a federal appeals court invalidated Hazleton's ordinances regarding the employment of and rentals to undocumented immigrants, the Supreme Court remanded the case back to the appeals court to consider that Court's ruling in 2011 upholding Arizona's e-verify employment law against a similar preemption challenge. See *City of Hazleton v. Lozano,* 131 S. Ct. 2958 (2011). On remand, the federal appeals court reached the same conclusion in striking down the Hazleton ordinances: that they were preempted by federal immigration law. *Lozano v. City of Hazleton,* 724 F.3d 297 (3d Cir. 2013).

102. Finding the criminal-penalty provisions of the ordinance preempted by federal law and inseparable from the rest of the ordinance, the federal appeals court for the 5th Circuit upheld the federal district court's permanent injunction invalidating the law. *Villas at Parkside Partners v. City of Farmers Branch, Tex.,* 726 F.3d 524 (5th Cir. 2013).

103. *Comite de Jornaleros de Redondo Beach v. Redondo Beach,* 657 F.3d 936 (9th Cir. 2011).

104. Arthur Brice, "Poor Latinos Are Victims of Abuse Nationwide, Activists Say," http://articles.cnn.com/2009-04-22/us/latino.abuse_1_poor-latinos-discrimination-immigrants?_s=PM:US (posted April 22, 2009; last visited June 20, 2012).

105. See Elizabeth McCormick and Patrick McCormick, "Hospitality: How a Biblical Virtue Could Transform United States Immigration Policy," *University of Detroit Mercy Law Review* 83 (2006): 857 (discussing how only five thousand immigrant visas, aside from farmworker visas, annually aim to accommodate the demand for low-skilled workers). Most other visas go toward family reunification. See Hiroshi Motomura, *Americans in Waiting: The Lost Story of Immigration and Citizenship in the United States* (New York: Oxford University Press, 2006), 7 (63 percent of immigrants are admitted based on family ties).

106. See also Ruben J. Garcia, *Marginal Workers: How Legal Fault Lines Divide Workers and Leave Them without Protection* (New York: New York University Press, 2012) (detailing abuses of temporary-worker programs and arguing for a labor-rights-as-human-rights orientation).

107. Bender, "Compassionate Immigration Reform," 121.

108. Quoted in ibid.

109. For example, the AgJOBS Act of 2009, S. 1038, 111th Cong. (2009).

110. But see Bender, *Run for the Border,* 119–120 (discussing how despite the existence of the Western Hemisphere exemption, various discretionary administrative restrictions, such as the literacy test and the prohibition against immigrants likely to become a public charge, were deployed or waived in the early twentieth century to make Mexican immigration consistent with U.S. labor needs).

111. 111 Cong. Rec. 18,244-83 (1965) (statement of Sen. Robert Kennedy).

112. Bender, *Run for the Border,* 159.

113. Bender, "Compassionate Immigration Reform," 116.

114. Ibid.

115. See generally Katherine Culliton-González, "Born in the Americas: Birthright Citizenship and Human Rights," *Harvard Human Rights Law Journal* 25 (2012): 127.

116. See Bender, *Run for the Border*, ch. 9 (detailing the pre-1960s entry of undocumented immigrants from Mexico who might elude administrative border-crossing requirements, such as taxes and the literacy test, and who might help U.S. farmers evade the wage protections of the formal Bracero Program entries).

117. But see Hing, *Deporting Our Souls*, 52–117 (decrying current immigration policies under which lawful permanent residents are deportable without relief upon conviction of a variety of crimes and supplying case studies of the unfairness of these policies).

118. Roberto Rodríguez, "Obama: No Human Being Is Illegal," http://www.yesmagazine.org/issues/columns/obama-no-human-being-is-illegal (posted November 14, 2008; last visited June 27, 2012).

119. Elise Foley, "Deportation Hits Another Record under Obama Administration," *Huff Post Politics,* http://www.huffingtonpost.com/2012/12/21/immigration-deportation_n_2348090.html (posted December 21, 2012; last visited April 4, 2014).

120. "10 Worst Immigrant Detention Centers Should Be Closed, Detention Watch Network Report Says," http://www.huffingtonpost.com/2012/11/16/worst-detention-centers-detention-watch-network_n_2138999.html (posted November 16, 2012; last visited December 4, 2012).

121. *United States v. Arizona*, 132 S. Ct. 2492, 2521 (2012).

122. Quoted in Tim Rutten, "Razing Arizona Law," http://articles.latimes.com/2010/may/01/opinion/la-oe-0501-rutten-20100501 (posted May 1, 2010; last visited June 27, 2012).

123. Robert S. Chang, *Disoriented: Asian Americans, Law, and the Nation-State* (New York: New York University Press, 1999), 27.

CHAPTER 4. BEASTS OF BURDEN

César Chávez, "1984 Address to the Commonwealth Club of California," http://www.chavezfoundation.org/_cms.php?mode=view&b_code=001008000000000&b_no=16&field=&key=&n=8 (last visited April 2, 2014). Former migrant worker quoted in Nancy Buirski, *Earth Angels: Migrant Children in America* (Portland, OR: Pomegranate Artbooks, 1994), 89.

1. Daniel Rothenberg, *With These Hands: The Hidden World of Migrant Farmworkers Today* (Berkeley: University of California Press, 1998), 44.

2. U.S. Department of Labor, *Findings from the National Agricultural Workers Survey, 2001–2002*, http://www.doleta.gov/agworker/report9/naws_rpt9.pdf (last visited December 3, 2012) (the survey was limited to crop workers and did not include, for example, those who work in poultry or dairy).

3. Southern Poverty Law Center, "Who Are Farmworkers?," http://www.splcenter.org/sexual-violence-against-farmworkers-a-guidebook-for-criminal-justice-professionals/who-are-farmworke (last visited July 18, 2012).

4. Rothenberg, *With These Hands*, 161.

5. Ibid.

6. Ibid., 62. This figure doesn't include workers in food preparation and distribution away from farms.

7. David Bacon, "Congress Must Face Reality—Immigrants Want Equality," http://news.newamericamedia.org/news/view_article.html?article_id=fab29f2cbea1fd5ac2b6fb37fbde9ffd (posted April 6, 2006; last visited June 29, 2012).

8. Lothrop Stoddard, *Re-Forging America: The Story of Our Nationhood* (New York: Scribner, 1927), 214.

9. Quoted in Susan Ferriss and Ricardo Sandoval, *The Fight in the Fields: Cesar Chavez and the Farmworkers Movement* (San Diego: Harcourt Brace, 1997), 150–151 (letter from César E. Chávez to E. L. Barr Jr., president of the California Grape & Tree Fruit League).

10. Quoted in Rothenberg, *With These Hands*, 243.

11. Cited in Southern Poverty Law Center, "Who Are Farmworkers?"

12. See Human Rights Watch, *Cultivating Fear: The Vulnerability of Immigrant Farmworkers in the US to Sexual Violence and Sexual Harassment* (May 2012), 18, http://www.hrw.org/sites/default/files/reports/us0512ForUpload_1.pdf (last visited November 9, 2013).

13. Rothenberg, *With These Hands*, 6.

14. Steven W. Bender, *One Night in America: Robert Kennedy, César Chávez, and the Dream of Dignity* (Boulder, CO: Paradigm, 2008), 90.

15. See Patrick H. Mooney and Theo J. Majka, *Farmers' and Farm Workers' Movements: Social Protest in American Agriculture* (New York: Twayne, 1995) (detailing the history of farm-labor insurgency).

16. Bender, *One Night in America*.

17. Rodolfo Acuña, *Occupied America: A History of Chicanos*, 3d ed. (New York: HarperCollins, 1988), 325.

18. Mooney and Majka, *Farmers' and Farm Workers' Movements*, 9.

19. Marc Cooper, "Sour Grapes," http://www.laweekly.com/content/printVersion/40574/ (posted August 11, 2005; last visited July 2, 2012).

20. See Gabriel Thompson, *Working in the Shadows: A Year of Doing the Jobs [Most] Americans Won't Do* (New York: Nation Books, 2010) (includes a description of grueling work picking lettuce in Arizona).

21. Ann Aurelia López, *The Farmworkers' Journey* (Berkeley: University of California Press, 2007), 51.

22. See Bill Ong Hing, *Ethical Borders: NAFTA, Globalization, and Mexican Migration* (Philadelphia: Temple University Press, 2010), and Carmen G. Gonzalez, "An Environmental Justice Critique of Comparative Advantage: Indigenous Peoples,

Trade Policy, and the Mexican Neoliberal Economic Reforms," *University of Penn-sylvania Journal of International Law* 32 (2011): 723.

23. López, *Farmworkers' Journey*, 9 (explaining that NAFTA has forced at least 1.75 million rural farmers off their land and into Mexican cities or the United States as economic refugees).

24. Bender, *One Night in America*, 96.

25. Rothenberg, *With These Hands*, 92

26. Bender, *Run for the Border*, 133; Shelley Cavalieri, "The Eyes That Blind Us: The Overlooked Phenomenon of Trafficking into the Agricultural Sector," *Northern Illinois University Law Review* 31 (2011): 501.

27. See Human Rights Watch, *Cultivating Fear*.

28. Dolores Huerta, "Keynote Address," *Hastings Race and Poverty Law Journal* 3 (2006): 203, 204.

29. Bender, *One Night in America*, 11. Only California guarantees agricultural workers the right to collectively bargain. Ronald L. Mize and Alicia C. S. Swords, *Consuming Mexican Labor: From the Bracero Program to NAFTA* (Toronto: University of Toronto Press, 2011), 239. Nonetheless, undocumented immigrants in protected occupations readily face the prospect of discharge for their union organizing, as illustrated by a Supreme Court decision holding that undocumented immigrants were not entitled to back pay for an otherwise unlawful retaliatory discharge. *Hoffman Plastic Compounds, Inc. v. NLRB*, 122 S. Ct. 1275 (2002).

30. Bender, *One Night in America*, 65.

31. Carey McWilliams, *Factories in the Field: The Story of Migratory Farm Labor in California* (Boston: Little, Brown, 1939), 316.

32. Bender, *Tierra y Libertad*, 30.

33. Quoted in Bender, *One Night in America*, 14.

34. Bender, *Greasers and Gringos*, 139.

35. Ibid.

36. Quoted in ibid.

37. Ibid., 140.

38. Bender, *Tierra y Libertad*, 14, 30.

39. Cited in ibid., 37.

40. Christopher Holden, "Bitter Harvest: Housing Conditions of Migrant and Seasonal Farmworkers," in *The Human Cost of Food: Farmworkers' Lives, Labor, and Advocacy*, ed. Charles D. Thompson Jr. and Melinda F. Wiggins (Austin: University of Texas Press, 2002), 178.

41. Glen Martin, "Napa Valley Celebrates the Good Life," *San Francisco Gate*, December 19, 2004, CM6.

42. Human Rights Watch, *Cultivating Fear*, 18.

43. Bender, *Tierra y Libertad*, 32.

44. Ilene J. Jacobs, "Farmworker Housing in California," *La Raza Law Journal* 9 (1996): 177, 180.

45. Bender, *Tierra y Libertad*, 33.

46. Cited in López, *Farmworkers' Journey*, 130–131.

47. Bender, *Greasers and Gringos*, 137.

48. López, *Farmworkers' Journey*, 132.

49. Ferriss and Sandoval, *Fight in the Fields*, 238. See also Joan D. Flocks, "The Environmental and Social Injustice of Farmworker Pesticide Exposure," *Georgetown Journal on Poverty Law and Policy* 19 (2012): 255, 272.

50. López, *Farmworkers' Journey*, 128.

51. See Human Rights Watch, *Cultivating Fear*, 59.

52. Bender, *One Night in America*, 65.

53. Ibid., 90.

54. López, *Farmworkers' Journey*, 143.

55. Ibid., 129.

56. Emily A. Spieler, "Risks and Rights: The Case for Occupational Safety and Heath as a Core Worker Right," in *Workers' Rights as Human Rights*, ed. James A. Gross (Ithaca, NY: Cornell University Press, 2003), 78, 111; Rothenberg, *With These Hands*, 214 (discussing how most field workers are uncovered by workers compensation, and their undocumented status may be an additional impediment in some states).

57. Ferriss and Sandoval, *Fight in the Fields*, 206–207.

58. See Human Rights Watch, *Cultivating Fear*.

59. Ibid., 23.

60. López, *Farmworkers' Journey*, 100.

61. Human Rights Watch, *Fingers to the Bone: United States Failure to Protect Child Farmworkers* (New York: Human Rights Watch, June 2000), 33.

62. Southern Poverty Law Center, "Who Are Farmworkers?," http://www.splcenter.org/sexual-violence-against-farmworkers-a-guidebook-for-criminal-justice-professionals/who-are-farmworke (last visited July 18, 2012).

63. Jessica Felix-Romero, "Farmworkers in the U.S.," http://www.harvestingjustice.org/index.php?option=com_content&view=category&layout=blog&id=53&Itemid=91 (posted March 20, 2012; last visited July 18, 2012). See also Human Rights Watch, *Fingers to the Bone*, 48 (reporting a national dropout rate for farmworker children of 45 percent in the early 1990s).

64. Estimates of the number of Mexican bracero workers ranged widely, with some sources claiming as few as 1 to 2 million, others claiming as many as 5 million, and most suggesting that the number exceeded 4 million and fell in the vicinity of 4.5 or 4.6 million.

65. Christopher David Ruiz Cameron, "Borderline Decisions: *Hoffman Plastic Compounds*, the New Bracero Program, and the Supreme Court's Role in Making Federal Labor Policy," *UCLA Law Review* 51 (2003): 1, 3.

66. See Bender, *Greasers and Gringos*, 143–147 (detailing segregationist practices for Latino/a residents), and Rothenberg, *With These Hands*, 38.

67. Quoted in Rothenberg, *With These Hands*, 38.

68. Ernesto Galarza, "The Braceros," in *The Fight in the Fields: Cesar Chavez and the Farmworkers Movement*, by Susan Ferriss and Ricardo Sandoval (San Diego: Harcourt Brace, 1997), 54.

69. Bender, *Run for the Border*, 124.

70. Quoted in Rothenberg, *With These Hands*, 244.

71. Quoted in Bender, *One Night in America*, 59.

72. Vincent Harding, "Interview with Dolores Huerta," in *Dolores Huerta Reader*, ed. Mario T. García (Albuquerque: University of New Mexico Press, 2008), 177, 185.

73. Rothenberg, *With These Hands*, 76.

74. Bender, *Greasers and Gringos*, 139.

75. Huerta, "Keynote Address," 203.

76. Rothenberg, *With These Hands*, xv.

77. See Human Rights Watch, *Cultivating Fear* (detailing reform recommendations).

78. Ibid., 50.

79. United Farm Workers, *Take Our Jobs*, 2010, http://www.takeourjobs.org/ (last visited July 9, 2012).

80. Rothenberg, *With These Hands*, 72.

81. Hing, *Ethical Borders*.

82. Mize and Swords, *Consuming Mexican Labor*, 56.

83. Frank Stricker, *Why America Lost the War on Poverty—and How to Win It* (Chapel Hill: University of North Carolina, 2007), 238.

84. The argument extends to clothing as another labor-intensive and often agriculturally sourced product. But it somehow fails to apply to constraining costs of other necessities such as health care, utilities, and transportation (gasoline), where costs keep spiraling.

85. Rothenberg, *With These Hands*, 325.

CHAPTER 5. THE WAGES OF POVERTY

1. John Iceland, *Poverty in America: A Handbook* (Berkeley: University of California, 2003), 95.

2. Cited in ibid.

3. Rae Gomes, "If You Own an Xbox—or an Air Conditioner—Can You Still Be Considered Poor?," http://www.alternet.org/story/151727/if_you_own_an_xbox_--_or_an_air_conditioner_--_can_you_still_be_considered_poor (posted July 21, 2011; last visited August 3, 2012).

4. Victor Davis Hanson, *Mexifornia: A State of Becoming* (San Francisco: Encounter Books, 2003), 67.

5. Barbara Ehrenreich, *Nickel and Dimed: On (Not) Getting By in America* (New York: Henry Holt, 2001), 216.

6. David K. Shipler, *The Working Poor: Invisible in America* (New York: Vintage Books, 2005), 9 (explaining flaws in the federal poverty-line calculation based on three times food costs when the average family spent one-sixth of its budget on food).

7. Carmen DeNavas-Walt, Bernadette D. Proctor, and Jessica C. Smith, "Income, Poverty, and Health Insurance Coverage in the United States: 2011" (Washington, DC: U.S. Census Bureau, September 2012), 13.

8. "U.S. Poverty on Track to Rise to Highest since 1960s," http://www.usatoday.com/news/nation/story/2012-07-22/poverty-in-america/56417780/1 (posted July 22, 2012; last visited August 1, 2012).

9. Peter Edelman, *So Rich, So Poor: Why It's So Hard to End Poverty in America* (New York: New Press, 2012), xvii.

10. Ibid.

11. Ibid., 32.

12. Glassdoor, "Walmart Wal Mart Cashier Hourly Pay," http://www.glassdoor.com/Hourly-Pay/Walmart-Stores-Wal-Mart-Cashier-Hourly-Pay-E715_D_KO15,31.htm (updated March 6, 2014).

13. Edelman, *So Rich*, 30.

14. DeNavas-Walt, Proctor, and Smith, "Income, Poverty."

15. William P. Quigley, *Ending Poverty as We Know It: Guaranteeing a Right to a Job at a Living Wage* (Philadelphia: Temple University Press, 2003).

16. Mark Robert Rank, *One Nation, Underprivileged: Why American Poverty Affects Us All* (New York: Oxford University Press, 2004), 32.

17. Tavis Smiley and Cornel West, *The Rich and the Rest of Us: A Poverty Manifesto* (New York: SmileyBooks, 2012), 52.

18. DeNavas-Walt, Proctor, and Smith, "Income, Poverty," 16.

19. Duncan Lindsey, *Child Poverty and Inequality: Securing a Better Future for America's Children* (New York: Oxford University Press, 2009), 5.

20. Smiley and West, *The Rich*, 53.

21. Edelman, *So Rich*, xiii.

22. Smiley and West, *The Rich*, 174. Compare López, *Farmworkers' Journey*, 9 (discussing epic poverty levels in Mexico's rural areas, due in part to NAFTA, where some 50 percent of Mexicans suffer "extreme poverty," and estimating that 158,000 Mexican children die each year before the age of five from malnutrition-related maladies).

23. Rank, *One Nation*, 39.

24. Evan McMorris-Santoro, "Racist Email Flap Blows Up Virginia Beach GOP," TPM, http://tpmdc.talkingpointsmemo.com/2010/10/racist-email-flap-blows-up-virgina-beach-gop.php (posted October 20, 2010; last visited August 3, 2012).

25. Cited in Kenneth J. Neubeck and Noel A. Cazenave, *Welfare Racism: Playing the Race Card against America's Poor* (New York: Routledge, 2001).

26. Martin Gilens, *Why Americans Hate Welfare: Race, Media, and the Politics of Antipoverty Policy* (Chicago: University of Chicago Press, 1999), 67 (discussing how images of urban blacks replaced those of Dust Bowl Okies and southern European and Irish immigrants; these immigrants were in fact "raced" as nonwhite but eventually became "white."); Ange-Marie Hancock, *The Politics of Disgust: The Public Identity of the Welfare Queen* (New York: New York University Press, 2004).

27. Ellen Reese, *Backlash against Welfare Mothers: Past and Present* (Berkeley: University of California Press, 2005), 27; Joe R. Feagin, *Subordinating the Poor: Welfare and American Beliefs* (Englewood Cliffs, NJ: Prentice-Hall, 1975), 109 (discussing a national survey in which six of ten respondents agreed that large numbers of welfare recipients have illegitimate babies to increase their draw).

28. Reese, *Backlash against Welfare Mothers*, 27.

29. Richard J. Herrnstein and Charles Murray, *The Bell Curve* (New York: Free Press, 1994), 548.

30. Gilens, *Americans Hate Welfare*, 61–62.

31. Ibid., 69 (discussing survey results in which only 35 percent of respondents chose "white" when asked whether welfare recipients are mostly white or black, despite the reality of white participation numbers); Sharon Hays, *Flat Broke with Children: Women in the Age of Welfare Reform* (New York: Oxford University Press, 2003), 23 ("Most people recognize that welfare has come to be associated with blacks, even though they have never been a majority of welfare recipients."). By 2013, however, blacks constituted a plurality (39.8 percent) of U.S. welfare recipients, with whites making up 38.8 percent and Latinas/os 15.7 percent of recipients. U.S. Department of Health and Human Services, U.S. Department of Commerce, CATO Institute, "Welfare Statistics," *Statistic Brain*, http://www.statisticbrain.com/welfare-statistics/ (last visited October 29, 2013).

32. Proposition 187 was ultimately gutted by a federal court. *League of United Latin Am. Citizens v. Wilson*, 908 F. Supp. 755 (C.D. Cal. 1995) (striking down the refusal to educate undocumented children); *League of United Latin Am. Citizens v. Wilson*, 997 F. Supp. 1244 (C.D. Cal. 1997) (invalidating the other benefit-denial provisions as preempted by the federal Personal Responsibility and Work Opportunity Reconciliation Act of 1996).

33. Bender, *Run for the Border*, 117–118.

34. For studies and arguments debunking the derogatory conception of the welfare queen, see Roberta Spalter-Roth, Beverly Burr, Heidi Hartmann, and Lois Shaw, "Few Welfare Moms Fit the Stereotypes," *Research in Brief* (Washington, DC: Institute for Women's Policy, 1995) (noting that half of single mothers collecting welfare worked); Reese, *Backlash against Welfare Mothers*, 28; Joel F. Handler and Yeheskel Hasenfeld, *Blame Welfare, Ignore Poverty and Inequality* (New York: Cambridge University Press, 2007), 30 (discussing why, given low pay, poverty rates for full-time working families of Latinos/as, female heads, and the lesser educated are high despite their "playing by the rules"); Neubeck and Cazenave, *Welfare Racism*, 139 (discussing data that women receiving welfare payments did not have significantly higher fertility rates than other women).

35. Quoted in Neubeck and Cazenave, *Welfare Racism*, 127 (noting that the *New York Times* debunked Reagan's facts); see also David Zucchino, *Myth of the Welfare Queen: A Pulitzer Prize-Winning Journalist's Portrait of Women on the Line* (New York: Scribner, 1997), 13 (concluding in his study of unmarried welfare mothers

in North Philadelphia that if "there were any Cadillac-driving, champagne-sipping, penthouse-living welfare queens in North Philadelphia, I didn't find them.").

36. Quoted in Reese, *Backlash against Welfare Mothers*, 175.

37. Quoted in Feagin, *Subordinating the Poor*, 5.

38. Jeff Nall, "Lies of Plutocracy, Exploding Five Myths That Dehumanize the Poor," http://www.sott.net/article/252959-Lies-of-Plutocracy-Exploding-five-myths-that-dehumanize-the-poor (October 26, 2012; last visited November 24, 2012).

39. Cong. Rec. 104th Cong., 1st Sess., March 24, 1995, H3766, H3772.

40. Mimi Abramovitz, *Under Attack: Fighting Back: Women and Welfare in the United States* (New York: Monthly Review Press, 2000), 19.

41. Reese, *Backlash against Welfare Mothers*, 16.

42. Solange Uwimana, "Ryan's Prescription for the Poor: End Anti-Poverty Programs," http://www.alternet.org/election-2012/ryans-prescription-poor-end-anti-poverty-programs (October 24, 2012; last visited November 24, 2012) (also describing how vice presidential candidate Paul Ryan stigmatized welfare as a "culture of dependency, wrecking families and communities").

43. Bill Clinton, "How We Ended Welfare, Together," *New York Times*, August 22, 2006, A19.

44. Bender, "Compassionate Immigration Reform," 120.

45. See generally Steven W. Bender, Raquel Aldana, Gilbert Paul Carrasco, and Joaquin G. Avila, *Everyday Law for Latinos/as* (Boulder, CO: Paradigm, 2008), 173–178.

46. Bender, *Tierra y Libertad*, 59.

47. Quoted in Kevin D. Hendricks, ed., *Open Our Eyes: Seeing the Invisible People of Homelessness* (Saint Paul, MN: Monkey Outta Nowhere, 2010), 49.

48. Michael Sullivan, "I Was Homeless; 'The Look' Judged Me Worthless," http://articles.cnn.com/2011-01-26/opinion/sullivan.homeless.writer_1_homeless-people-e-train-queens-church?_s=PM:OPINION (posted January 26, 2011; last visited August 4, 2012) (describing the experience of the writer as a homeless man during the winter of 1983–1984).

49. Randall Amster, *Lost in Space: The Criminalization, Globalization, and Urban Ecology of Homelessness* (New York: LFB Scholarly Publishing, 2008), 82–84.

50. Joseph Dillon Davey, *The New Social Contract: America's Journey from Welfare State to Police State* (Westport, CT: Praeger, 1995), 30, 39.

51. Cited in Melissa J. Doak, *Social Welfare: Fighting Poverty and Homelessness* (Farmington Hills, MI: Thomson Gale, 2008), 12.

52. Martha F. Davis and Susan J. Kraham, "Beaten, Then Robbed," *New York Times*, January 13, 1995.

53. Shannon Moriarty, "Five Things You Absolutely Must Know about Homelessness," in *Open Our Eyes: Seeing the Invisible People of Homelessness*, ed. Kevin D. Hendricks (Saint Paul, MN: Monkey Outta Nowhere, 2010), 19, 20.

54. Steve Kastenbaum, "NYC Hit with Huge Wave of Homelessness," http://cnnradio. cnn.com/2013/01/28/nyc-budget-cuts-cause-homeless-crisis/ (posted January 28, 2013; last visited April 7, 2013).

55. John Derbyshire, "Welfare Programs for the Homeless Exacerbate the Problem," in *Poverty and Homelessness*, ed. Noël Merino (Farmington Hills, MI: Greenhaven Press, 2009), 132, 136–137.

56. In 2012, the federal Ninth Circuit Court of Appeals upheld an injunction issued against the City of Los Angeles, preventing the city from seizing and destroying the unabandoned property of the homeless, even when left on sidewalks in violation of a local ordinance. *Lavan v. City of Los Angeles*, 693 F.3d 1022 (9th Cir. 2012).

57. National Law Center on Homelessness & Poverty and National Coalition for the Homeless, *Homes Not Handcuffs: The Criminalization of Homelessness in U.S. Cities* (Washington, DC: National Law Center on Homelessness & Poverty and National Coalition for the Homeless, July 2009), 10. See this publication also for discussions of court decisions challenging these various approaches to criminalizing the homeless.

58. Tana Ganeva, "10 Unbelievably Sh**ty Things America Does to Homeless People," http://www.alternet.org/story/154830/10_unbelievably_sh**ty_things_america_does_to_homeless_people (posted April 5, 2012; last visited August 5, 2012).

59. For international human rights law, see National Law Center, *Homes Not Handcuffs*.

60. Devin Dwyer, "Violence against the Homeless: Is It Growing?," http://abc-news.go.com/Politics/hate-crimes-law-senators-add-attacks-homeless/story?id=11754964#.UB2TSmAW9P4 (posted September 29, 2010; last visited August 5, 2012).

61. National Coalition for the Homeless, "'Kicked, Set on Fire, Beaten to Death': Shocking Rise of Violence against America's Homeless," http://www.alternet.org/story/148486/%22kicked,_set_on_fire,_beaten_to_death%22%3A_shocking_rise_of_violence_against_america's_homeless?page=entire (posted October 20, 2010; last visited August 5, 2012).

62. Article 25.

63. Rank, *One Nation*, 125–132; see also C. Melissa Snarr, *All You That Labor: Religion and Ethics in the Living Wage Movement* (New York: New York University Press, 2011) (exploring the intersection of religion and the living-wage movement).

64. For day-in-the-life discussions of the inadequacies of minimum-wage employment opportunities in the United States, see Ehrenreich, *Nickel and Dimed*, and Thompson, *Working in the Shadows*.

65. For background on the economic theory behind, and the calculation of, living wages, see Robert Pollin, Mark Brenner, Jeannette Wicks-Lim, and Stephanie Luce, *A Measure of Fairness: The Economics of Living Wages and Minimum Wages in the United States* (Ithaca, NY: Cornell University Press, 2008); for broader

perspectives, see Oren M. Levin-Waldman, *Wage Policy, Income Distribution, and Democratic Theory* (New York: Routledge, 2011).

66. Snarr, *All You That Labor*, 24.

67. United States Department of Labor, http://www.dol.gov/whd/minwage/america. htm (last visited April 4, 2014).

68. Edelman, *So Rich*, 65.

69. Schiff later disputed the context of his remarks made on television's *Daily Show*, http://www.schiffradio.com/b/The-Daily-Show:-A-Call-To-Action/98027245398783791.html (last visited February 6, 2014).

70. Quigley, *Ending Poverty*, 22, 86 (stating that women are the largest group that would benefit from a one dollar increase in the minimum wage).

71. Holly Sklar and Paul Sherry, "Raising the Minimum Wage Is Necessary to Combat Poverty," in *Poverty and Homelessness*, ed. Noël Merino (Farmington Hills, MI: Greenhaven Press, 2009), 161.

72. Jack Temple, "How McDonald's Sends Taxpayers the Bill," http://www.cnn. com/2013/10/29/opinion/temple-hidden-fast-food-taxes/index.html?hpt=hp_bn7 (posted October 29, 2013; last visited October 29, 2013).

73. Catherine Ruetschlin, "Retail's Hidden Potential: How Raising Wages Would Benefit Workers, the Industry and the Overall Economy," http://www.demos.org/ sites/default/files/publications/RetailsHiddenPotential.pdf (last visited December 6, 2012).

74. Ibid.

75. Center for American Progress, "A Variety of Approaches Are Needed to Cut Poverty," in *Poverty and Homelessness*, ed. Noël Merino (Farmington Hills, MI: Greenhaven Press, 2009), 144.

76. Iceland, *Poverty in America*, 65, 69.

77. Doak, *Social Welfare*, 115.

78 . Gwen Sharp, "The Minimum Wage and the Cost of Housing," http://thesoci-etypages.org/socimages/2012/06/04/the-minimum-wage-and-the-cost-of-hous-ing/ (posted June 4, 2012; last visited August 4, 2012).

79. Bender, *Tierra y Libertad*, 157 (supplying ideas for a government emphasis on low-income housing).

80. Douglas A. Timmer, D. Stanley Eitzen, and Kathryn D. Talley, "Making Home-lessness Go Away: Politics and Policy," in *Social Solutions to Poverty: America's Struggle to Build a Just Society*, ed. Scott J. Myers-Lipton (Boulder, CO: Para-digm, 2006), 281 (researchers found that almost half of shelter users complained of lack of security and privacy and perceived shelters as demoralizing and dangerous).

81. See Gilbert Paul Carrasco and Congressman Peter W. Rodino Jr., "'Unalienable Rights,' the Preamble, and the Ninth Amendment: The Spirit of the Constitu-tion," *Seton Hall Law Review* 20 (1990): 498 (arguing that, despite the absence of housing as a fundamental right protected under the Equal Protection Clause, those government policies keeping people in abject poverty, such as subsidies

to agribusiness, may be vulnerable to challenge under the Ninth Amendment's protection of such retained fundamental rights as a minimum quality of life).

82. Timmer, Eitzen, and Talley, *Making Homelessness Go Away*, 278.

83. Bender, *Tierra y Libertad*, 183 (statistic based on a four-year college degree).

84. Lindsey, *Child Poverty*, 5.

85. See Bender, *Tierra y Libertad*, 183–184, for additional ideas about educational investment.

86. Nall, "Lies of Plutocracy."

87. Hays, *Flat Broke*.

88. Maureen Farrell, "The Highest Earning Hedge Fund Manager Is . . . ," http://money.cnn.com/2012/03/30/markets/top-earning-hedge-fund-managers/index.htm (posted March 30, 2012; last visited August 5, 2012).

89. Les Leopold, *How to Make a Million Dollars an Hour: How Hedge Funds Get Away with Siphoning Off America's Wealth* (Hoboken, NJ: Wiley, 2013).

90. Edelman, *So Rich*, 33.

91. Daniel Tencer, "Study: Most Americans Want Wealth Distribution Similar to Sweden," http://www.rawstory.com/rs/2010/09/25/poll-wealth-distribution-similar-sweden/ (posted September 25, 2010; last visited August 5, 2012).

92. Timothy Noah, *The Great Divergence: America's Growing Inequality Crisis and What We Can Do about It* (New York: Bloomsbury Press, 2012), 4.

93. Ibid., 151 (discussing a *New York Times* survey of two hundred corporations with revenues of $10.78 billion or more).

94. Ibid.

95. Ronald J. Sider, *Just Generosity: A New Vision for Overcoming Poverty in America* (Grand Rapids, MI: Baker, 1999), 45.

96. Feagin, *Subordinating the Poor*, 137.

97. David B. Grusky and Tamar Kricheli-Katz, eds., *The New Gilded Age: The Critical Inequality Debates of Our Time* (Stanford, CA: Stanford University Press, 2012), 2.

98. Tencer, "Most Americans."

99. Noah, *Great Divergence*, 18.

100. Warren E. Buffett, "Stop Coddling the Super-Rich," *New York Times*, http://www.nytimes.com/2011/08/15/opinion/stop-coddling-the-super-rich.html/ (posted August 14, 2011; last visited August 6, 2012).

101. Stricker, *Poverty*, 211 (based on 1997 to 1998 figures of poverty and growth in net worth).

CHAPTER 6. SEXUALITY AND DEHUMANIZATION

Ex parte H.H., 830 So. 2d 21, 26 (Ala. 2002) (concurring opinion) (arguing that a same-sex relationship creates a strong presumption of unfitness as a parent and alone justifies the denial of custody of children). "God Hates Fags," http://www.godhatesfags.com/ (last visited April 5, 2014). "Eminem—Criminal Lyrics," http://rapgenius.com/Eminem-criminal-lyrics (last visited April 5, 2014). Dan Loumena, "NBA Fines Roy Hibbert $75,000 for Using Gay Slur," http://articles.latimes.

com/2013/jun/02/sports/la-sp-sn-roy-hibbert-fined-gay-slur-20130602 (posted June 2, 2013; last visited April 5, 2014).

1. Quoted in Murdoch and Price, *Courting Justice*, 202.

2. Quoted in Shannon Gilreath and Lydia E. Lavelle, *Sexual Identity Law in Context: Cases and Materials* (St. Paul, MN: West, 2012), 67.

3. *Lawrence v. Texas*, 539 U.S. 558, 590 (2003) (dissenting opinion).

4. Sean Loughlin, "Two Republicans Criticize Santorum for Remarks about Gays," http://www.cnn.com/2003/ALLPOLITICS/04/24/santorum.gays/ (posted April 24, 2003; last visited April 4, 2014).

5. William N. Eskridge Jr., *Gaylaw: Challenging the Apartheid of the Closet* (Cambridge, MA: Harvard University Press, 1999), 133.

6. Jonathan Katz, "Treatment," in *Cases and Materials on Sexual Orientation and the Law*, ed. William B. Rubenstein, Carlos A. Ball, Jane S. Schacter (St. Paul, MN: West, 2011), 47, 48; Anthony C. Infanti, *Everyday Law for Gays and Lesbians and Those Who Care about Them* (Boulder, CO: Paradigm, 2007), 12.

7. Quoted in Murdoch and Price, *Courting Justice*, 355.

8. The federal Ninth Circuit Court of Appeals upheld California's law against a challenge that it violated the constitutionally protected free speech rights, among others, of practitioners, patients, or parents. *Pickup v. Brown*, 728 F.3d 1042 (9th Cir. 2013).

9. Family Research Council, "Testimony of Peter Sprigg before the Maryland Senate Judicial Proceedings Committee," http://www.frc.org/testimony/testimony-of-peter-sprigg-before-the-maryland-senate-judicial-proceedings-committee (posted February 26, 2013; last visited March 16, 2013).

10. Martha C. Nussbaum, *From Disgust to Humanity: Sexual Orientation and Constitutional Law* (New York: Oxford University Press, 2010), 1 (quoting Paul Cameron).

11. Duke, "Paris Hilton Apologizes."

12. Jim Brown, "Duquesne Sophomore Challenges 'Sexual Orientation' Harassment Charge," http://www.freerepublic.com/focus/f-news/1513662/posts (posted November 1, 2005; last visited April 30, 2014).

13. Ron Dicker, "Transgender Player Gabrielle Ludwig Mocked by ESPN Radio Hosts," http://www.huffingtonpost.com/2012/12/11/gabrielle-ludwig-transgender-basketball-mocked-espn-radio_n_2276979.html (posted December 11, 2012; last visited April 4, 2014).

14. Sara Bufkin, "Bachmann's Husband Calls Homosexuals 'Barbarians' Who 'Need to be Educated' and 'Disciplined,'" http://thinkprogress.org/lgbt/2011/06/29/257646/bachmanns-husband-calls-homosexuals-barbarians-who-need-to-be-educated-and-disciplined/ (posted June 29, 2011; last visited April 4, 2014).

15. Steve Williams, "Pope Decides Gay People Aren't Fully Developed Humans," http://www.care2.com/causes/pope-decides-gay-people-arent-fully-developed-humans.html (posted September 27, 2012; last visited November 24, 2012).

16. Joseph Ratzinger, "Letter to the Bishops of the Catholic Church on the Pastoral Care of Homosexual Persons," October 1, 1986, http://www.vatican.va/roman_curia/congregations/cfaith/documents/rc_con_cfaith_doc_19861001_homosexual-persons_en.html (last visited April 14, 2014).

17. David Badash, "Genocide? Pastor Says Kill All 'Queers and Homosexuals' by Airlifting into Electric Pen," http://thenewcivilrightsmovement.com/genocide-pastor-says-kill-all-queers-and-homosexuals-by-airlifting-into-electric-pen/politics/2012/05/21/39917 (posted May 21, 2012; last visited August 9, 2012).

18. Susan Gluck Mezey, *Gay Families and the Courts: The Quest for Equal Rights* (Lanham, MD: Rowman & Littlefield, 2009), 153.

19. Gilbert Paul Carrasco, *Sexuality and Discrimination: A Rights and Liberties Perspective* (Durham, NC: Carolina Academic Press, 2005), 89.

20. Quoted in ibid., 12.

21. Eskridge, *Gaylaw*, 66 (reporting that between 40 and 85 percent of the arrests were for consensual, same-sex adult relations).

22. Joey L. Mogul, Andrea J. Ritchie, and Kay Whitlock, *Queer (In)Justice: The Criminalization of LGBT People in the United States* (Boston: Beacon Press, 2011), 53–54.

23. Eskridge, *Gaylaw*, 74.

24. *Bowers v. Hardwick*, 478 U.S. 186, 197 (1986) (upholding Georgia law).

25. *Lawrence v. Texas*, 539 U.S. 558 (2003).

26. Mogul, Ritchie, and Whitlock, *Queer (In)Justice*, 56–57 (describing discriminatory, selective enforcement against gay men of these vague laws); *Singson v. Commonwealth*, 621 S.E.2d 682 (2005) (upholding the conviction under the Virginia Crimes against Nature law of a man who solicited an undercover police officer for fellatio in a department-store restroom stall).

27. *Boy Scouts of America v. Dale*, 530 U.S. 640 (2000) (requiring the Boy Scouts to accept an openly gay scoutmaster would violate its constitutionally protected freedom of association).

28. Carrasco, *Sexuality and Discrimination*, 12.

29. Katie Miller and Jeff Krehely, "New Data Demonstrates Unique Needs of Gay and Transgender Families," http://www.americanprogress.org/issues/lgbt/news/2012/10/31/43383/new-data-demonstrate-the-unique-needs-of-gay-and-transgender-families/ (posted October 31, 2012; last visited March 25, 2013).

30. Nan D. Hunter, Courtney G. Joslin, and Sharon M. McGowan, *The Rights of Lesbians, Gay Men, Bisexuals, and Transgender People* (New York: New York University Press, 2004), 39–40 (noting a trend toward equality in the treatment of teachers, including antidiscrimination laws and the fact that some districts actively recruit LGBT teachers).

31. *Board of Education of Oklahoma City v. National Gay Task Force*, 470 U.S. 903 (1985) (a 4-4 decision without the participation of Justice Powell affirmed the appellate court invalidation).

32. *Romer v. Evans*, 517 U.S. 620 (1996).

33. "Don't Ask, Don't Tell," http://en.wikipedia.org/wiki/Don't_ask,_don't_tell (last visited August 9, 2012).

34. See U.S. Department of State, "Briefing on Lesbian, Gay, Bisexual, and Transgender (LGBT) Resolution at UN Human Rights Council," http://www.state.gov/p/io/rm/2011/166470.htm (posted June 17, 2011; last visited April 6, 2014).

35. Carrasco, *Sexuality and Discrimination*, 443.

36. Ibid., 448.

37. Ontario Consultants on Religious Tolerance, "Legal and Economic Benefits of Marriage," http://www.religioustolerance.org/mar_bene.htm (posted July 4, 2011; last visited August 9, 2012).

38. In several states, such as New Jersey, progress toward same-sex equality has come through the courts rather than through the legislature or voters. See *Garden State Equality v. Dow*, 79 A.3d 1036 (N.J. 2013) (applying an earlier decision of the same court that the New Jersey Constitution guaranteed committed same-sex couples the same rights as opposite-sex couples, finding a lack of probability of success to challenge a trial court ruling rejecting the resulting legislative compromise of same-sex civil unions, and ordering same-sex civil marriages to commence).

39. Joan M. Burda, *Gay, Lesbian, and Transgender Clients: A Lawyer's Guide* (Chicago: American Bar Association, 2008), 13. Adopted by ballot initiative in 2008, California's Proposition 8 amended the state's Constitution to outlaw same-sex marriage. Ultimately, a federal district court struck down the ballot initiative as violating federal constitutional dictates of due process and equal protection, and the Supreme Court let the ruling stand for want of standing after the named state official defendants refused to defend the law and the ballot initiative proponents took over the defense. *Hollingsworth v. Perry*, 133 S. Ct. 2652 (2013).

40. *United States v. Windsor*, 133 S. Ct. 2675, 2696 (2013) (uncertainty remains about whether the federal government must accord equal benefits when a same-sex couple, while lawfully married in a state recognizing same-sex marriage, resides elsewhere).

41. Infanti, *Everyday Law*, 205.

42. Ibid.

43. Ibid., 206.

44. *Bottoms v. Bottoms*, 457 S.E.2d 102 (Va. 1995).

45. *Florida Dept. of Children and Families v. Adoption of X.X.G.*, 45 So.3d 79 (Fla. Dist. Ct. App. 2010) (appellate court concludes adoption law violates the equal-protection clause of the Florida constitution). See Mezey, *Gay Families*, 24–25 (describing remaining states with constraints on gay adoption).

46. GLADD, "Sean Penn Wins the Big Prize," http://www.glaad.org/2009/02/23/sean-penn-wins-the-big-prize (posted February 22, 2009; last visited April 4, 2014).

47. Adam Nagourney, "Political Shifts on Gay Rights Lag behind Culture," *New York Times*, June 28, 2009, A1.

48. "Washington State Begins Issuing Same-Sex Marriage Licenses," *theguardian*, http://www.guardian.co.uk/world/2012/dec/06/

washington-state-same-sex-marriage (posted December 6, 2012; last visited December 6, 2012).

CHAPTER 7. DEHUMANIZING CRIMINALS

Concurrences of Justices Marshall and Brennan in *Furman v. Georgia*, 408 U.S. 238, 371 (Marshall) and 305 (Brennan) (1972).

1. Adam Liptak, "Group Gives Up Death Penalty Work," *New York Times*, January 5, 2010, A11.

2. See Bender, *Greasers and Gringos*, 128, and Howard W. Allen and Jerome M. Clubb, *Race, Class, and the Death Penalty: Capital Punishment in American History* (Albany: State University of New York Press, 2008), 81–82 (describing how crowds attended lynchings in which the victims were burned, tortured, and mutilated, with body parts sold as souvenirs).

3. Christopher Berry-Dee and Tony Brown, *Monsters of Death Row: Dead Men and Women Walking* (London: Virgin Books, 2003), ix.

4. Sandy Friend, "Forever Fighting in Memory of Michael Lyons," https://www. change.org/petitions/forever-fighting-in-memory-of-michael-lyons (last visited September 10, 2012).

5. Quoted in Sarah Hoye and Sunny Hostin, "Doctor Found Guilty of First-Degree Murder in Philadelphia Abortion Case," http://www.cnn.com/2013/05/13/justice/ pennsylvania-abortion-doctor-trial (posted May 14, 2013; last visited October 25, 2013).

6. Raymond Paternoster, Robert Brame, and Sarah Bacon, *The Death Penalty: America's Experience with Capital Punishment* (New York: Oxford University Press, 2008), 7–8; see also Richard Francis, *Judge Sewall's Apology: The Salem Witch Trials and the Forming of an American Conscience* (New York: HarperCollins, 2005) (story of one of the Salem witch-trial judges who apologized five years later for his role).

7. David Garland, *Peculiar Institution: America's Death Penalty in an Age of Abolition* (Cambridge, MA: Belknap Press, 2010), 116.

8. Allen and Clubb, *Race, Class*, 91.

9. *Coker v. Georgia*, 433 U.S. 584 (1977).

10. *Kennedy v. Louisiana*, 554 U.S. 407 (2008).

11. *Enmund v. Florida*, 458 U.S. 782 (1982).

12. *Atkins v. Virginia*, 536 U.S. 304, 316 (2002) (leaving to states the determination of mental deficiency; although the defendant, Daryl Atkins, was later adjudged as not being mentally deficient and therefore fit for execution, his sentence was later commuted to life in prison based on prosecutorial misconduct in his first trial).

13. *Roper v. Simmons*, 543 U.S. 551 (2005).

14. *Miller v. Alabama*, 132 S. Ct. 2455 (2012) (the Court struck down a sentencing scheme that mandated life without the possibility of parole and did not consider the argument that the Constitution's bar on cruel and unusual punishment

categorically barred all sentences of life without the possibility of parole for juvenile offenders).

15. *Campbell v. Wood*, 18 F.3d 662, 687 (9th Cir. 1994) (the lower court determined that "the mechanisms involved in bringing about unconsciousness and death in judicial hanging occur extremely rapidly, that unconsciousness was likely to be immediate or within a matter of seconds, and that death would follow rapidly thereafter."). Washington law now supplies the optional method of lethal injection. See Wa. Rev. Code §10.95.180 ("The punishment of death shall be supervised by the superintendent of the penitentiary and shall be inflicted by intravenous injection of a substance or substances in a lethal quantity sufficient to cause death and until the defendant is dead, or, at the election of the defendant, by hanging by the neck until the defendant is dead.").

16. Berry-Dee and Brown, *Monsters of Death Row*, 10 (noting that Florida now allows the alternate method of lethal injection).

17. Ibid.

18. *Dawson v. State*, 554 S.E.2d 137, 143 (Ga. 2001).

19. Scott Christianson, *The Last Gasp: The Rise and Fall of the American Gas Chamber* (Berkeley: University of California Press, 2010) (discussing how Americans designed and built the gas chamber that later served as the model for the Final Solution).

20. Ibid., 2.

21. See *Fierro v. Gomez*, 77 F.3d 301 (9th Cir. 1996) (holding that the California protocol for the gas chamber constitutes cruel and unusual punishment). The Supreme Court then vacated the decision in light of California's subsequent granting to prisoners the option of execution by lethal injection. 519 U.S. 918 (1996).

22. Garland, *Peculiar Institution*, 118.

23. *Wilkerson v. Utah*, 99 U.S. 130 (1878). See also *Louisiana ex rel. Francis v. Resweber*, 329 U.S. 459 (1947) (plurality of Supreme Court permitted second attempt at executing a prisoner by electrocution after mechanical malfunction in the electric chair frustrated the first attempt).

24. *Baze v. Rees*, 553 U.S. 35, 50 (2008).

25. Dana Ford and Ashley Fantz, "Controversial Execution in Ohio Uses New Drug Combination," http://www.cnn.com/2014/01/16/justice/ohio-dennis-mcguire-execution/ (last visited February 4, 2014).

26. Lindsey Bever, "Botched Oklahoma Execution Reignites Death Penalty Debate," *Washington Post*, http://www.washingtonpost.com/news/morning-mix/wp/2014/04/30/botched-oklahoma-execution-reignites-death-penalty-debate/ (posted April 30, 2014; last visited May 2, 2014).

27. *Furman v. Georgia*, 408 U.S. 238 (1972).

28. Paternoster, Brame, and Bacon, *Death Penalty*, 108; Death Penalty Information Center, "History of the Death Penalty" in *The Death Penalty: Debating the Moral, Legal, and Political Issues*, ed. Robert M. Baird and Stuart E. Rosenbaum (Amherst, NY: Prometheus Books, 2011), 28.

29. Jackson et al., *Legal Lynching*, 13.

30. Garland, *Peculiar Institution*, 218.

31. Ibid., 218–219 (thirty-three executions for rape and eight for armed robbery).

32. The Supreme Court refused to hear the case and to overturn capital punishment. *Buck v. Thaler*, 130 S. Ct. 2096 (2010). Earlier, the Texas Court of Criminal Appeals had upheld the death sentence of a Latino defendant despite expert testimony that his Argentine background was "a factor weighing in favor of future dangerousness." Although the Texas attorney general relented before the U.S. Supreme Court and agreed to a new sentencing hearing, the defendant was ultimately denied this hearing because the court ruled his lawyers had failed to object in a timely fashion to the expert's prejudicial testimony at the original sentencing. *Saldano v. State*, 70 S.W.3d 873 (Tex. Ct. Crim. App. 2002).

33. Allen and Clubb, *Race, Class*, 81, 83.

34. Ibid., 69.

35. Innocence Project, "The Innocent and the Death Penalty," http://www.innocenceproject.org/Content/The_Innocent_and_the_Death_Penalty.php (last visited April 2, 2014) (detailing how eighteen death-row inmates were exonerated by DNA evidence); see also Jackson et al., *Legal Lynching*, 117 (stating that more than one-third of Illinois capital convictions were reversed from 1977 to 1999 because of "fundamental error.").

36. For example, Paternoster, Brame, and Bacon, *Death Penalty*, 110 (detailing the case of Earl Washington Jr., a mentally disabled black man, scheduled for execution in Virginia for the rape and murder of a white woman, who was exonerated by DNA evidence and later found to have been convicted using a confession deliberately falsified by a Virginia state police investigator); *Brown v. Mississippi*, 297 U.S. 278 (1936) (the Supreme Court reversed the death sentences of black defendants who had been convicted based on their confessions procured by torture; the sheriff had whipped them and strung one from a tree).

37. "Report of the Council to the Membership of the American Law Institute on the Matter of the Death Penalty," http://www.ali.org/doc/Capital%20Punishment_web.pdf (posted April 15, 2009; last visited September 10, 2012).

38. Christianson, *Last Gasp*, 223.

39. Helen Jung, "Gov. John Kitzhaber: Oregon Death Penalty Fails 'Basic Standards of Justice,'" *Oregonian*, http://www.oregonlive.com/pacific-northwest-news/index.ssf/2011/11/gov_john_kitzhaber_oregon_deat.html (posted November 22, 2011; last visited September 12, 2012).

40. See *Gregg v. Georgia*, 428 U.S. 153 (1976) (joint opinion of Justices Stewart, Powell, and Stevens, identifying "retribution and deterrence of capital crimes by prospective offenders" as the two social purposes the death penalty serves).

41. *Furman v. Georgia*, 408 U.S. 238, 301 (concurrence of Justice Brennan, relying on Justice Marshall's finding).

42. Bender, *Run for the Border*, 21–22 (discussing the widespread public opinion in Mexico in the midst of the wrenching drug war that kidnappers who murder their

victims face the death penalty, an outcome so far resisted by Mexican officials); Jackson et al., *Legal Lynching*, 23.

43. Bender, *Run for the Border*, 22–23.

44. Bender, *Run for the Border*, 22 (citing figures from Death Watch International that suggest the true China count might be even higher).

45. Paternoster, Brame, and Bacon, *Death Penalty*, xi.

46. Keith A. Findley and John Pray, "Lessons from the Innocent," https://media.law. wisc.edu/m/ngm9y/findleywarfall01.pdf (last visited October 26, 2013).

47. *Gregg v. Georgia*, 428 U.S. 153 (1976).

48. Garland, *Peculiar Institution*, 43.

49. Quoted in ibid., 63.

50. Tamara Rice Lave, "Shoot to Kill: A Critical Look at Stand Your Ground Laws," *University of Miami Law Review* 67 (2013): 827, 849–850 (describing Florida's law).

51. Ibid.

52. Ibid., 855.

53. Ibid., 850–851.

54. Dream Defenders, Community Justice Project of Florida Legal Services, Inc., and the National Association for the Advancement of Colored People, "Written Statement on Stand Your Ground Laws" (2013), http://dreamdefenders.org/wp-content/uploads/2013/08/SYG_Shadow_Report_ICCPR.pdf (last visited April 4, 2014).

55. "NRA: Stand Your Ground Is a 'Fundamental Human Right,'" http://www. dailykos.com/story/2013/07/17/1224466/-NRA-Stand-Your-Ground-is-a-fundamental-human-right# (posted July 17, 2013; last visited October 28, 2013).

56. Thomas Hobbes, *Leviathan: Or, the Matter, Forme & Power of a Commonwealth Ecclesiasticall and Civill* (reprint, London: Cambridge University Press, 1904), ch. 24.

CHAPTER 8. FLYING WHILE MUSLIM

Coulter quote from February 2006 in Christine Tamer, "Note, Arab Americans, Affirmative Action, and a Quest for Racial Identity," *Texas Journal on Civil Liberties & Civil Rights* 16 (2010): 101, 114. Savage quote from September 2008 in same source, p. 108. Cooksey quote from September 17, 2011, in "Apology from Congressman," http://www.nytimes.com/2001/09/21/us/national-briefing-south-louisiana-apology-from-congressman.html (posted September 21, 2001; last visited April 4, 2014). Quote from Mississippi judge in Scott Kaufman, "Mississippi Judge Ejects Sikh from Court for Refusing to Remove 'That Rag' from His Head," http://www.rawstory.com/rs/2013/09/27/mississsppi-judge-ejects-sikh-from-court-for-refusing-to-remove-that-rag-from-his-head/ (September 17, 2013; last visited October 24, 2013).

1. Jack G. Shaheen, *Reel Bad Arabs: How Hollywood Vilifies a People* (New York: Olive Branch Press, 2001), 11.

2. Michael Welch, *Scapegoats of September 11th: Hate Crimes & State Crimes in the War on Terror* (New Brunswick, NJ: Rutgers University Press, 2006), 74.

3. Liaquat Ali Khan, "The Essentialist Terrorist," *Washburn Law Journal* 45 (2005): 47; see also Jasbir K. Puar and Amit S. Rai, "Monster, Terrorist, Fag: The War on Terrorism and the Production of Docile Patriots," *Social Text* 20 (2002): 117.

4. Quoted in Smith, *Less Than Human*, 23.

5. Amany R. Hacking, "A New Dawn for Muslims: Asserting Their Civil Rights in Post-9/11 America," *Saint Louis University Law Journal* 54 (2010): 917, 919.

6. "Anti-Muslim Subway Posters Prompt NYPD to Increase Security in Stations," http://www.huffingtonpost.com/2012/09/25/anti-muslim-subway-posters-nypd-increase-security_n_1912239.html (posted September 25, 2012; last visited April 4, 2014) (the American Freedom Defense Initiative funded the ads).

7. French, "Native American," 244.

8. Quoted in Christine Tamer, "Note, Arab Americans, Affirmative Action, and a Quest for Racial Identity," *Texas Journal on Civil Liberties & Civil Rights* 16 (2010): 101, 123. The Libertarian Party withdrew its nomination of Landham based on these remarks.

9. Welch, *Scapegoats of September 11th*, 65.

10. Muneer I. Ahmad, "A Rage Shared by Law: Post–September 11 Racial Violence as Crimes of Passion," *California Law Review* 92 (2004): 1259, 1263.

11. Shoba Sivaprasad Wadhia, "Business as Usual: Immigration and the National Security Exception," *Penn State Law Review* 114 (2010): 1485, 1504.

12. Jerome Taylor, "I Never Hated Mark. My Religion Teaches That Forgiveness Is Always Better Than Vengeance," *Independent*, http://www.independent.co.uk/news/world/americas/i-never-hated-mark-my-religion-teaches-that-forgiveness-is-always-better-than-vengeance-2309526.html (posted July 9, 2011; last visited September 19, 2012). The backlash against Arabs was not limited to post–September 11th, as violence targeted Arab Americans in retaliation for the TWA terrorist hijacking in 1985, the Gulf War, and other events.

13. For a list of incidents since September 11th, see "History of Hate: Crimes against Sikhs since 9/11," http://www.huffingtonpost.com/2012/08/07/history-of-hate-crimes-against-sikhs-since-911_n_1751841.html (posted August 7, 2012; last visited April 4, 2014).

14. Sahar F. Aziz, "From the Oppressed to the Terrorist: Muslim American Women Caught in the Crosshairs of Intersectionality," *Hastings Race and Poverty Law Journal* 9 (2012): 191.

15. "Park51 Controversy," http://en.wikipedia.org/wiki/Park51_controversy (last visited April 4, 2014).

16. Hacking, "New Dawn," 926; see generally Sahar F. Aziz, "Sticks and Stones, the Words That Hurt: Entrenched Stereotypes Eight Years after 9/11," *New York City Law Review* 13 (2009): 33.

17. Holly Huffman, "Researcher Recounts Poor Treatment While at A&M," http://www.theeagle.com/news/a_m/article_623e5065-d437-5197-99ef-cf6c2ca6b560.html?mode=jqm (posted February 7, 2009; last visited April 4, 2014).

18. Scott Keyes, "Herman Cain Tells ThinkProgress 'I Will Not Appoint' a Muslim in My Administration," http://thinkprogress.org/politics/2011/03/26/153625/herman-cain-muslims/ (posted March 26, 2011; last visited April 4, 2014).

19. Huma Khan and Amy Bingham, "GOP Debate: Newt Gingrich's Comparison of Muslims and Nazis Sparks Outrage," http://abcnews.go.com/Politics/gop-debate-newt-gingrichs-comparison-muslims-nazis-sparks/story?id=13838355 (posted June 14, 2011; last visited April 4, 2014).]

20. Tamer, "Arab Americans," 105–106.

21. Wadhia, "Business as Usual," 1499–1501.

22. Hilal Elver, "Racializing Islam before and after 9/11: From Melting Pot to Islamophobia," *Transnational Law & Contemporary Problems* 21 (2012): 119, 171.

23. *Awad v. Ziriax*, 670 F.3d 1111 (10th Cir. 2012) (affirming a preliminary injunction against the constitutional amendment), 2013 WL 4441476 (W.D. Okla. 2013) (issuing a permanent injunction); see generally Yaser Ali, "Comment, Shariah and Citizenship: How Islamophobia Is Creating a Second-Class Citizenry in America," *California Law Review* 100 (2012): 1027.

24. Ali, "Shariah and Citizenship," 1045.

25. See Margaret Chon and Donna E. Arzt, "Walking While Muslim," *Law and Contemporary Problems* 68 (2005): 215, 221 n. 27 (discussing the fact that many Muslims would consider the terrorist acts as inconsistent with religious teachings).

26. Ali, "Shariah and Citizenship," 1044.

27. Ahmad, "Rage Shared by Law," 1270.

28. Khan, "Essentialist Terrorist," 74–75.

29. Wadhia, "Business as Usual," 1487. See also *Ashcroft v. Iqbal*, 556 U.S. 662 (2009) (the Supreme Court ruled on Iqbal's lawsuit to clarify and heighten the pleading standard required to survive a motion to dismiss).

30. Wadhia, "Business as Usual," 1493–1495.

31. Further, Article 5 of the Universal Declaration of Human Rights provides that no one shall be subjected to torture or degrading treatment.

32. The Supreme Court rejected the Bush administration's views, in part, on the applicability of the Geneva Convention, see *Hamdan v. Rumsfeld*, 548 U.S. 557 (2006) (holding Article 3 of the Geneva Conventions applicable to Guantánamo detainees, thus guaranteeing trial by a "regularly constituted court affording all the judicial guarantees which are recognized as indispensable by civilized peoples," and finding that the U.S. military commission failed to satisfy this standard).

33. Quoted in Marjorie Cohn, ed. *The United States and Torture: Interrogation, Incarceration, and Abuse* (New York: New York University Press, 2011), 13.

34. Ibid., 7.

35. Quoted in Elver, "Racializing Islam," 145.

36. Tom Malinowski, "Banned State Department Practices," in *Torture: Does It Make Us Safer? Is It Ever OK? A Human Rights Perspective*, ed. Kenneth Roth and Minky Worden (New York: New Press, 2005), 142–144.

37. Welch, *Scapegoats of September 11th*, 119.

38. Ibid., 120.

39. Muneer I. Ahmad, "Resisting Guantánamo: Rights at the Brink of Dehumanization," *Northwestern University Law Review* 103 (2009): 1683, 1691.

40. Ibid., 1687.

41. Anne-Marie Cusac, *Cruel and Unusual: The Culture of Punishment in America* (New Haven, CT: Yale University Press, 2009), 249–250; Cohn, *United States and Torture*, 2–3.

42. Quoted in Smith, *Less Than Human*, 22.

43. Charlie Savage, "Election to Decide Future Interrogation Methods in Terrorism Cases," *New York Times*, September 27, 2012.

44. Although the United States finally adopted this covenant, which was approved by the UN General Assembly, it supplied the reservation that this provision does not restrict rights of free speech protected under the U.S. Constitution. For discussion of the extent to which courts may permissibly restrict hate speech consistent with the guarantee of free speech, see Bender, *Greasers and Gringos*, ch. 13.

45. Chon and Arzt, "Walking While Muslim," 230.

46. Welch, *Scapegoats of September 11th*, 121.

47. Scott Shane, "U.S. Practiced Torture after 9/11, Nonpartisan Review Concludes," http://www.nytimes.com/2013/04/16/world/us-practiced-torture-after-9-11-non-partisan-review-concludes.html?pagewanted=all&_r=0 (posted April 16, 2013; last visited April 26, 2013) (noting that the report compared the torture of suspected terrorist detainees to the internment of Japanese Americans and further suggested torture as a candidate for historical regret).

48. Among the court challenges contested by the government and ultimately holding that the War on Terror detainees were entitled to certain constitutional and other rights are *Boumediene v. Bush*, 553 U.S. 723 (2008) (enemy combatant detainees are entitled to habeas corpus actions to challenge the legality of their detentions), and *Hamdan v. Rumsfeld*, 548 U.S. 557 (2006) (holding Article 3 of the Geneva Conventions applicable to Guantánamo detainees, thus guaranteeing trial by a "regularly constituted court affording all the judicial guarantees which are recognized as indispensable by civilized peoples," and finding that the U.S. military commission failed to satisfy this standard).

49. Quoted in Lance Tapley, "Mass Torture in America: Notes from Supermax Prisons," in *The United States and Torture: Interrogation, Incarceration, and Abuse*, ed. Marjorie Cohn (New York: New York University Press, 2011), 215, 232.

50. Ibid., 219.

51. Lance Tapley, "Americans Face Guantanamo-Like Torture Everyday in a Super-Max Prison Near You," http://www.alternet.org/story/149233/ameri-cans_face_guantanamo-like_torture_everyday_in_a_super-max_prison_near_you?page=0%2Co (posted January 18, 2011; last visited September 19, 2012).

52. Ibid.

53. Andrew Gumbel, "How Did a Form of Torture Become Policy in America's Prison System?," http://www.alternet.org/civil-liberties/

how-did-form-torture-become-policy-americas-prison-system (posted October 11, 2013; last visited October 26, 2013) (explaining that the current system of long-term solitary confinement aims to address prison gangs and noting that the U.N.'s Human Rights Council declared solitary confinement for more than fifteen days unjustifiable).

54. Tapley, "Americans Face Guantanamo."

55. Cusac, *Cruel and Unusual*, 249.

56. Jamie Fellner, "Torture in U.S. Prisons," in *Torture: Does It Make Us Safer? Is It Ever OK? A Human Rights Perspective*, ed. Kenneth Roth and Minky Worden (New York: New Press, 2005), 176.

CHAPTER 9. FROM SLAVERY TO THE NEW JIM CROW OF MASS INCARCERATION

"After Obama Victory, Most Racist Tweets Ever," http://rollingout.com/entertainment/after-obama-victory-most-racist-tweets-ever/attachment/twitter14/ (last visited April 5, 2014). Kirsten West Savali, "GOP Arizona Radio Host: 'Obama Is the First Monkey President,'" http://newsone.com/2021269/barbara-espinosa-obama-monkey/ (June 17, 2012; last visited November 10, 2012).

1. Ian Haney López and Michael Olivas, "Jim Crow, Mexican Americans, and the Anti-Subordination Constitution: The Story of *Hernandez v. Texas*," in *Race Law Stories*, ed. Rachel F. Moran and Devon W. Carbado (New York: Foundation Press, 2008), 273, 295.

2. Bender, *Greasers and Gringos*, 144–145.

3. Ferriss and Sandoval, *Fight in the Fields*, 35.

4. Bender, *Greasers and Gringos*, 143.

5. NBC News, "AP Poll: Majority Harbor Prejudice against Blacks," October 27, 2012, http://usnews.nbcnews.com/_news/2012/10/27/14740413-ap-poll-majority-harbor-prejudice-against-blacks?lite [hereinafter AP Poll] (last visited December 4, 2012) (when measuring implicit anti-Latino/a sentiments, the number jumped to 57 percent from 52 percent expressing explicit anti-Latino/a sentiments).

6. See generally Michael L. Perlin, *The Hidden Prejudice: Mental Disability on Trial* (Washington, DC: American Psychological Association, 2000).

7. Ray Sanchez, "Feds: No Charges in Michigan Police Shooting of Homeless Man," http://www.cnn.com/2014/02/25/justice/michigan-police-shooting/ (posted February 25, 2014; last visited April 4, 2014).

8. Casey McNerthney, "Woodcarver's Family to Get $1.5 Million from City," http://www.seattlepi.com/local/article/Woodcarvers-family-to-get-1-5-million-from-city-1359018.php (posted August 30, 2011; last visited April 4, 2014).

9. For example, Derrick Bell, *Faces at the Bottom of the Well: The Permanence of Racism* (New York: Basic Books, 1992).

10. Bootie Cosgrove-Mather, "AIDS Drugs Tested on Foster Kids," http://www.cbsnews.com/news/aids-drugs-tested-on-foster-kids/ (posted May 4, 2005; last visited April 13, 2014).

11. See generally Steven Pinker, *The Better Angels of Our Nature: Why Violence Has Declined* (New York: Viking Press, 2011).

12. Keith Edwards, "Hard Truths for Hispanic and African-American Voters," http://www.americanthinker.com/2012/09/hard_truths_for_hispanic_and_african-american_voters.html (posted September 15, 2012; last visited November 22, 2012).

13. "Subprime in Black and White," http://www.nytimes.com/2007/10/17/opinion/17wed2.html (posted October 17, 2007; last visited April 6, 2013) (Latinos/as were similarly targeted by subprime lenders).

14. AP Poll.

15. See AP Poll (implicit antiblack sentiments jumped from 49 to 56 percent from 2008 to 2012).

16. For a map depicting the origin of these racist tweets, see Jorge Rivas, "Map Shows You Where Those Racists Tweeting after Obama Election Live," http://colorlines.com/archives/2012/11/a_new_map_shows_you_where_those_racists_tweeting_after_obamas_re-election_live.html (posted November 9, 2012; last visited April 4, 2012).

17. Dana Bash, "Ted Nugent Hits Campaign Trail after Calling Obama 'Subhuman Mongrel,'" http://politicalticker.blogs.cnn.com/2014/02/18/ted-nugent-hits-campaign-trail-for-texas-gop-candidate/ (February 18, 2014; last visited April 2, 2014).

18. John Blake, "Parallels to Country's Racist Past Haunt Age of Obama," http://inamerica.blogs.cnn.com/2012/11/01/parallels-to-countrys-racist-past-haunt-age-of-obama/ (posted November 1, 2012; last visited November 11, 2012) (remarks of Nsenga Burton).

19. An Internet copy of this book, embraced by some of today's white supremacists, can be found at http://www.lvulvu.us/pdf/carroll.pdf; Brennan, *Dehumanizing the Vulnerable*, 6.

20. Tsesis, *We Shall Overcome*, 23.

21. *Dred Scott v. Sandford*, 60 U.S. 393 (1857).

22. *Mitchell v. Wells*, 37 Miss. 235 (1859) (known then as the High Court of Errors and Appeals of Mississippi).

23. Quoted in Tsesis, *We Shall Overcome*, 54.

24. Smith, *Less Than Human*, 122–123 (discussing how Benga killed himself years after his display).

25. "Ota Benga," Wikipedia, http://en.wikipedia.org/wiki/Ota_Benga (last visited November 12, 2012).

26. Quoted in Wilma King, "'Suffer with Them Till Death': Slave Women and Their Children in Nineteenth-Century America," in *More Than Chattel: Black Women and Slavery in the Americas*, ed. David Barry Gaspar and Darlene Clark Hine (Bloomington: Indiana University Press, 1996), 147. See generally Adrienne Davis, "'Don't Let Nobody Bother Yo' Principle': The Sexual Economy of American Slavery," in *Still Brave: The Evolution of Black Women's Studies*, ed. Stanlie M. James, Frances Smith Foster, and Beverly Guy-Sheftall (New York: Feminist Press, 2009); F. Michael Higginbotham, *Ghosts of Jim Crow: Ending Racism in Post-Racial*

America (New York: New York University Press, 2013), 55 (describing the murder conviction and hanging of a black woman in Missouri after the court rejected her proffered defense of resisting rape by her master; slave women were regarded as property without the right to defend themselves).

27. Douglas A. Blackmon, *Slavery by Another Name: The Re-Enslavement of Black Americans from the Civil War to World War II* (New York: Doubleday, 2008); see also Paternoster, Brame, and Bacon, *Death Penalty*, 167–168.

28. Blackmon, *Slavery by Another Name*, 57.

29. Ibid., 72.

30. Ibid., 381.

31. *Plessy v. Ferguson*, 163 U.S. 537 (1896).

32. Tsesis, *We Shall Overcome*, 130.

33. Finally, in *Shelley v. Kraemer*, 334 U.S. 1 (1948), the Supreme Court invalidated racially restrictive covenants.

34. Earlier, starting in 1917, the Supreme Court struck down as unconstitutional the racially discriminatory zoning ordinances many municipalities had adopted to prevent blacks from moving into white neighborhoods, in the supposed interest of preventing racial conflict. See *Buchanan v. Warley*, 245 U.S. 60 (1917); *Harmon v. Tyler*, 273 U.S. 668 (1927) (the ordinance prevented black occupancy in a white neighborhood absent majority white-resident consent).

35. *Loving v. Virginia*, 388 U.S. 1 (1967). Earlier, the California Supreme Court had relied on the Fourteenth Amendment to strike down California's law prohibiting marriage between a white person and a "Negro, mulatto, Mongolian, or member of the Malay race," finding the law unconstitutionally vague and a violation of equal protection. *Perez v. Sharp*, 198 P.2d 17 (Cal. 1948) (this case is also known as *Perez v. Lippold*).

36. Quoted in Tsesis, *We Shall Overcome*, 273.

37. See generally Derrick Bell, *And We Are Not Saved: The Elusive Quest for Racial Justice* (New York: Basic Books, 1987), 207 (suggesting that antimiscegenation laws were based more on preventing blacks from making economic and cultural gains than on an abhorrence of interracial sex).

38. Jon Terbush, "Nearly Half of Mississippi Republicans Think Interracial Marriage Should Be Illegal," http://tpmdc.talkingpointsmemo.com/2011/04/nearly-of-mississippi-republicans-think-interracial-marriage-should-be-illegal.php (posted April 7, 2011; last visited November 22, 2012).

39. *Richardson v. Ramirez*, 418 U.S. 24 (1974).

40. "Exhibit Traces History of Voting Rights Act," http://www.nbcnews.com/id/8839169/ns/us_news-life/t/exhibit-traces-history-voting-rights-act/#.UXrsl-WAW9P4 (posted August 5, 2005; last visited April 26, 2013).

41. Quoted in John Hope Franklin and Alfred A. Moss Jr., "The Triumph of White Supremacy," in *When Sorry Isn't Enough: The Controversy over Apologies and Reparations for Human Injustice*, ed. Roy L. Brooks (New York: New York University Press, 1999), 401, 403–404.

42. The Supreme Court has recognized federal constraints on state identification laws. See *Arizona v. Inter Tribal Council of Arizona, Inc.*, 133 S. Ct. 2247 (2013) (invalidating an Arizona requirement that registering voters prove citizenship as contrary to the federal National Voter Registration Act). At the same time, the Supreme Court struck down a key section of the Voting Rights Act that required certain jurisdictions with notorious records of voting suppression to obtain, in advance, federal clearance of nondiscrimination for voting changes such as redistricting or even moving polling locations. *Shelby County, Ala. v. Holder*, 133 S. Ct. 2612 (2013).

43. *Palmer v. Thompson*, 403 U.S. 217 (1971).

44. Bender, *One Night in America*, 100.

45. Frontline, "Thirty Years of America's Drug War: A Chronology," n.d. http://www. pbs.org/wgbh/pages/frontline/shows/drugs/cron/ (last visited April 2, 2014).

46. Quoted in "War on Drugs," http://en.wikipedia.org/wiki/War_on_Drugs (last visited November 8, 2013).

47. Paul Butler, *Let's Get Free: A Hip-Hop Theory of Justice* (New York: New Press, 2009), 44.

48. Bender, *Run for the Border*, 97.

49. *Reefer Madness*, Motion Picture Ventures, 1936 (original title: *Tell Your Children*). Quoted in Steven W. Bender, "Joint Reform?: The Interplay of State, Federal, and Hemispheric Regulation of Recreational Marijuana and the Failed War on Drugs," *Albany Government Law Review* 6 (2013): 359, 363.

50. See generally andré douglas pond cummings, "President Obama Signs Bill Lowering Crack-Powder Cocaine Sentencing Disparity," http://www.saltlaw.org/blog/2010/09/22/president-obama-signs-bill-lowering-crack-powder-cocaine-sentencing-disparity/ (posted September 22, 2010; last visited November 14, 2012).

51. James P. Gray, *Why Our Drug Laws Have Failed and What We Can Do about It: A Judicial Indictment of the War on Drugs* (Philadelphia: Temple University Press, 2001).

52. Michelle Alexander, *The New Jim Crow: Mass Incarceration in the Age of Colorblindness* (New York: New Press, 2010).

53. Bender, *Run for the Border*, 165.

54. Bender, *Greasers and Gringos*, 52 (among other things, the training film instructed officers to seek out "males of foreign nationalities, mainly Cuban, Colombians, Puerto Ricans, or other swarthy outlanders").

55. *Illinois v. Caballes*, 543 U.S. 405 (2005).

56. Frank Rudy Cooper, "The Un-Balanced Fourth Amendment: A Cultural Study of the Drug War, Racial Profiling and *Arvizu*," *Villanova Lew Review* 47 (2002): 851, 879 (also arguing that law enforcement's call for a drug war influenced the Supreme Court to authorize racial profiling).

57. *Whren v. United States*, 517 U.S. 806 (1996).

58. See generally Kevin R. Johnson, "The Song Remains the Same: The Story of *Whren v. United States*," in *Race Law Stories*, ed. Rachel F. Moran and Devon W. Carbado (New York: Foundation Press, 2008), 419, 438–439.

59. See *Terry v. Ohio*, 392 U.S. 1 (1968). A legal challenge to the discriminatory stop-and-frisk practices of New York City police, which targeted black and Latino/a residents, as constitutional violations resulted in a permanent injunction and other remedies, *Floyd v. City of New York*, 2013 WL 4046209 (S.D.N.Y. 2013); these were later stayed from taking effect pending appeal by the city to the federal appeals court. In 2014, New York City's new mayor dropped the appeal.

60. Nate Blakeslee, *Tulia: Race, Cocaine, and Corruption in a Small Texas Town* (New York: Public Affairs, 2005).

61. See Bender, *Greasers and Gringos*, 55–57 (discussing the permissibility of racial profiling in immigration enforcement).

62. Alexander, *New Jim Crow*, 59.

63. Ibid., 6.

64. NAACP, *Misplaced Priorities: Over Incarcerate, Under Educate,* May 2011, 2nd ed., http://naacp.3cdn.net/01d6f368edbe135234_bq0m68x5h.pdf (last visited November 14, 2012).

65. Ibid., 10.

66. Alexander, *New Jim Crow*, 60.

67. Ibid., 59–60.

68. Human Rights Watch, "United States: Stark Race Disparities in Drug Incarceration," http://www.hrw.org/news/2000/06/07/united-states-stark-race-disparities-drug-incarceration (posted June 8, 2000; last visited April 4, 2014).

69. Ibid.

70. Bender, *Run for the Border*, 164–165.

71. Alexander, *New Jim Crow*, 6–7.

72. Ibid., 138.

73. See also *Department of Housing and Urban Development v. Rucker*, 535 U.S. 125 (2002) (upholding a federal law construed to allow public-housing evictions for drug-related activity by household members such as children or guests of the tenant, regardless of whether the tenant knew or should have known of the activity).

74. Nine of the states have lifetime bans for drug felons, and the other twenty-three impose partial bans, such as barring just those convicted of trafficking.

75. Alexander, *New Jim Crow*, 154.

76. NAACP, "Misplaced Priorities," 12.

77. Ibid., 3.

78. See Higginbotham, *Ghosts of Jim Crow*, 184–187 (proposing a federal constitutional amendment guaranteeing a right to education as a basis for imposing constitutionally mandated equity in public school funding at the state level).

79. Alexander, *New Jim Crow*, 175.

80. NAACP, "Misplaced Priorities," 4.

81. Although I sometimes use the terms *decriminalization* and *legalization* interchangeably, I use the term *decriminalization* to refer to the retention of government regulation over a particular substance, such as through controlled sales or allowed possession of regulated quantities, criminal restrictions on possession by

minors and driving while intoxicated, and the possibility of violations carrying the sanction only of mandatory admission to treatment programs.

82. Bender, *Run for the Border*, 166.

83. Alexander, *New Jim Crow*, 138.

84. "Officer Who Sent 'Jungle-Monkey' E-mail: 'I Am Not a Racist,'" http://www.cnn.com/2009/US/07/30/gates.police.apology/ (posted July 30, 2009; last visited April 4, 2014).

85. Quoted in Gordon W. Allport, *The Nature of Prejudice*, 25th anniversary ed. (Reading, MA: Addison-Wesley, 1979), 326.

CHAPTER 10. YOU'VE COME A LONG WAY, BABY?

1. In contrast to social-contract theory, which posits that we exchanged the brutal and insecure state of nature for government-protected freedoms, consider this account of the failure of social-contract theory to address the subordinate freedoms of women: Carole Pateman, *The Sexual Contact* (Stanford, CA: Stanford University Press, 1988). For discussion of the similar gap between social-contract theory and the reality of unaddressed color-line subordination, see Charles W. Mills, *The Racial Contract* (Ithaca, NY: Cornell University Press, 1997).

2. *Bradwell v. State*, 83 U.S. 130, 141 (1872) (Justice Bradley concurrence).

3. Ephesians 5:22 (King James Bible translation).

4. *Frontiero v. Richardson*, 411 U.S. 677, 684 (1973).

5. Ibid., 685.

6. See Debran Rowland, *The Boundaries of Her Body: The Troubling History of Women's Rights in America* (Naperville, IL: Sphinx, 2004), 17; Joseph William Singer, *Property Law: Rules, Policies, and Practices* (New York: Wolters Kluwer, 2010), 82.

7. Singer, *Property*, 689–690 (discussing the shortcomings of these laws with regard to income earned inside the home, among other things).

8. *Minor v. Happersett*, 88 U.S. 162 (1874).

9. Alex Kane, "Female Tea Party Leader Says Women Are Too 'Diabolical' to Vote," http://www.alternet.org/news-amp-politics/female-tea-party-leader-says-women-are-too-diabolical-vote (posted October 16, 2012; last visited April 4, 2014).

10. *Commonwealth v. Welosky*, 177 N.E. 656 (Mass. 1931).

11. Colleen Walsh, "Hard-Earned Gains for Women at Harvard," *Harvard Gazette*, http://news.harvard.edu/gazette/story/2012/04/hard-earned-gains-for-women-at-harvard/ (posted April 26, 2012; last visited November 20, 2012).

12. Michelle Fabio, "The Ongoing Battle over Equal Pay for Women in the Workplace," http://www.legalzoom.com/business-law/employment-law/ongoing-battle-over-equal (last visited November 20, 2012).

13. Caroline A. Forell and Donna M. Matthews, *A Law of Her Own: The Reasonable Woman as a Measure of Man* (New York: New York University Press, 2000), 232–234 (detailing how the essence of the spousal-rape exemption remains despite law reform, given, among other things, the almost insurmountable presumption of consent attendant to marriage).

14. Chris Hedges, *Empire of Illusion: The End of Literacy and the Triumph of Spectacle* (New York: Nation Books, 2009).

15. See Brennan, *Dehumanizing the Vulnerable*.

16. William Brennan, *The Abortion Holocaust: Today's Final Solution* (St. Louis, MO: Landmark Press, 1983).

17. Brennan, *Dehumanizing the Vulnerable*, 90 (discussing an April 22, 1990, article in *Parade Magazine*).

18. *Roe v. Wade*, 410 U.S. 113 (1973); see also *Doe v. Bolton*, 410 U.S. 179 (1973) (a companion case allowing abortion at any time when necessary to protect a woman's health).

19. *Planned Parenthood of Southeastern Pa. v. Casey*, 505 U.S. 833 (1992).

20. *Isaacson v. Horne*, 716 F.3d 1213 (9th Cir. 2013). The Supreme Court refused to consider the appeal, thus leaving in place the federal appellate court's invalidation of the law as unconstitutional.

21. *Griswold v. Connecticut*, 381 U.S. 479 (1965).

22. John Eligon and Michael Schwirtz, "Senate Candidate Provokes Ire with 'Legitimate Rape' Comment," *New York Times*, http://www.nytimes.com/2012/08/20/us/politics/todd-akin-provokes-ire-with-legitimate-rape-comment.html?_r=0 (posted August 19, 2012; last visited April 4, 2014).

23. Annie Groer, "Indiana GOP Senate Hopeful Richard Mourdock Says God 'Intended' Rape Pregnancies," *Washington Post*, http://www.washingtonpost.com/blogs/she-the-people/wp/2012/10/24/indiana-gop-senate-hopeful-richard-mourdock-says-god-intended-rape-pregnancies/ (posted October 24, 2012; last visited May 2, 2015).

24. "Joe Walsh on Abortion: No Exception for 'Life of the Mother' Thanks to 'Advances in Science and Technology,'" http://www.huffingtonpost.com/2012/10/18/joe-walsh-abortion-exception_n_1983701.html (posted October 18, 2012; last visited April 4, 2014).

25. "Transcript, Tom Hartmann: Surging Republican Santorum Thinks Condoms Should Be Outlawed," http://www.thomhartmann.com/blog/2012/01/transcript-thom-hartmann-surging-republican-santorum-thinks-condoms-should-be-outlawed- (posted January 29, 2012; last visited November 21, 2012).

26. National Institute for Reproductive Health, "Quick Sheet: Barriers to Contraceptive Access for Low-Income Women," n.d., http://www.nirhealth.org/sections/publications/documents/contraceptiveaccessquicksheetFINAL.pdf (last visited November 21, 2012).

27. Bell, *Not Saved*, 229 (suggesting that before *Roe* wealthy women were nonetheless able to obtain relatively safe, albeit expensive, abortions).

28. For example, in 2013 Congress reauthorized the Violence against Women Act, albeit after a prolonged legislative fight.

29. Center for Reproductive Rights, "Bill of Reproductive Rights," http://www.drawtheline.org/sign-now/ (last visited April 5, 2014).

30. Convention on the Elimination of All Forms of Discrimination against Women, http://www.un.org/womenwatch/daw/cedaw/text/econvention.htm (last visited April 5, 2014).

CHAPTER 11. INTERNATIONAL DEHUMANIZATION

Tim O'Brien, *The Things They Carried* (New York: Houghton Mifflin, 1990), 225–226 (collection of stories centered on the Vietnam War).

1. Bender, *Run for the Border*, 135; Evelyn H. Cruz, "Through Mexican Eyes: Mexican Perspectives on Transmigration," *Valparaiso University Law Review* 46 (2012): 1019 (discussing the risks that Central and South Americans face in migrating through Mexico to the United States and noting that the typical crossing takes a month).

2. "Central America Edges Out Mexico for Leader in Undocumented Immigrants," http://latino.foxnews.com/latino/politics/2012/12/22/central-america-is-new-leader-for-undocumented-immigrants-in-us/ (posted December 22, 2012; last visited December 22, 2012).

3. Bender, *Run for the Border*, 132–133.

4. Bender, *Run for the Border*, 22–25.

5. Ibid., 81.

6. Smith, *Less Than Human*, 83.

7. Ibid., 84.

8. Goldhagen, *Worse Than War*, 201.

9. Smith, *Less Than Human*, 19; see also ibid., 17 (discussing how, in turn, the Japanese depicted American and British leaders as subhuman enemies with horns, tails, claws, or fangs).

10. Goldhagen, *Worse Than War*, 201.

11. Smith, *Less Than Human*, 20.

12. Goldhagen, *Worse Than War*, 201.

13. Captain Steven P. Gibb, "The Applicability of the Laws of Land Warfare to U.S. Army Aviation," *Military Law Review* 73 (1976): 25, 59.

14. Rush Limbaugh, "Japan Nixed Bam's A-Bomb Apology," http://www.rushlimbaugh.com/daily/2011/10/12/japan_nixed_bam_s_a_bomb_apology (posted October 12, 2011; last visited December 7, 2012) (transcript of a Rush Limbaugh show discussing a Wikileaks disclosure of government documents revealing the offer of an apology).

15. Charles Babington, "Clinton: Support for Guatemala Was Wrong," *Washington Post*, March 11, 1999, A1.

16. George E. Bisharat, "Sanctions as Genocide," *Transnational Law & Contemporary Problems* 11 (2001): 379 (concluding that a prima facie case may be made under the U.N. Convention, which addresses killing or causing serious bodily or mental harm or deliberately inflicting conditions of life calculated to bring about the physical destruction of a national, ethnic, racial, or religious group).

17. Matthew Lee, "Clinton: Mexico Violence Fueled by America's 'Insatiable' Demand for Drugs," http://www.huffingtonpost.com/2009/03/25/clinton-mexico-trip-agend_n_178983.html (posted March 25, 2009; last visited April 4, 2014).

18. Sara Miller Llana, "Mexico Birthday Party Massacre Bears Resemblance to Juarez Killings," http://www.csmonitor.com/World/Americas/2010/0719/Mexico-birth-day-party-massacre-bears-resemblance-to-Juarez-killings (posted July 19, 2010; last visited April 4, 2014).

19. Richard Delgado, "Norms and Normal Science: Toward a Critique of Normativity in Legal Thought," *University of Pennsylvania Law Review* 139 (1991): 993, 945.

20. For background, see Frank H. Wu, "Why Vincent Chin Matters," http://www.nytimes.com/2012/06/23/opinion/why-vincent-chin-matters.html (posted June 22, 2012; last visited April 4, 2014).

21. See Steven W. Bender, "Gringo Alley," *University of California, Davis Law Review* 45 (2012): 1925, 1933 (discussing the implications of the use of drone technology in immigration and border control).

22. Finally enacted in 2014, the Ugandan bill, while failing to impose the death penalty, did toughen penalties against gay people and imposed punishments that include life imprisonment.

CONCLUSION

Pope Francis on Vatican Radio, September 24, 2013.

1. *Brown v. Board of Education*, 347 U.S. 483 (1954); *Plessy v. Ferguson*, 163 U.S. 537 (1896); *Lawrence v. Texas*, 539 U.S. 558 (2003); *Bowers v. Hardwick*, 478 U.S. 186 (1986).

2. See IIya Somin, "How Empathy Can Distort Judges' Thinking and Lead to Bad Decisions," http://www.latimes.com/news/opinion/opinionla/la-oew-chemerin-sky-somin28-2009may28,0,4921073.story (posted May 28, 2009; last visited April 7, 2013); Bender, "Compassionate Immigration Reform," 110–111.

3. See Bender, "Joint Reform?"

4. See Bender, *Greasers and Gringos*, 222.

5. Sharyn Jackson, "Iowa Gay Marriage Ruling a Turning Point for Justices," http://www.usatoday.com/story/news/nation/2014/04/02/iowa-gay-marriage-ruling-a-turning-point-for-justices/7237453/ (posted April 2, 2014; last visited April 4, 2014).

6. Bender, *Greasers and Gringos*, 222.

7. Shaheen, *Reel Bad Arabs*.

8. The commercial is available at AdRespect, http://www.adrespect.org/common/adlibrary/adlibrarydetails.cfm?QID=9&ClientID=11064 (last visited April 6, 2014).

9. See Bender, *Greasers and Gringos*.

10. See *Greenbelt Cooperative Publishing Association, Inc. v. Bresler*, 398 U.S. 6 (1970); *Old Dominion Branch No. 496, National Association of Letter Carriers, AFL-CIO v. Austin*, 418 U.S. 264 (1974).

11. See generally "Adios, Lou Dobbs," http://news.newamericamedia.org/news/view_article.html?article_id=427ccb3621f86e9a443fb77c44dd2077 (posted November 13, 2009; last visited November 24, 2012) (interview of the co-founder of Presente.org, Roberto Lovato).

12. Paul Colford, "'Illegal Immigrant' No More," http://blog.ap.org/2013/04/02/illegal-immigrant-no-more/ (posted April 2, 2013; last visited April 6, 2013).

13. Judy Faber, "CBS Fires Don Imus over Racial Slur," http://www.cbsnews.com/news/cbs-fires-don-imus-over-racial-slur/ (posted April 12, 2007; last visited April 4, 2014).

14. See generally Steven W. Bender, "Knocked Down Again: An East L.A. Story on the Geography of Color and Colors," *Harvard Latino Law Review* 12 (2009): 109.

15. Bender, *One Night in America.*

16. Richard Rorty, *Truth and Progress: Philosophical Papers,* vol. 3 (New York: Cambridge University Press, 1998), 185.

17. Bender, "Compassionate Immigration Reform," 112.

18. Lynn Hunt, *Inventing Human Rights: A History* (New York: Norton, 2007); see also Richard Delgado, "Watching the Opera in Silence: Disgust, Autonomy, and the Search for Universal Human Rights," *University of Pittsburgh Law Review* 70 (2008): 277 (reviewing Hunt's work); Thomas R. Rochon, *Culture Moves: Ideas, Activism, and Changing Values* (Princeton, NJ: Princeton University Press, 1998), 227 (explaining that the cultural conversion against slavery was in part attributable to the publication of the sympathetic *Uncle Tom's Cabin,* which became part of popular culture); Pinker, *Better Angels,* 589–590 (discussing studies and opposing views on whether reading fiction fosters empathy).

19. Delgado, "Watching the Opera," 295.

20. Bender, *Tierra y Libertad,* ch. 4.

21. Linda A. Jackson, *Stereotypes, Emotions, Behavior, and Overall Attitudes toward Hispanics by Anglos,* Michigan State University Research Report 10, 1995, http://www.jsri.msu.edu/pdfs/rr/rr10.pdf (last visited November 24, 2012).

22. Carrasco, *Sexuality and Discrimination,* 9 (finding that only 55 percent of those who did not know a gay person favored equality).

23. CNN, "CNN Poll: 'Rob Portman Effect' Fuels Support for Same-Sex Marriage," http://politicalticker.blogs.cnn.com/2013/03/25/cnn-poll-rob-portman-effect-fuels-support-for-same-sex-marriage/ (posted March 25, 2013; last visited April 6, 2013).

24. The Pew Research Center poll in 2013 also confirmed the shift in support for same-sex marriage, finding 49 percent supporting same-sex marriage and 44 percent opposed, in contrast to an earlier poll, in 2003, finding most U.S. residents (58 percent) opposed and only 33 percent in favor. Pew Research Center for the People & the Press, "Growing Support for Gay Marriage: Changed Minds and Changing Demographics," http://www.people-press.org/2013/03/20/growing-support-for-gay-marriage-changed-minds-and-changing-demographics/ (posted March 20, 2013; last visited April 6, 2013) (the second most given reason, 18

percent, for a shift to support same-sex marriage was that the person had thought more about the issue or had grown older).

25. Richard Socarides, "Rob Portman and His Brave, Gay Son," http://www.newyorker.com/online/blogs/newsdesk/2013/03/rob-portman-and-his-brave-gay-son.html (posted March 15, 2013; last visited April 4, 2014).

26. Smith, *Less Than Human*, 273.

27. John Shuford, "Meet the Director," n.d., http://connect.gonzaga.edu//shuford/ (last visited April 2, 2014).

28. John F. Kennedy, *A Nation of Immigrants* (New York: Harper & Row, 1964), 68.

29. Ibid., 8.

30. See generally Bender, *One Night in America*, 106–107.

31. Ibid., 152. Earlier, the Catholic Church and other denominations orchestrated the 1980s' sanctuary movement, which supplied a safe haven in the United States to Central American refugees fleeing the upheaval in their countries.

32. Bender, *One Night in America*, 152.

33. Terry Coonan, "There Are No Strangers among Us: Catholic Social Teachings and U.S. Immigration Law," *Catholic Lawyer* 40 (2000): 105.

34. DefineAmerican.org. See also Jose Antonio Vargas, "My Life as an Undocumented Immigrant," *New York Times*, June 22, 2011.

35. Quoted in Bender, *One Night in America*, 59.

36. Sumbul Ali-Karamali, "Opinion: American Muslims Live in Fear 11 Years after 9/11," http://religion.blogs.cnn.com/2012/09/11/opinion-american-muslims-live-in-fear-11-years-after-911/ (posted September 11, 2012; last visited November 24, 2012).

37. Richard Delgado, "Prosecuting Violence: A Colloquy on Race, Community, and Justice," *Stanford Law Review* 52 (2000): 751 (critiquing the restorative-justice movement).

38. A possible alternate approach for creating sympathy for convicted murderers is found in a study by psychologists in which participants were told a background story for a murder that explained the provocation for the crime. The study revealed that listening to a story (although not face-to-face) enhanced sympathies for the murderer as well as for the class of murderers. See Pinker, *Better Angels*, 587–588. Still, in comparison to the supplied script of a murderer taunted by his neighbor, who also set fire to his car, most death-row murderers have a much less sympathetic story or at least not one that involves an evil-doing victim, and so their already scant chances for sympathy are dimmed.

39. For example, *Garcia v. Gloor*, 618 F.2d 264 (5th Cir. 1980) (an English-only rule in the workplace did not disparately affect a bilingual Mexican American employee whose language was a matter of choice and not an immutable characteristic, such as skin color, sex, or place of birth).

40. Attacking same-sex marriage through shaming churchgoers, the archbishop of Detroit, Allen Vigneron, said in 2013 that Catholics who receive Communion but support same-sex marriage are effectively perjuring themselves by

contradicting holy teachings. "Gay Marriage Supporters Should Avoid Taking Communion, Says Allen Vigneron, Detroit Catholic Archbishop," http://www. huffingtonpost.com/2013/04/08/gay-marriage-supporters-communion-catholic-allen-vigneron_n_3037109.html (posted April 8, 2013; last visited April 4. 2014). In a similar vein, a 2013 bulletin issued by Cardinal Timothy Dolan, president of the U.S. Conference of Catholic Bishops, called for prayer, fasting, and personal sacrifice by parishioners toward the goal of defeating same-sex marriage. Stephen C. Webster, "America's Top Catholic Calls for Renewed Wave of Anti-LGBT Sentiment," http://www.rawstory.com/rs/2013/05/26/americas-top-catholic-calls-for-renewed-wave-of-anti-lgbt-sentiment/ (posted May 26, 2013; last visited April 5, 2014).

41. The video is available at https://www.youtube.com/watch?v=omsr4AHtk9g&feature=youtu.be (posted October 1, 2012; last visited April 5, 2014).

42. Quoted in Bender, *One Night in America*, 151.

43. For example, Derrick A. Bell Jr., "*Brown v. Board of Education* and the Interest-Convergence Dilemma," *Harvard Law Review* 93 (2000): 518; Richard Delgado, "Rodrigo's Roundelay: *Hernandez v. Texas* and the Interest-Convergence Dilemma," *Harvard Civil Rights–Civil Liberties Law Review* 41 (2006): 23; Mary L. Dudziak, *Cold War, Civil Rights: Race and the Image of American Democracy* (Princeton, NJ: Princeton University Press, 2000).

44. Martínez, "Rise of the Market State."

45. Richard Delgado, "Rodrigo's Homily: Storytelling, Elite Self-Interest, and Legal Change," *Oregon Law Review* 87 (2008): 1259, 1278.

46. Butler, *Let's Get Free*, 29–40 (detailing these and other interest convergences for ending mass incarceration).

47. Delgado, "Rodrigo's Homily."

ABOUT THE AUTHOR

Steven W. Bender is Professor of Law and Associate Dean for Research and Faculty Development at Seattle University School of Law. He writes in diverse areas: real estate, race relations, politics, history, and culture. His published books include *Greasers and Gringos: Latinos, Law, and the American Imagination* (NYU Press, 2003), *One Night in America: Robert Kennedy, César Chávez, and the Dream of Dignity* (2008), *Tierra y Libertad: Land, Liberty, and Latino Housing* (NYU Press, 2010), and *Run for the Border: Vice and Virtue in U.S.-Mexico Border Crossings* (NYU Press, 2012).